BUTLER'S
LIVES OF THE SAINTS

NEW
FULL EDITION

OCTOBER

BUTLER'S
LIVES OF THE SAINTS

NEW FULL EDITION

Patron
H. E. CARDINAL BASIL HUME, O.S.B.
Archbishop of Westminster

BUTLER'S LIVES OF THE SAINTS

NEW
FULL EDITION

OCTOBER

Revised by
PETER DOYLE

BURNS & OATES

THE LITURGICAL PRESS
Collegeville, Minnesota

First published 1996 in Great Britain by
BURNS & OATES
Wellwood, North Farm Road,
Tunbridge Wells, Kent TN2 3DR

First published 1996 in North America by
THE LITURGICAL PRESS
St John's Abbey, Collegeville,
Minnesota 56321

ISBN 0 86012 259 X   Burns & Oates
ISBN 0-8146-2386-7   The Liturgical Press

Library of Congress Catalog Card Number: 95-81671

Typeset by Search Press Limited
Printed in the United States of America

CONTENTS

(Entries in Capital Letters indicate that the saint or feast is commemorated throughout the Roman Catholic Church with the rank of Solemnity, Feast, Memorial or
Optional Memorial, according to the 1969 revised calendar of the Latin [Roman]
Rite of the Catholic Church, published in the Roman Missal of 1970, or that the
saint is of particular importance for the English-speaking world. These entries are
placed first on their dates. All others are in chronological order, by date of death.)

Contents

Contents

PREFACE

The month of October illustrates the diversity and richness of the Calendar of Saints of the Roman Catholic Church. It has traditionally been the month of the rosary, because the feast of Our Lady of the Rosary is celebrated on 7 October. It also has the feast-days of some of the most popular of the saints, with St Francis (4 Oct.), St Thérèse of Lisieux, "The Little Flower," (1 Oct.), and St Teresa of Avila (15 Oct.). For English readers there is also St Edward (13 Oct.), the founder of Westminster Abbey, and the Forty Martyrs of England and Wales (25 Oct.). The last-named feast commemorates the group of martyrs canonized in 1970, and a general background account is given in this volume; each of them also has an individual feast-day, where details of their lives and sufferings will be found.

For what may be termed major saints, it is difficult for the present-day editor to keep up with the devotional and scholarly literature that is multiplying in many languages. An attempt has been made in the bibliography attached to each saint to point the reader toward some of the more recent literature available. For other saints the editor's problem is the reverse: while the existence of the saint is beyond doubt, little exists in the way of trustworthy historical material to tell us more than the barest of facts, and here a line has to be steered between a too-easy acceptance of legend and the minutiae of scholarship.

Changes in the Calendar of Saints since 1969 have meant that some saints have lost their universal status (like St Hilarion, 21 Oct.), some have been moved from October to other months (like St Remigius, from 1 Oct. to 13 Jan.), and some have been dropped altogether because there is now too much doubt about their existence. Among these last may be mentioned St Ursula and her eleven thousand maiden companions, formerly venerated on 21 October. Cardinal Wiseman, writing in the middle of the last century, judged a person who doubted their existence to be suspect of heresy, evidence in itself, of course, that there was some doubt about it. The previous edition of this work gave a critical account of the development of Ursula's legend and noted that the feast was treated with considerable reserve in the Roman liturgy; the story illustrates very well the mixture of historical embroidery, sham relics, and it has to be said, unscrupulous use by mercenary monks of holy people to support the legend that characterizes some medieval writing about the saints. Not that we should feel too superior to our ancestors in this regard: every age creates its myths to support and explain its beliefs, and medieval people could be quite sceptical about miracle stories, as they seem to have been about those attributed to St Gerald of Aurillac (13 Oct.). What surprises us more, perhaps, is how certain saints captured the medieval imagination and remained universally popular for centuries, such as St Faith (6 Oct.), when there seemed to be little to distinguish them from others; the current academic study of popular culture might serve a useful purpose here. The month of October has been enriched by new additions to the Calendar, especially of those beatified in recent years. Some of these are noteworthy for their involvement in the social problems of their day, such as Bd Bartholomew Longo (5 Oct.) and Bd Louis Guanella (24 Oct.). It is good to see an increasing number of laypeople among the saints and *beati,* and Bd Contardo Ferrini (27 Oct.) provides a timely ideal for present-day Christians.

No one can become involved in studying or reading about the saints without realizing the outstanding work done over recent centuries by the Bollandists, first of all in their monumental series, *Acta Sanctorum,* and more recently in their bi-annual publication, the *Analecta Bollandiana.* Their balanced approach to distinguishing fact from fiction in the accounts of saints and *beati* is a model for others to follow, and so most entries in this volume contain a reference to these works. There is also the Italian *Bibliotheca Sanctorum,* a multi-volume work based on authoritative scholarship and with the added attraction of being well illustrated and containing sections on the iconography of all the major saints. It has been used extensively for the entries on Bd Bartholomew Longo (5 Oct.), St John Baptist Turpin du Cormier (17 Oct.), Bd Joseph Baldo (24 Oct.), and Bd Louis Guanella (24 Oct.). Information about some of those recently beatified or canonized is not always easy to find, but recourse may be had to the official publications *Notitiae* and *A.A.S.* In English there is the very useful *Oxford Dictionary of Saints* by David Hugh Farmer, and the *Oxford Dictionary of the Christian Church,* which is particularly helpful for information about people, movements, and events in the Church's history.

The allocation of saints to particular days poses some problems. There may be differences between the Church's Calendar, which fixes the day on which a particular saint is celebrated or remembered liturgically, and the Roman Martyrology, the Church's official complete list of saints and *beati,* which assigns saints and *beati* to the dates of their death. The latter practice is followed here. A new edition of the Roman Martyrology is being prepared, and drafts for some months have appeared in *Notitiae.* That for October is not yet ready, and so references to the Roman Martyrology in this volume are to the former edition.

There are a few exceptions to the general editorial practice regarding the order of the saints for each day: St Wilfrid (12 Oct.) and The Forty Martyrs of England and Wales (25 Oct.) have been listed first on their respective days although they are not in the universal Calendar, because of their particular interest to English readers. The same has happened to St Francis Borgia (10 Oct.), simply because he seems to deserve it!

I wish to thank all who have helped me in editing this volume: Paul Burns as managing editor for his patience, understanding, and support; Fr Philip Caraman, S.J., for suggestions about the entry on the English Martyrs; Brother Austin Chadwick, F.S.C., for extremely useful material on the Brothers of the Christian Schools who were martyred in Spain during the Civil War and for materials on Bd Arnold Rèche, F.S.C.; John Harwood for help with the saints of the Eastern Church, and especially for his advice about how to portray St Ignatius of Constantinople; Nancy McDarby of Minnesota for keeping me on a politically correct line with the North American martyrs; Dom Henry Wansbrough, O.S.B., for help with the gospel saints Luke, Simon, and Jude. The general consultants, English and American, have read and commented on much of the volume, and I have benefited especially from the advice of David Hugh Farmer.

I feel I should also acknowledge a debt of gratitude to Alban Butler himself, who in the dog days of the mid-eighteenth century was inspired to start the process which has led to the present edition. An account of his life and the various editions of his great work can be found in the January volume of this series. The present editor can only note Butler's warning that "authors who polish the style, or abridge the histories of others, are seldom to be trusted," and hope that the saintly old president of Douai College will not be too upset by his efforts. Finally, I would not have been able to undertake and complete the work involved in editing this volume without the constant support and encouragement of my wife, Barbara.

14 May 1996, Feast of St Matthias, Apostle

Peter Doyle

Abbreviations and Short Forms

A.A.S.	*Acta Apostolicae Sedis.* Rome, 1909– .
AA.SS.	*Acta Sanctorum.* 64 vols. Antwerp, 1643– .
Anal.Boll.	*Analecta Bollandiana* (1882–).
Anal.Eccles.	*Analecta Ecclesiastica* (1893–).
Anal.Franc.	*Analecta Franciscana* (1885–).
Archiv. Fratrum Praed.	*Archivum Fratrum Praedicatorum* (1931–).
A.S.C.	*The Anglo-Saxon Chronicle,* in *E.H.D.,* 1 and 2.
Baring-Gould and Fisher	S. Baring-Gould and J. Fisher. *The Lives of the British Saints.* 4 vols., 1907–13.
Bede, *H.E.*	The Venerable Bede. *Historia Ecclesiastica.* (ed. L. Sherley–Price and D. H. Farmer) 1955; revised ed. 1990.
Bibl.SS.	*Bibliotheca sanctorum.* 13 vols. Rome, 1960–70; Suppl. 1, *Prima Appendice.* Rome, 1987.
B.T.A.	H. Thurston and D. Attwater (eds.). *Butler's Lives of the Saints.* 4 vols., London and New York,1953–4; the previous edition of this work.
Catholic Encyclopaedia	C. Herbermann (ed.). *The Catholic Encyclopaedia.* 17 vols. New York, 1907–14.
Catholicisme	G. Jacquemet *et al.* (eds.). *Catholicisme: hier, aujourd'hui, demain.* Paris 1948– .
C.M.H.	H. Delehaye. *Commentarius Perpetuus in Martyrologium Hieronymianum* (*AA.SS.*, 65). 1931.
C.R.S.	*Catholic Record Society.* London, 1905– .
D.A.C.L.	H. Cabrol and H. Leclerq (eds.). *Dictionnaire d'Archéologie Chrétienne et de Liturgie.* 15 vols. Paris, 1907–53.
D.C.B.	W. Smith and H. Wace (eds.). *Dictionary of Christian Biography.* 4 vols. London, 1877–87.
Dict.Sp.	M. Viller, S.J., *et al.* (eds.). *Dictionnaire de Spiritualité.* 1937– .
Diz. dei Papi	B. Mondin. *Dizionario enciclopedico dei Papi: storia e insegnamenti.* Rome, 1995.
D.H.G.E.	A. Baudrillart *et al.* (eds.), *Dictionnaire d'Histoire et de Géographie Ecclésiastiques.* 1912– .
D.N.B.	L. Stephen and S. Lee (eds.). *Dictionary of National Biography.* 63 vols. London, 1885–1900.

D.T.C.	A. Vacant, E. Mangenot, and E. Amman (eds.). *Dictionnaire de Théologie Catholique.* 15 vols. Paris, 1903–50.
Duchesne, *Fastes*	L. Duchesne. *Fastes épiscopaux de l'ancienne Gaule.* 3 vols. 2d ed., Paris, 1907–15.
E.H.D.	D. C. Douglas *et al.* (eds.). *English Historical Documents.* London, 1953– .
E.H.R.	*English Historical Review* (1886–).
Irish Saints, The	D. P. Mould. *The Irish Saints.* 1964.
Jedin–Dolan	H. Jedin and J. Dolan (eds.). *History of the Church*, Eng. trans. 10 vols. London and New York, 1965–81.
J.E.H.	*Journal of Ecclesiastical History* (1950–).
K.S.S.	A. P. Forbes (ed.). *Kalendars of Scottish Saints.* 1872.
L.E.M.	E. H. Burton and J. H. Pollen (eds.). *Lives of the English Martyrs.* 2d series, London, 1915.
M.G.H.	*Monumenta Germaniae Historica.* The *Scriptores* series is split into sub-series, of which the following are referred to: *Auctores antiquissimi; Scriptores rerum merovingicarum; Scriptores.*
M.M.P.	R. Challoner. *Memoirs of Missionary Priests.* London, 1741–2; new ed. by J. H. Pollen, 1924.
N.C.E.	*New Catholic Encyclopedia.* 14 vols. New York, 1967.
N.J.B.C.	*The New Jerome Biblical Commentary.* London, 1989.
Notitiae	*Congregatio de Cultu Divino et Disciplina Sacramentorum. Notitiae.* Rome, 1965– .
O.D.C.C.	F. L. Cross and E. A. Livingstone (eds.). *The Oxford Dictionary of the Christian Church.* Oxford, New York, and Toronto, 1957; 2d ed., 1974.
O.D.S.	D. H. Farmer. *The Oxford Dictionary of Saints.* 3d ed., Oxford and New York, 1993.
Office of Readings	*The Divine Office. The Liturgy of the Hours According to the Roman Rite.* 3 vols., London, Sydney, and Dublin, 1974; vol. 3: *The Weeks of the Year.*
P.L.	J. P. Migne (ed.). *Patrologia Cursus Completus. Series Latina.* 221 vols., Paris, 1844–64.
Propylaeum	*Propylaeum ad Acta Sanctorum Decembris.* Brussels, 1940.
Rev. Ben.	*Revue Bénédictine* (1885–).

R.H.E.	*Revue d'Histoire Ecclésiastique* (1900–).
S.C.	*Sources Chrétiennes*. Paris, 1940– .
S.S.	*Surtees Society* (1834–).
Stanton	R. Stanton. *A Menology of England and Wales*. 1892.
Vies des Saints	J. Baudot et P. Chaussin (eds.). *Vies des Saints et des Bienheureux*. 13 vols. Paris, 1935–59.
V.S.H.	C. Plummer (ed.). *Vitae Sanctorum Hiberniae*. 2 vols., 1910; 2d ed., 1968.

THE
ELIZABETHAN
PERSECUTION
····◇····
TOWNS WHERE THERE
WERE EXECUTIONS
····◇····

NEWCASTLE
2
•1 GATESHEAD
CARLISLE •1
•9 DURHAM
•1 DARLINGTON

•6 LANCASTER
40
• YORK

1• BEAUMARIS

2
• LINCOLN

WREXHAM •1
DERBY
•3
1•
STAFFORD
OAKHAM •1

WARWICK
•1

IPSWICH
1•

• GLOUCESTER
3
• OXFORD 4
1• CHELMSFORD
2
76 •LONDON
ISLEWORTH • 2•
ROCHESTER 2
2• KINGSTON
CANTERBURY
4

1
SALISBURY • ANDOVER
1• • WINCHESTER
5
CHICHESTER
•2

EXETER
1•
6 DORCHESTER
2
ISLE OF WIGHT
LAUNCESTON
1•

THE FIGURES SHOW THE NUMBER OF VICTIMS PUT TO DEATH
IN EACH PLACE

See: "The Forty Martyrs of England and Wales," 25th October.
Source: Philip Hughes, The Reformation in England, *Vol. 3 (1950, 1963).*

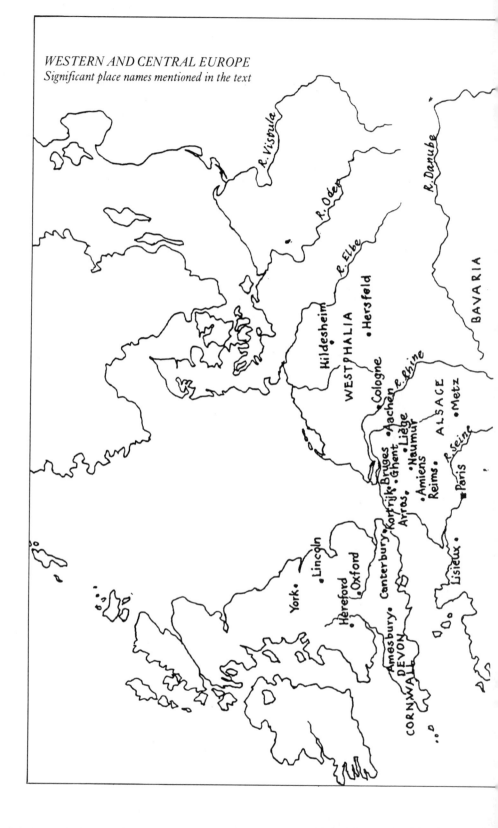

WESTERN AND CENTRAL EUROPE
Significant place names mentioned in the text

R. Vistula

R. Oder

R. Danube

R. Elbe

Hildesheim

WESTPHALIA

Hersfeld

BAVARIA

Cologne

Aachen

R. Rhine

Liège

Namur

ALSACE

Metz

Bruges

Ghent

Kortrijk

Arras

Amiens

Reims

R. Seine

Paris

Lincoln

Hereford

Oxford

Canterbury

Amesbury

DEVON

York

Lisieux

CORNWALL

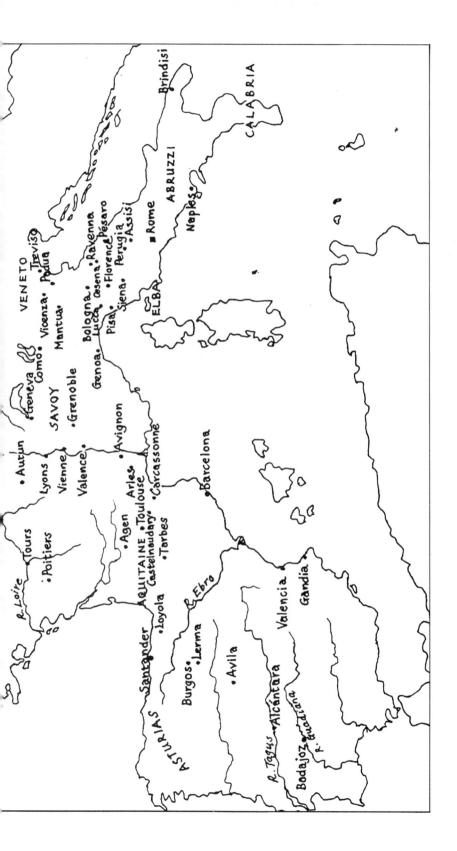

1

ST THÉRÈSE OF LISIEUX (1873-97)

Thérèse was born on 2 January 1873, the youngest of the five surviving children of Louis Martin, a watchmaker of Alençon, and Azélie-Marie Guérin. Her baptismal names were Marie Françoise Thérèse. Her parents were comfortably off and very devout, and Thérèse was brought up in a close, loving atmosphere and was, perhaps a little spoilt as the youngest child. Her earliest memories, she wrote in her autobiography, were of "smiles and tender caresses."

After her mother died in 1877 and the family moved to Lisieux, Thérèse looked to her eldest sister, Pauline, as a second mother. Pauline, however, entered the local Carmel when Thérèse was nine, and the latter developed a nervous disorder, regressing to some extent to earlier years in a subconscious search for security and love. She also became hypersensitive and for some years was given to frequent bouts of weeping for no apparent reason. She later claimed that the overcoming of this condition was part of the "conversion" she underwent after her Christmas Communion when she was thirteen.

By that time a second sister, Marie, had also entered the Carmel, and Thérèse herself was being drawn more and more to follow her sisters' example. While her father agreed to her request to be allowed to become a Carmelite, both the convent authorities and the local bishop refused out of hand because she was still only fourteen. She was determined, however, to try her vocation. A few months later she went to Rome with her father on pilgrimage and took advantage of a papal audience to ask Leo XIII to intervene on her behalf so that she would be able to enter the convent at fifteen. He upheld the decision of the local superiors but was impressed by her earnestness and told her, "You shall enter if it be God's will." She had been hoping for a positive reply, and in a letter to her sister Pauline she expressed her disappointment: "I felt as if I had been crushed to powder. I felt abandoned. . . . As I write to you I could cry my heart out. It's fit to burst. But don't mind. God can't try me more than I can bear. He has given me the courage I need to stand this last trial. . . . I am the child Jesus' little ball. If he wants to smash his toy he can do so. Yes, I want all and everything he wants."

Eventually the bishop gave his permission and Thérèse entered Carmel in April 1888, still only fifteen years of age. Her name in religion was Thérèse of the Infant Jesus; later on she was allowed to add to this "and of the Holy Face," as a reminder of Jesus' suffering. Thus she began her famous "little way" to perfection, which she claimed to be something new. There was nothing extraordinary in her life as a nun, if by "extraordinary" is meant severe bodily mortifications or the ecstasies of the

1

mystic, such as her namesake, Teresa of Avila (15 Oct.), experienced. On the other hand, it is important to understand what she meant by "little," for there was nothing unheroic or undemanding in it. She believed very strongly that everyone was called to perfection and so it must be attainable by all—it was not the preserve of great souls practising superhuman virtue but was open to "little" souls like herself. She also stressed the littleness of the creature in the presence of the Creator and believed that it was by acknowledging her littleness in this sense that she recognized and became dependent on the greatness of God and totally reliant on God's freely offered love.

Thérèse never used the phrase "spiritual childhood" about her "way"; this was added to her writings later by Mother Agnes of Jesus in 1907 when she was preparing a new edition of the autobiography. Nor did Thérèse ever refer to Christ's words in St Matthew's Gospel, "unless you become as little children," in this context. While there was a childlike simplicity about her decision to become a saint and the single-minded determination with which she went about it, one must be just as clear about her references to childlike qualities as about her use of the word "little" in connection with her spirituality. She wanted to prevent any feelings of pride growing in the mind of the seeker after God, and to stress again the free gift of God's love. What the soul had to do was to respond in as straightforward a way as possible to the simplicity of Christ's invitation to approach him and his Father with complete trust, the trust of the child who knows it is loved and responds by loving as ardently as possible in return.

There could, indeed, be nothing childish about a spirituality nurtured on the scriptures, the *Imitation of Christ*, the writings of St John of the Cross (14 Dec.) and St Teresa of Avila—and on the Rule and the liturgical life of Carmel. She had a commonsense directness in her spirituality, perhaps owing something to another inspiration, St Francis de Sales (24 Jan.), who taught the superiority of hidden and humble acts of charity over all the bodily mortifications then held in high esteem in many convents (including, for example, the taking of the discipline with bunches of nettles at Lisieux). Her reliance on the scriptures and the daily liturgy and her intense concentration on Christ have made some commentators see in her a modern saint ahead of her time. Perhaps her modern appeal lies as much in the simplicity of her approach. She was able to cut through the rigid formalism that marked so much nineteenth-century religion and its complexities. She wrote, for example, "When I read some spiritual treatises which show perfection as difficult to attain and liable to many illusions, my poor little spirit tires very quickly; I shut the learned book which is giving me a headache and drying up my heart, and I open the holy Scriptures. Then everything seems clear; one word opens up infinite horizons, perfection seems easy. I see that it is sufficient to acknowledge one's nothingness and to abandon oneself like a child to God's arms." Thérèse believed that perfection was attainable by every Christian; the negative and exclusive rigorism of Jansenism (not entirely absent from the way of life in the Lisieux Carmel) had no place in her make-up.

In this respect it is worth stressing that she was far from seeing spirituality and holiness as preserves of the priest or religious. Toward the end of her life she wrote a delightful letter of congratulation to a cousin who was getting married, in which she said, "We have both said good-bye to carefree childhood days. Now we have to face the responsibilities of life. We all take a different road but each one leads to the same goal. You and I must have a single aim: to grow in holiness while following the way that God in his goodness has laid down for us." Thérèse's early years in Carmel were not easy ones—as she put it, she found more thorns than roses; she was treated with some severity by Mother Mary of Gonzaga, the prioress, and suffered doubts about her vocation. There were unfortunate divisions within the community. There were family trials, too. Her father suffered a number of strokes which affected his mind, and he had to spend three years in an institution. Thérèse's clothing ceremony had to be postponed, as did her profession of vows. Her father never recovered fully and died in 1894. A third sister, Céline, who had been nursing him, now entered Carmel.

Thérèse stated that her reasons for entering the convent were to save souls and, especially, to pray for priests. She lived a life of prayer and sacrifice, devoted to the faithful keeping of the daily Rule. The only office she held was that of assistant to the novice-mistress. The task of guiding the novices was for her a matter of cooperating in a divine work which was only possible if she did it "ensconced in the arms of Jesus."

It was customary at the time for one or two of the nuns who had reached a high level of spirituality to be allowed by their superior to consecrate themselves as victims to divine justice, to suffer in themselves the punishments due to sinners. This practice was regarded as the pinnacle of Carmelite spirituality. When Thérèse was twenty-two, she asked the prioress for permission to offer herself in this way, but with a key difference. She wanted to become a victim of God's merciful love, a love which was, she said, "a thousand times more demanding than his justice." Her act of consecration was: "My God, I desire to love you and make you loved by others . . . but I know my own weakness and ask you to be my holiness. To live out an act of perfect love I offer myself as a holocaust victim to your merciful love, asking you to consume me entirely . . . in that way I will become a martyr of your love, O my God."

Like St Teresa of Avila, Thérèse had been attracted to work as a missionary as a way of spreading God's love throughout the world and saving souls. In the last years of her life she wanted to become a member of the new Carmel established in Hanoi in French Indochina, but her health, apart from any other considerations, made such a transfer impossible. Instead, she took under her spiritual wing two foreign missionaries, and some of her most moving spiritual letters from 1896 and 1897 were written to encourage them in their work. To one she wrote, "I am perfectly sure that I shall not stay inactive in heaven; my desire is to go on working for the Church and for souls." The year before she died she promised, "If I go to heaven soon, I shall ask Jesus' permission to visit you at Su-Chuen, and we shall continue our apostolate together." It was just before she died that she developed this idea further: "I will spend my heaven doing good upon earth. . . . I shall not be able to take any rest until the end of the world, as long as there are souls to be saved," and she promised to let fall from heaven a shower of roses.

The first signs of the tuberculosis which was to kill her appeared in Holy Week 1896, and she hoped that it was an indication that God would soon call her to himself. But she did not die until September of the following year, and in the intervening months her faith was tested to such an extent that she understood for the first time the plight of people who had no faith to live by. In trying to explain the spiritual suffering that she went through in those final months she wrote, "God allowed my soul to be overrun by an impenetrable darkness, which made the thought of heaven, hitherto so welcome, a subject of nothing but conflict and torment. And this trial was not to be a matter of a few days or a few weeks. . . . I get tired of the darkness all around me, [and the voice which says] death will make nonsense of your hopes; it will only mean a night darker than ever, the night of mere non-existence. . . . It isn't just a veil, it's a great wall which reaches to the sky and blots out the stars!" These trials were accepted by Thérèse as a sharing in Christ's suffering and as the final preparation for heaven, the result of her dedication of herself as a sacrifice to divine love. She lived through them by trust and constant prayer, as she wrote, "I don't suppose I've made so many acts of faith in all the rest of my life as I have during this last year." These last months were also marked by severe physical suffering as breathing became more difficult, and she was given neither morphine nor oxygen to relieve the pain. On one occasion she cried out to Our Lady, "Holy Virgin, you know how I am suffocating! I can't get any earthly air, when will the Lord give me that of heaven?" She died on 30 September 1897 after a long and very painful agony.

Thérèse left a relatively large body of writings for one who had died so young. These include her famous autobiography, *The Story of a Soul*, which had been written under obedience (and some of it only in the last two months of her life), over two hundred letters, sixty-two poems, prayers, plays to be performed in the convent, and a collection of "Last Words." The autobiography in particular suffered at the hands of its first editors in the convent, who had their own ideas about how Thérèse should be portrayed to the world. Later facsimile editions showed how extensive the "corrections" and rewriting had been—but the saint's fundamental message had not been altered.

Popular devotion to Thérèse began so soon after her death and spread so widely as to be truly remarkable, given that she had lived an obscure life as an enclosed nun. The publication of her autobiography was, in human terms, responsible for this. First published by the Carmel a year after Thérèse's death, 47,000 copies had been sold by 1910; in the next five years over 150,000 copies were sold, and the convent was receiving about five hundred letters a day. So many people claimed to have received favours through her intercession that the authorities began the cause of her canonization without waiting for the usual interval. Pope Pius X announced the introduction of her cause in 1914, and in 1921 Benedict XV pronounced that her virtues had been heroic. Two years later she was beatified, and finally she was canonized by Pius XI in 1925. In 1927 she was proclaimed a principal patron of all missionaries, men and women, and in 1947 a secondary patron of France.

Pictures and statues of the saint abound; more, probably, than any other her image has suffered from plaster saintliness and sentimentality. In appearance she was slight, with blonde hair and grey-blue eyes; there are original photographs which show more of her true character and a much stronger face than the re-touched and usually insipid copies. A very good bronze in Westminster Cathedral shows her in a striking pose, hurrying forward joyfully, as it were, to meet her Lord. She was, of course, a child of her times—of that ultra pious world of the bourgeois Catholic family and its withdrawal from the world, a culture foreign to the modern English or American mind (though it should be remembered that the family's regular spiritual reading included Guéranger's *Année Liturgique*). Some of those closest to her and some of her followers would have restricted her within this mould, but Thérèse's strength lay in her ability to cut through the superficial and concentrate on the basics of the Christian call to perfection through a simple but total trust in God and an acceptance of the demands of divine love.

Autobiography of a Saint, Thérèse of Lisieux, trans. R. A. Knox (1958) with useful intro. by Fr François, O.C.D., editor of the facsimile edition; J.Dubois, "Une Sainte Moderne, Thérèse de L'Enfant-Jesus," *D.H.G.E.*, 23, fasc. 132; *Bibl.SS.*, 12, 379-94; *Dict. Sp.*, 15 (1991), pp. 576-611; J.Longchampt (ed.), *St Thérèse de L'Enfant-Jésus et de la Sainte-Face, Oeuvres Complètes*: new centenary edition in eight vols. (Paris, 1992), and a shorter one-volume edition, *ibid.;* A. Sicari, *Nuovi ritratti di santi*, 2 (1992); A. Combes, *St Therese and Her Mission* (1956). Of the many lives and studies see those by H. Petitot (1927), H. U. von Balthasar (1953), I. Görres (1959), J. Norbury (1966). Selections from her writings in T. Carey (ed.), *Thérèse of Lisieux - A Discovery of Love* (1992). There is a critical edition of her poems, *Un Cantique d'Amour*, 2 vols. (1979); the forty poems from the autobiography were translated by A. Bancroft (1996). The letter to her sister and the marriage letter are quoted from J. Cumming (ed.), *Letters from Saints to Sinners* (1996), pp. 148-9, 167-8.

St Romanus the Melodist (Mid-Sixth Century)

Romanus was born about the end of the fifth century at Emesa (present-day Homs) in central Syria and was a convert from Judaism. He studied at Beirut, where he became a deacon, and then moved to Constantinople during the reign of Anastasius I (491-518). He was assigned to the church of the Most Holy Mother of God at Blacherne, and achieved great fame as a composer of the *Kontakia*, or liturgical hymns, used in the Eastern liturgy; these are a type of metrical sermon or commentary on a particular feast, such as Christmas or the Presentation, or on passages from the scriptures. He was not the originator of this type of hymn, as has some-times been claimed, but he perfected its style, inspired partly by his native Syrian poetic traditions. His compositions are considered to be among the most beautiful ever written and are still used today, although in a much shortened form. Some eighty of his works are extant, but there is some doubt about the authenticity of all of them. They are marked by a vividness of feeling and a dramatic style; the most popular of his Marian hymns, for example, features a lament of Our Lady at the foot of the cross.

There is a legend that Our Lady appeared to him one Christmas Eve at her shrine, where he loved to pray. She gave him a roll of paper to eat, and as a result, when he was deacon at the Christmas liturgy, he was inspired to extemporize a hymn which began, "On this day the Virgin gives birth to him who is transcendent, and earth offers a shelter to the unattainable. Angels join with shepherds to glorify him and the Magi follow the star. For a new child is born to us, who was God before all ages." This *Kontakion*, one of Romanus' best-loved compositions, is still used in the Byzantine rite as a summary of the feast of Christmas, and as a strictly orthodox statement of the doctrine of the Incarnation.

Another of his compositions is the famous Akathist hymn, described in a recent work as: "Theologically, poetically, and musically, one of the most profound and beautiful compositions bequeathed to us" by Byzantine hymn writers (Preface to *The Service of the Akathist Hymn*). Most of the hymn consists of praises addressed to Our Lady, each beginning with the angel's greeting, "Hail," and it deals with the main events of the Incarnation from the Annunciation to the Presentation in the Temple. According to tradition, the hymn was sung on a number of occasions when Constantinople was saved from its enemies through the help of Our Lady. To mark these events a later *Kontakion*, beginning with the words "To thee, our leader in battle and defender" was added. The hymn became associated with the feast of the Annunciation (25 Mar.); in the Greek church parts of it are sung on the first four Fridays of Lent.

We do not know when Romanus died, but there are enough references to current events in his hymns to show that he was still alive in 548, when the empress Theodora died, but not in 565, when the emperor Justinian died. The Greek Church has a complete office in his honour; the date of his feast-day varies in different traditions.

In art Romanus is portrayed in three ways: as a deacon, either alone or with other deacons; asleep, with Our Lady giving him the roll of paper to eat; or, in a sixteenth-century Russian icon called *The Protection of the Mother of God*, with a picture of the Blacherne shrine, where the apparition is said to have taken place, and insets of Romanus receiving the paper roll and singing his famous hymn to Mary.

For a critical edition of his works, P. Maas and C. A. Trypanis, *Sancti Romani Melodi Cantica*, I, *Cantica genuina* (1963), and II, *Cantica dubia* (1970); a French translation by J. Grosdidier de Matons, *Romanos le Melode. Hymnes*, is in *S.C.*, 99, 110, 114, 128 (1964-7). See also *The Service of the Akathist Hymn*, trans. from the Greek by the Holy Transfiguration Monastery, Boston (1991); Mother Mary and Arch. Kallistos Ware, *The Lenten Triodion, Translated from the Original Greek* (1978); *Bibl.SS.*, 11, 319-23; *O.D.C.C.*, pp. 341, 1196; E. Wellesz, *A History of Byzantine Music and Hymnography* (1949); A. de Halleux, *R.H.E.* 62 (1967), pp. 459-62; G. Gharib, *Icone Di Santi: Storia e Culto* (1990), pp. 208-13.

St Mylor, *Martyr* (date unknown)

The medieval life of this saint (also called Melor, Melar) was abridged from a French original and was probably written at the Wiltshire abbey of Amesbury, which claimed to have his relics. It tells the story of the son of a Breton duke whose uncle, after murdering the duke, tried to prevent him from ever being a threat by cutting off his right hand and left foot and banishing him to a monastery. There the boy gained a reputation for holiness and miracle-working, and so his uncle had him beheaded. The body was the cause of several miracles, including the deaths of the murderers, and was buried with great honour. The story of the death of the boy-prince had strong appeal. After many years the relics were taken to Amesbury.

As Farmer says, the life of this obscure saint has been "obfuscated by hagiographers who have confused names, dates and places almost irretrievably." When the legend was written down in England the events of the saint's life and martyrdom were transferred to Cornwall and Devon; the original Breton version contains bits of folklore and Celtic fabulous elements, including the replacement of the boy's severed limbs by ones in gold and silver, which grew in the same way as his natural ones would have done. It is impossible to disentangle the true parts of the story from the false, and bits of the lives of more than one saint have almost certainly been conflated. We know that during the reign of King Athelstan (*c.* 894–939) the relics of some Breton saints were brought to England, amongst which may have been those which were given to Amesbury. According to Doble, the Cornish St Mylor was probably not Melor or Melar the boy-martyr but the Breton St Meloir, a bishop. There is also a Breton St Magloire (24 Oct.), whose name is philologically the same as both Melar and Meloir but who was a different person. There are three Cornish dedications to St Mylor.

St Melor was represented in the pictures of martyrs on the walls of the English College chapel in Rome.

G. H. Doble, *The Saints of Cornwall*, 3 (1964), pp. 20-52, is the best attempt to establish an identity for the saint and an excellent example of the detective work required in such reconstructions; *Anal. Boll.*, 46 (1928), pp. 411-2; *O.D.S.*, p. 350.

St Bavo (*c.* 655)

Bavo (also called Allowin) was a nobleman of Brabant in the Low Countries. He led a life that was far from exemplary until the death of his wife, when he was converted to a life of prayer and penance by St Amand (6 Feb.). After giving his wealth to the poor he became a monk and accompanied Amand on missionary journeys in France and Flanders. He then became a hermit, living at first in the trunk of a tree and later in a cell at Mendonck; after a return to the monastic life at Ghent he was given permission by his abbot to become a hermit once more. Despite this seclusion his fame spread and he was especially noted for the penance he did for his earlier irregular life. He died about the year 655. He is one of the diocesan patrons of Ghent and Haarlem, and his feast-day is featured in the Old English Sarum missal.

AA.SS., Oct., 1, pp. 198-303, gives a number of early Lives; the earliest was edited by B. Krusch, *M.G.H. Scriptores rerum merov.*, 4, pp. 527-46, where it is dismissed as of little historical value; E. de Moreau, *St Amand* (1927), pp. 220-2; R. Podevijn, *Bavo* (1945); M. Coens, *Anal. Boll.* 63 (1945), pp. 220-41, discusses whether Bavo was a bishop; *Bibl.SS.*, 2, 982-3.

Bd Francis of Pesaro (*c.* 1270-1350)

Francis was born in Pesaro, on the eastern coast of Italy south of Rimini, about 1270. His parents left him well off while he was still young, and he decided to devote his wealth to helping the poor and to dedicate his life to God. In the year 1300 he joined the Third Order of St Francis and then retired to a hermitage he had built on the slopes of Monte San Bartolo, near his native town, along with Bd Peter of Foligno. Francis had a very strong devotion to Our Lady and built two chapels in her honour. He soon attracted a number of disciples, and in order to support them he begged from place to place, making himself known over quite a wide area, and gaining a reputation for kindness and sanctity. He set up a house for them to live in near Pesaro and devoted himself to prayer and works of charity, such as restoring hospitals and churches, very much in the spirit of St Francis (4 Oct.). He lived in this way for about fifty years, and a number of remarkable happenings were reported of him, including impossibly rapid movement from place to place. As the previous edition of this work took care to point out, this does not necessarily mean anything more than that he had a better knowledge than his companions of short cuts across country: "Such simple incidents as this in the lives of the saints have been too easily magnified into miracles by enthusiastic biographers."

Francis helped Bd Michelina Metelli (9 Sept.), who was also a Franciscan tertiary, to found the Confraternity of the Most Holy Annunciation, whose main work was to look after the sick and dying and to bury the dead. This was in 1347 at Pesaro. He also built a hospice for tramps and pilgrims at Almetero. He died about 1350; his tomb was such a favourite place of pilgrimage that his body was moved to a shrine in Pesaro cathedral. His cult was approved in 1859.

AA.SS., Aug., 1, pp. 658-62, gives a short medieval biography; see also *Vies des Saints*, 8, p. 83; *Bibl.SS.*, 5, 1183-4.

Bd Nicholas of Forca Palena, *Founder* (*c.* 1349-1449)

Nicholas was born in Forca Palena in the Abruzzi region of southern Italy, about the year 1349. He became a priest and worked for several years in his native town but then decided to devote himself to a life of greater austerity. About the beginning of the fifteenth century he went to Rome, perhaps at the time that Innocent VII became pope (1404), since Innocent was from the same diocese as Nicholas. He joined a community of hermits under the direction of Rinaldo of Piedmont, near the church of San Salvatore, and so impressed Rinaldo that the latter made him his successor as both leader of the community and parish priest of the church. There is some debate about when the hermits adopted a separate Rule; at first they may have lived as members of the Third Order of St Francis. After Rinaldo's death the number of hermits had grown so large that Nicholas went to Naples with some of them and set up another community there.

Nicholas was in Florence in 1434 and 1437, and Pope Eugenius IV (1431-47), who was also in the city, gave him two nearby monasteries to reform. He seems to have acquired other monastic houses over the next few years, and in 1444 a new monastery was opened in Rome, on the Janiculum, with its church dedicated to Sant' Onofrio, and Nicholas went to live there. At some stage he had put his various groups of hermits under the patronage of St Jerome (30 Sept.) and had formed them into a Congregation. There was at the time another Congregation of hermits with St Jerome as their patron, the Poor Brothers of St Jerome, founded by Bd Peter of Pisa (17 June) in 1380. Nicholas and Peter had become close friends, and they decided it would be better to have only one Congregation as their two foundations were so similar. It is not clear when the union took place, but it was given papal approval in 1446 (Peter had died in 1435). Nicholas died in 1449 at the age of one hundred. His cult started very shortly after his death and was strong in the sixteenth and seventeenth centuries; in 1712 his body was transferred to a tomb under the high altar of Sant' Onofrio, where it still rests. The Hieronymites, as the combined Congregation became known after the name of its patron, obtained official approval of the cult in 1771. Pope Benedict XIV (1740-58), an acknowledged expert on the processes of beatification and canonization, refused to beatify Nicholas formally without all the due processes being carried out.

There does not appear to have been a contemporary Life. *AA.SS.*, Sept., 8, pp. 235-58, puts together a full account from various sources, especially the *Historica Monumenta* of the Hieronymite Sajanello, published in 1728. See also *Bibl.SS.*, 9, 918-20.

2

St Eleutherius of Nicomedia, *Martyr* (*c.* 300)

According to the Roman Martyrology, Eleutherius, a soldier, and many other Christians were accused of burning down the palace of Diocletian and as a result were executed by various means. Eleutherius achieved "his victorious martyrdom as gold tried in fire." This story, however, has no historical foundation, and all we know about the saint is contained in a Syriac list of saints of the fifth century, which says that he suffered in Nicomedia. He is also mentioned in the martyrology of St Jerome, which claims that a set of *acta* existed. He is sometimes identified with the saint of the same name whose feast-day used to be 4 August according to the Roman Martyrology.

AA.SS., Oct., 1, pp. 321-3; *Bibl.SS.*, 4, 1009; H. Quentin, *Les Martyrologes historiques du Moyen-âge* (1908), pp. 615-6; *S.C.*, 55, p. 13.

St Leger, *Bishop* (*c.* 616-79)

Leger, or Leodegar, was born about the year 616 of a noble Alsatian family and educated at the royal court and at Poitiers, where his uncle was bishop. After ordination he was put in charge of the nearby abbey of Saint-Maxence, which he reformed on the general lines of the Rule of St Benedict (11 July). He had a reputation at this time of being severe and demanding, and seems to have inspired awe and respect rather than love or affection. He was called to the court and later, about the year 663, made bishop of Autun in Burgundy, a diocese which had been torn apart by rival factions. Leger restored peace and firm government, reforming the clergy, building churches, and helping the poor. He also reformed the monasteries, saying that if monks lived as they were supposed to by their rule, their prayers would be sufficient to preserve the world from natural disasters.

Leger became heavily involved in the politics of the court. For a time King Childeric II was his protégé but then turned against him because of Leger's opposition to the king's unlawful marriage. Inevitably in such a situation he made enemies, one of whom was Ebroin, a powerful figure intent on uniting the Frankish kingdoms. When Arthaud was restored to Autun after a period in exile, Ebroin decided to take revenge. He laid siege to Autun, and Leger, after defending his city for a time, surrendered to avoid further bloodshed. Leger and his brother were accused of complicity in the death of the king, who had been assassinated, and they were tortured to try to make them confess. His brother was murdered (the Roman Martyrology names him as a martyr), and Leger was severely mutilated but recovered. He later wrote to his mother, who had become a nun, saying that the death of her son should be an occasion for rejoicing, not sorrow, and that their enemies should be forgiven. Two years later he was again taken by Ebroin, and this time he was murdered, after having been deposed by a local synod of bishops. The reasons for the quarrel between Ebroin and Leger were political and complex, and some good people at the time supported the former against the saint. His murder seems to have been a political act, and it is not clear why he should be regarded as a martyr.

Leger's relics were moved to the monastery of Saint-Maxence in 682, and his cult became popular in France, especially around Poitiers, in Alsace, and in Arras, where he had been tortured, and, of course, in Autun itself. Many monasteries claimed to have part of his relics, and a large number of churches were dedicated to him. His cult spread to England, where a few churches were dedicated to him, and he featured in monastic calendars. He was prayed to for eye disorders and blindness and was one of the patron saints of millers.

AA.SS., Oct., 1, pp. 355-491, prints two early Lives, based on a near-contemporary Life which is still partially extant—see B. Krusch, *M.G.H., Scriptores rerum merov.*, 5, 249-362, for a reconstructed version; H. Leclerq, *D.A.C.L.*, 8, 2460-92; *Bibl.SS.*, 7, 1190-3; *O.D.C.C.*, p. 814.

Bd Antony Chevrier, *Founder* (1826-79)

Antoine-Marie Chevrier was born in Lyons on 16 April 1826. He made his First Communion when he was eleven and from then on was a frequent communicant, which was unusual at the time. He studied for the priesthood in Lyons, where he was a very able scholar, and was ordained in 1850. He was appointed curate in the parish of St Andrew, in a working-class area on the edge of the city, and impressed everyone by his holiness, zeal, and prudence. On Christmas night 1856, while praying before the crib, he had a revelation of the meaning of divine poverty which was to affect the rest of his life and give him a new vocation, and he vowed "to follow Jesus Christ as closely as possible, to make himself able to work effectively for the salvation of souls."

When the river Rhone overflowed he worked heroically to save the people threatened by the floods. Afterward, two wealthy people opened a house of refuge for those ruined by the floods and called it "The Town of the Infant Jesus." Antony was encouraged by St John Vianney (4 Aug.) to become its chaplain and worked there for three years; the idea behind the initiative was twofold: to encourage the children of the poor to make their First Communions and to prepare them to do so, and to provide lodgings for the very poor and homeless.

In 1859 he decided the work was so great that he needed to set up a new movement to help abandoned children and the poor. The following year he was able to acquire a disused ballroom called "The Prado," and here he established The Providence of the Prado. He lived there for twenty years, helped in the work by a number of priests, whom he eventually formed into the Society of Priests of the Prado. Its members were very few in number by the time of his death but grew

11

steadily thereafter and reached a peak of about a hundred by the middle of the present century. They lived in community but remained secular priests, following the Rule of the Third Order of St Francis. A society of Sisters was also formed; they followed the same Rule, taught the catechism to girls in a number of parishes, and looked after the sick.

Antony had a particular interest in the spiritual formation of priests and wrote a number of books on the subject. For him the ideal priest would imitate Christ in both his spiritual life and an active apostolate in a poor parish. Secular priests had two ways to choose from: what he called "the ordinary way" and the way of the evangelical counsels of perfection; priestly sanctity lay in choosing the second of these. He believed that priests should leave as much as possible of the temporal work of a parish to laypeople so that they would be free to carry out their essentially spiritual function. Their preaching must be simple and direct, "a conversation between priest and congregation." They should live in community as far as was possible, though he recognized that parochial life would limit the extent to which this ideal could be achieved. He did not develop a mystical theology in any of his writings, but put great emphasis on prayer and on the guidance of the Holy Spirit. He was fond of repeating the words "to know, to love, to act": through prayer we get to know God, this leads on to our loving him, and that in turn must lead us to action, directed by the Holy Spirit. He set the highest standard for the degree of sanctity the secular priest should aspire to. He should, he wrote, "astonish the world by his virtues" so that he could win it over to God.

For the last year of his life he was afflicted by painful ulcers; he died on 2 October 1879 and was buried in the chapel of the Prado. He was beatified in 1986 while Pope John Paul II was visiting Lyons.

As well as his involvement in works of charity and his interest in social questions, Antony published a number of books. Among these were *The Priest According to the Gospel, or the True Disciple of Christ* (this went into a third edition in 1922); *A Spiritual Testament*; *The Priestly Ministry Today*; *Subjects for Prayer*; and *In the School of Jesus Christ*. Some of his letters were also published; those to priests, nuns, and seminarians are particularly instructive.

Notitiae, 22 (1986), pp. 870-1; H. Waltz, *Le P. Chevrier* (1942); *Dict.Sp.*, 2, 835-7; *Bibl.SS.*, 3, 1198-1200. Another Chevrier, Claude- Marie, was beatified in Lyons in 1986; he had also died in 1879, as a martyr in China—see 17 Feb.

3

ST THOMAS OF HEREFORD, *Bishop* (*c.* 1218-82)

Thomas was born about 1218 at Hambledon near Great Marlow in Buckingham-shire. His father, William, was second baron Cantilupe and steward of the royal household; his mother, Millicent, was the daughter of a Norman lord and widow of the count of Evreux, while his uncle, Walter, was bishop of Hereford. Thomas went to Oxford in 1237 to begin his university studies; he then went to Paris, where he became Master of Arts in 1245. It seems he was ordained about the same year and then moved on to Orleans to study civil law; he was back in Oxford studying and teaching canon law in the mid-1250s and was elected chancellor of the univer-sity in 1261. During his term of office he was respected for his strictness and impartiality in dealing with the unruly student body. Despite his university suc-cesses he was not a scholar or a noted teacher, and he left no treatises or other writings. His was the career of the capable ecclesiastical administrator, scrupulous in carrying out his duties, but not above holding a number of benefices at the same time by papal dispensation.

Thomas joined the cause of the rebel barons against Henry III and was one of their envoys to the French king, St Louis (25 Aug.), who had been asked to arbitrate between the two sides. This failed, and after the barons had defeated the king at Lewes they chose Thomas to be chancellor of England in 1265, an office he held for a few months before Henry finally defeated Simon de Montfort and the barons at Evesham later in the same year. Even in the short period of his chancel-lorship Thomas gained a reputation for refusing bribes, standing up to the king, and reforming the office.

After the barons' defeat Thomas withdrew to Paris but was later reconciled to the king and returned to Oxford, where he was elected for a second period of office as chancellor in 1273. He lived for much of the time in London, where he gained a reputation for his lavish hospitality and general sociability, although those who knew him well testified to his own abstemious way of life. He still held a number of other posts, being archdeacon of Stafford, precentor at York, and the holder of four canonries and seven or eight parishes; he was conscientious in choosing suitable vicars to look after these benefices, visiting and preaching in them when he could and using his wealth to repair and maintain the church buildings. In 1275 he was appointed bishop of Hereford and was consecrated at Canterbury.

As might have been expected, Thomas took up his duties as diocesan bishop with vigour and determination. Hereford had not been served well by his immediate predecessors, and both lay and ecclesiastical lords had encroached on its territory and its rights. Some of his opponents he excommunicated, others he forced to do public penance; he even fought hard to regain his hunting rights from the Earl of Gloucester. At the same time he carried out his spiritual duties, confirming, preaching, rebuking public sinners, and depriving pluralists, among them the dean of St Paul's, who did not have the necessary dispensation. He was highly regarded by King Edward I and was a member of the royal council; he was one of the regents during the king's absence in 1279.

His last years were marked by serious quarrels with John Pecham, archbishop of Canterbury, over rights of appeal and jurisdiction. In the end the archbishop excommunicated him, in 1282, and so Thomas set out for Rome to put his case to Pope Martin IV. He was warmly received by the pope at Orvieto but became seriously ill; he retired to Montefiascone and died there on 25 August. His bones and heart were brought back to England; the former were buried in the cathedral in Hereford, the latter at Ashridge in Buckinghamshire.

Miracles were reported as soon as his relics were moved to a new tomb in the north transept in 1287 (the fine base of which can still be seen); between then and 1312 no fewer than five hundred were carefully recorded as the cathedral became a major place of pilgrimage. Petitions for his canonization were made by his successor in 1290 and 1299; in 1305 the king himself presented another petition, and a commission of inquiry was set up in 1307 with the task first of all of examining the matter of Thomas' excommunication. He was eventually canonized by John XXII in 1320 after the most exhaustive and well-documented inquiries. His relics were moved to a new shrine in the Lady Chapel in 1349.

St Thomas is an outstanding example of the responsible exercise of authority in the cause of religion and the reform of the Church. In an age noted for litigation he was as litigious as anyone and a stickler for his rights as diocesan bishop; to have acted otherwise would have been regarded at the time as a dereliction of duty. Good administration was not an end in itself, however, and he was concerned to ensure proper pastoral care of his people and high standards of conduct among his clergy. He led an austere personal life but was gracious and amiable in manner; he had a particular devotion to Our Lady, fasting on the vigils of her feast-days and choosing the feast of her Nativity as his consecration day. One of his former servants, giving evidence to the 1307 commission, said that Thomas' fear of God was noticeable in his hatred of liars, and of those who loved luxury, or were unjust and evil.

AA.SS., Oct., 1, pp. 539-705, makes use of the canonization material; T. F. Tout, *D.N.B.*, 3; R. G. Griffiths and W. W. Capes (eds.), *Registrum Thomae de Cantilupe* (1906) is invaluable for his diocesan administration; D. L. Douie, *Archbishop Pecham* (1952); M. Jancey (ed.), *St Thomas Cantilupe Bishop of Hereford* (1982); J. R. Maddicott, *Simon De Montfort* (1994).

St Hesychius (Fourth Century)

Hesychius was a disciple of St Hilarion (21 Oct.) and accompanied his master from Gaza in Palestine to Egypt to live a life of solitude and penance. When Hilarion, to avoid the fame he was beginning to attract, fled secretly to Sicily, the faithful

Hesychius eventually found his retreat after a three-year search. The two monks then withdrew to Dalmatia and, later, to Cyprus. Hesychius was sent back to Palestine to visit their former monastery in Gaza. Before he died in Cyprus about the year 370, Hilarion is said to have written a short will in Hesychius' favour, leaving him his Gospel book, his clothes, and a hairshirt. The local people wanted to keep the body for veneration, but Hesychius managed to take it back to Palestine, where it was buried in the monastery at Majuma; here Hesychius himself died and was buried. Most of what we know about this holy monk comes from St Jerome's Life of Hilarion, which is not regarded as altogether reliable historically.

AA.SS., Oct., 2, pp. 141-9; *Bibl.SS.*, 5, 86.

SS Hewald the White and Hewald the Black, *Martyrs* (*c.* 695)

The two brothers Hewald, or Ewald, were Northumbrian priests who spent some years in Ireland as exiles "for the sake of the eternal kingdom," according to Bede, who is also the source for our knowledge of the epithets given to them because of the colour of their hair. While both were devout and religious, Hewald the Black was more learned in the scriptures. They followed the example of St Willibrord (7 Nov.) and went to work among the Old Saxons, choosing to settle in Westphalia. While waiting to be introduced to the local lord they spent the time in prayer and saying Mass; this frightened the people, who thought that the two missionaries would try to convert their lord so that they would lose the protection of their gods. The two were murdered in a village near Dortmund, one straightaway and the other after a long torture, and their bodies were thrown into the Rhine. Bede tells us that the local lord was incensed at what had happened and had the villagers slain and their houses burned down.

The bodies of the two martyrs were recovered and buried with honour. Later Pepin III, ruler of the Franks, had them removed to Cologne and enshrined in the church of St Cunibert, where they still are. They are venerated as patrons of Westphalia, and their feast is also kept by the Premonstratensians, for whom St Norbert (6 June) obtained part of their relics in the twelfth century. Two other churches, at Xanten and Gorze, also claim to have some relics.

AA.SS., Oct., 2, pp. 180-207; Bede, *H.E.*, 5, 10; *Bibl.SS.*, 5, 401-2.

St Gerard of Brogne, *Abbot* (959)

Gerard was born toward the end of the ninth century in the region of Namur in modern Belgium. He was a noble who devoted his life to religion, especially the cause of reforming the monastic Order. Legend has it that he was advised by St Peter in a vision to have the relics of St Eugenius brought to his estates at Brogne from the famous abbey of Saint-Denis and that he later joined that abbey as a monk; it is, however, doubtful that he was ever a member of that community.

He was ordained and in 919 was allowed to found a monastery at Brogne; after running the community for some time he retired to a nearby cell to ensure the seclusion he desired for prayer. Some time later, however, he was asked to reform the abbey of Saint-Ghislain, near Mons, which he did by restoring discipline and introducing the Rule of St Benedict. Gerard was then asked to reform all the monastic houses in the lands of the count of Flanders, as well as some in Normandy, a task which occupied him for about twenty years. Some of the monks who objected to his reforms went to England, where they were welcomed by King Edmund and allowed to live in the abbey at Bath. His reforms were slow and in several cases of short duration. It may be that he was not forward-looking enough, preferring to rely on models from the past, especially the ancient eremitical tradition, instead of creating something new to suit his age; it may be that he failed to get the support of lay patrons and local bishops for what he was doing. It is to his credit that he did not allow himself to be discouraged in what was by any reckoning a huge undertaking and that he continued to live a very austere life which would be, he hoped, an example to his brethren.

After making a general visitation of all the monasteries he had reformed, Gerard retired to his cell at Brogne, where he died on 3 October 959. The abbey quickly became a place of pilgrimage and was renamed Saint Gerard. His feast is celebrated in the dioceses of Namur, Ghent, and Liège. Relics, considered authentic, are venerated at Saint-Gérard, nearby Maredsous, and Ghent.

AA.SS., Oct., 2, pp.220-320, gives a Life written about one hundred years after Gerard's death, of no historical value; *Anal.Boll.* 3 (1884), pp. 29-57, and 5 (1887), pp. 385-95; *D.H.G.E.*, 10, 829-32; *Bibl.SS.*, 6 , 178-80; a major conference was held at Maredsous in 1959, with papers published in *Rev.Ben.* 70 (1960), pp. 5-240.

ST FRANCIS OF ASSISI
Silver cross, red marks of stigmata, on brown field.

4

ST FRANCIS OF ASSISI, *Founder* (1182-1226)

Francis was born in Assisi in Umbria in the early months of 1182. His father was Pietro di Bernardone, a well-to-do merchant, and his mother was Giovanna, nick-named "Pica." Both parents were Italian and probably citizens of Assisi; attempts to make Giovanna a native of Piccardy or Provence seem to have no historical justification, and "Pica" probably means "odd" or "unusual"; she chose to give birth to her first-born in a makeshift manger on the ground floor of the house in deliberate imitation of the birth of Christ. She had her baby christened Giovanni in honour of John the Baptist, but when his father returned from France where he had been on business, he added the unusual name Francesco, to mark his own love of France. As Francis grew up he learned some French and Provençal from his father and, perhaps from the same source, got to know the courtly and troubadour stories and songs of the day. He also learned his father's trade and became a skillful buyer and seller of cloth, but he seems to have been more interested in spending than in making money. As his earliest biographer, Thomas of Celano, put it, he was a "cautious businessman but a very showy spender." He led the life of a wealthy young man about town, keen to excel and be accepted as the leader of his friends but noted also for his generosity to the poor and sensitivity to the feelings of other people.

When Francis was twenty, Assisi became involved in a war with neighbouring Perugia, and Francis joined the town's army, no doubt hoping for adventure and some glory. But the army was defeated and he was taken prisoner; after a year in prison he was released, only to be struck down by a serious illness which lasted for about another year. He seems to have undergone some change of heart during this long period of inactivity, but he still saw himself as a soldier and volunteered to fight in southern Italy in support of the papal army. He fitted himself out with the best armour and horses but stopped when he got to Spoleto, where he had a dream in which a voice invited him to "follow the master rather than the man." Taking heed of this obscure message, he returned to Assisi, gave up his former way of life, and began to meditate and pray a great deal. He was later to date his conversion from this period and in particular from when he met a leper while out riding; at first he was put off and backed away from the man, but then he dismounted and gave him some money, kissing his hand as he did so. Francis referred to this incident as the occasion when he "left the world." After this he visited the leper houses and the hospitals frequently, giving money and clothes to help the poor and the sick.

In the autumn of 1205, while he was praying one day in the church of San Damiano outside Assisi, he seemed to hear a voice from the crucifix say to him three times, "Francis, go and repair my church, which as you can see is in ruins." He took this literally and sold some of his father's cloth to raise the money. His father had already tried to get him to change his way of life and return to the family business; this action by Francis brought the issue to a head, and Bernardone took his son to the bishop's court to have the money paid back, threatening to disinherit Francis as well. The bishop urged Francis to pay back the money, as it belonged in law to his father; Francis did so, renounced his inheritance, and also took off his clothes and gave those back as well. A labourer's smock was found for him to wear, and this public renunciation of his inheritance and of the world marked his conversion to a life of poverty and dedication of himself to God. He spent the next two years living as a solitary, dividing his time between prayer, helping the poor and sick, wandering about the town to beg alms, and working manually to rebuild three ruined churches— St Damian's, St Peter's, and St Mary of the Angels, or Portiuncula. It was while he was hearing Mass in this last church, sometime in 1208, that he understood what his vocation should be. The Gospel reading was Matthew 10:7-19, the sending out of the disciples to preach the gospel, and the command that they should take no possessions with them, no money, not even shoes or a staff. Francis followed the words literally. He gave away his shoes, tunic, and staff, and wore only the simple tunic and hood of the local shepherds, which he tied round his waist with a cord.

He began straightaway to preach in the streets of Assisi, a simple message of repentance and peace based on his obvious concern for the salvation of souls. The impact was immediate, and within a few weeks he had been joined by a dozen or so disciples; among these were Bernardo da Quintavalle, a well-to-do merchant, Pietro Cattani, a lawyer and canon of the cathedral, and the future Brother Giles. The group became known as the Penitentiaries of Assisi; Francis preferred the name *frati minores*, or "lesser brothers," as it was more humble: hence their later official name of Friars Minor. They lived together in a tumbledown cottage outside the town, where Francis instructed them in the ideals of the religious life and drew up a simple set of rules based on the evangelical counsels of perfection. He took this Rule to Rome to get official recognition, and in 1210 Innocent III gave it verbal approval, at the same time investing the members of the group with the clerical tonsure and authorizing them to preach their message of repentance wherever there was a need.

Francis was ordained deacon about this time but out of humility and the high regard in which he held the priesthood did not proceed any further in Holy Orders. Back in Assisi they were given the chapel of the Portiuncula as their headquarters, but Francis, with his strict views on poverty and the holding of possessions, refused to accept its ownership and insisted on paying a yearly rent in kind for it. Religious poverty for Francis meant more than the traditonal non-owning of goods by individual monks; there had to be corporate poverty as well, so that the Order and its houses owned nothing. This poverty was reflected in the places where the early friars lived. As his first biographer put it, "He taught his brothers to make poor dwellings, of wood, not of stone, and to erect small 'places' according to a humble plan. Often, indeed, speaking of poverty, he would propose . . . this saying of the gospel: The foxes have dens and the birds of the air have nests, but the Son of Man has nowhere to lay his head."

The years 1209-24 were years of intense activity for Francis and the new Order. They travelled throughout Italy as itinerant preachers, drawing huge crowds and impressing people with their austere way of life and simple call to conversion; miracles were reported wherever Francis himself went. The number of those wishing to join the friars grew very quickly, and Francis had to spend time re-organizing and legislating for what was becoming a major body, something which he had not intended. The friars were divided into provinces, with a minister in charge of each one, and annual general chapters were held from 1217 to ensure the Rule was being properly observed. In 1212 Francis founded a second Order in cooperation with St Clare (11 Aug.); she received the religious habit from him at the Portiuncula and by 1215 had become abbess of a new house of "Poor Ladies of St Damian," or Poor Clares, as they became known. They followed an extremely strict way of life in enclosed communities, interpreting Francis' ideals of poverty and simplicity as rigorously as possible.

To be appreciated properly, Francis' activity needs to be judged in the context of its time. The late twelfth and early thirteenth centuries were a time of crisis for the Church, and concerned observers deplored the decline of standards and practice in the religious life throughout Europe; towns were growing and presenting particular problems to a Church that was largely rural in its pastoral mission; heresy was rife among groups who were sincerely trying for reform; and the first signs of alternative religious practice outside the control of church authorities were appearing. To some extent Francis' preaching and ideals met with a ready response because they were seen to answer an obvious need for reform and because a return to a simpler and purer form of religion had already been called for. But Francis (and his contemporary, St Dominic [8 Aug.], who was establishing his own Order of friars at the same time), did much more than just develop a movement already in being. His contribution was that of "one of the great originals of history, who opened windows on unfamiliar prospects in the world around, in the mind of men, in the gospel message and in the personal religion of multitudes of Christians" (Knowles). In the older Orders of monks and canons the primary concern was the spiritual advance of the individual through a life of liturgical and monastic observance, usually in a setting deliberately chosen for its remoteness from the bustle of the world; the new friars, on the other hand, were a dynamic force directly involved in the needs of that world. "The new warmth of devotional life, the preaching, the confessing and the daily counsel of the friars gave a new strength to the lower levels of Christian society" (Knowles), and despite Francis' reservations about theologians and book-learning, they played a major part in the flowering of university life and the revival of theology in the thirteenth century.

Given Francis' concern to spread the gospel message of repentance and bring people to a knowledge of Christ "our brother who laid down his life for his sheep," it is not surprising that he turned his mind to missionary work outside Europe, and especially to those lands where Islam, the traditional enemy of Christianity, had control. He set out for Palestine in 1212 but ended up shipwrecked in Dalmatia; in 1214 he set out for Morocco but was taken ill in Spain and had to return. In 1219 he sailed for Egypt and landed at Damietta on the Nile Delta, which an army of Crusaders was beseiging; he thought the Christian soldiers as much in need of repentance as the Muslims but had little success with them and less with the Sultan, by whom, however, he was received courteously and allowed to preach. He visited Palestine before returning to Italy. His friars continued and developed this missionary activity. The first Franciscan martyrs died in Morocco in 1227 (see St Daniel, 10 Oct.), and by the middle of the century they were being sent to Mongolia and China, where they established a flourishing Christian community which lasted for more than a century.

In 1221 Francis completed the foundation of the Franciscan family by establishing the Third Order of Penitents, or Franciscan tertiaries. This allowed men and women who wished to follow the Franciscan spiritual ideal in the world to do so; they could either continue to live at home or become members of communities as "regular tertiaries." Those who live in the world still undergo a novitiate and are clothed in the habit of the Order, though this is not worn in public; a small scapular worn under the clothes takes its place. They recite a liturgical office or other prayers and are bound by a solemn promise instead of vows. The Third Orders (there was a Dominican one as well) met the need many laypeople were experiencing at the time for a deeper, more personal spiritual life than seemed available within the formal structures of the Church and encouraged them to play an active role in works of charity.

Francis had not intended to found a new Order and was probably surprised at the rapid growth in the numbers of his friars—there were about five thousand of them by 1220. He is reported as saying, "Would that there were fewer Friars Minor, and that the world should so rarely see one as to wonder at their fewness!" As we have seen, he was faced with having to organize them into provinces, and it was not long before the problems of rapid expansion brought other, more fundamental problems for him to deal with, which caused dissensions and, ultimately, bitter divisions among his followers. The original simple Rule was no longer enough by itself to guide those friars who did not have Francis by their side; there was no novitiate to test the quality of entrants; their cardinal protector in Rome wanted to make some of them into bishops to spread the reform more effectively, and most seriously of all for Francis, there were differences over the interpretation of his insistence on absolute poverty, so that he had to upbraid in the severest terms the friars at Bologna, who were living in a proper stone house and planning to open a school in connection with the university. Some historians have seen the dead hand of Roman officialdom behind all this, wanting to curb the excesses of Francis' early enthusiasm and ensure proper control of the wandering friars, but there is no evidence to support this view. Once Francis had drawn up a new Rule and this had been approved in 1223 by Pope Honorius III, it was accepted by all sides and settled the arguments for the time being. It contained some compromises which Francis made reluctantly, and it welded the friars into an intimate union with the Church, which caused no problems for Francis, who was completely devoted to the institutional Church as the continuation of Christ's presence on earth. Francis had already resigned from the office of minister general of the Order at the general chapter of 1220, handing over its running to Brother Elias of Cortona.

Francis spent the Christmas of 1223 at a place named Grecchio, where he decided, in his own words, "to make a memorial of that Child who was born in Bethlehem and in some sort behold with bodily eyes the hardships of his infant state, lying on hay in a manger with the ox and the ass standing by." So he made a crib; he was probably not the first to do so, but his use of it is thought to have made it popular. He remained for some months at Grecchio in semi-retirement, giving his time to prayer and contemplation; his secretary and confessor, Brother Leo, reported on the physical signs that accompanied his meditations, especially the ecstasies and levitations that Francis always tried to keep secret. In August 1224 he moved to La Verna, an isolated place high in the mountains to the north of Arezzo, where he made a simple cell for himself. It was there while in ecstasy that he received the stigmata, or marks of the wounds of Christ's passion on his hands, feet, and side; these were visible lesions which bled at times and were painful. This is the first recorded case of a phenomenon that became more common as devotion to the physical sufferings of Christ increased in popularity. While Francis did all he could to keep them hidden, covering his hands with his habit and even wearing shoes and stockings, it was inevitable that they became known; their existence is well documented, and we have several detailed descriptions of them. For Francis the stigmata marked the closest possible symbolic configuration of himself with his suffering Lord, so often the focus of his meditation and contemplation.

For the remaining two years of his life Francis experienced acute physical suffering; he was going blind with a painful eye infection and had a chronic stomach complaint. Attempts to ease the pain in his eyes through primitive surgery and cauterization only made things worse. He paid a final visit to St Clare at San Damiano and while there composed his famous *Canticle of the Sun,* in which he praises God for giving us all the things we need for living and which people so often forget to thank God for. He improvized a tune for the *Canticle* so that it could be sung by the friars in troubadour fashion, to instruct the people. Just a few days before he died he added some verses thanking God "for our Sister, Bodily Death." After a particularly severe attack of stomach trouble, the friars who were with him in Siena thought he was about to die and asked him for a final message; he dictated a brief statement urging them to love one another, to love and observe "the Lady Poverty," and to love and honour the clergy of the Church. He recovered a little and was taken back to Assisi, where he dictated his *Testament,* in which he retold the story of his conversion and exhorted the friars to observe the Rule faithfully. In the circumstances it could not be a carefully prepared and structured document, but it contains the essentials of Francis' thought and may reflect his continued anxiety about how his original ideal was being watered down in the interests of a more practicable realism. He stresses that the churches and houses of the brethren must reflect their promise of poverty, and they must live in them as pilgrims and visitors, not owners; they must not seek any privileges for the Order from Rome; they must obey completely the minister general and the local guardians and be faithful to the official teaching of the Church; above all, they must follow Christ in his redeeming passion and in the Eucharist, which for Francis was the continuation of the Incarnation.

Toward the end of September 1226 Francis was taken to the Portiuncula, as he had requested. He sent a last message to St Clare and her nuns and asked the friars to sing the verse about "Sister Death" from his *Canticle*. He called for bread, broke it, and gave a piece to each of those who were present as a sign of mutual peace, saying, "I have done my part; may Christ teach you to do yours." He was laid out on the ground and covered with an old habit; the Passion of Our Lord from the Gospel of St John was read aloud, and Francis died about seven o'clock in the evening of 3 October. He had asked to be buried in the criminals' cemetery, but his body was taken instead to the church of San Giorgio in Assisi; in 1230 it was reburied in the new basilica built by order of Brother Elias. The fact that he was canonized so quickly, in 1228, only two years after his death, witnesses to the impact he had made and the way he had captured the religious imagination of the time through his simple approach to the essentials of Christianity. He has been hailed as "the one saint whom all succeeding generations have agreed in canonizing."

There are so many attractive traits in Francis that there is a danger of choosing the one that appeals most to us in the late twentieth century and neglecting other, perhaps less attractive characteristics. Francis has been praised for his stress on poverty and his practical concern for the poor, for his brushing aside of learned theologians to get to the heart of the gospel, for his humility and self-effacement, for his love of animals and obvious empathy with the natural world—he has even been hailed as the first environmentalist. He has appealed to some because he preached peace and tried to bring about reconciliation, to others because he placed so much importance on the humanity of Jesus and gave us the crib. The previous edition of this work said, "Religious and social cranks of all sorts have appealed to him for justification, and he has completely won the hearts of the sentimental." That is a harsh judgment, but it does have to be remembered that Francis is a saint because he single-mindedly followed the gospel and because he struggled with the needs of the twelfth-century Church and society; because he is a saint, he should challenge us to change our lives and make us not feel too comfortable in our beliefs and attitudes.

For all that he was lovable, Francis must also have been somewhat terrifying in the sense that all fanatics are terrifying. His was a life guided by a single vision, to become as like Christ as was humanly possible; every word of Christ had to be obeyed, every action tested to see if it conformed to his will. As Pius XII said in 1962, Francis succeeded so well in this quest that he can truly be called an *"alter Christus"* ("a second Christ"). That Christ was so much the focus and centre of his spiritual life is obvious from Francis' devotion to the passion, his reverence for the humanity of Christ in the crib, his obedience to the Church as the official keeper of Christ's word, and his adoration of the Eucharist because it continued Christ's presence on earth. In one of his *Admonitions* to the friars he wrote, "Every day Jesus humbles himself just as he did when he came from his heavenly throne into the Virgin's womb; every day he comes to us and lets us see him in abjection, when he descends from the bosom of the Father into the hands of the priest at the altar. He shows himself to us in this sacred bread just as he once appeared to his apostles in real flesh" (quoted in Moorman).

It was because of the Eucharist that Francis had such a high opinion of the priesthood. One might have expected him, as a reformer, to be severe toward those whose priestly lives gave scandal or failed to reach an acceptable level of dedication. But there are enough examples related of his attitude in such cases to show that his reverence for the office always overcame any possible condemnation of the individual. When confronted with a priest who was living in concubinage, and asked what should be done with the offender, Francis replied, "Whether you are a sinner I do not know, but what I do know is that your hands can touch the Word of God"; he then knelt and kissed the priest's hands. Thomas of Celano recounts how Francis often said, "If it happened that I met a saint who had come from heaven and a poor priest, I would salute the priest first of all and kiss his hands. I would say, 'Oh dear, St Laurence, wait a bit, because his (the priest's) hands can touch the Word of life and possess a superhuman power'" (quoted in Sicari).

The other direct way in which Francis felt he was in touch with Christ was through the scriptures, because they related his words and commands and told us about his life. Francis had never studied the scriptures in any formal sense, but his feeling for them and his ability to quote from them show how deeply he must have both studied and prayed over them. In the six letters of his that we have there are fifteen Old Testament and thirty-eight New Testament quotations, but his reverence went beyond this: he venerated the writings themselves, urging his friars "wherever they found the divine words written down to venerate them as much as possible . . . and look after them carefully, honouring in the words the Lord who had spoken them." There were other groups and movements at the time that sought to live according to the gospel, but outside or at least independently of the Church. This could never be the case for Francis, because he believed the Church was a continuation of Christ's incarnation, another manifestation of the Saviour who had died for us: there could not be any division between the Christ accessible to us in the scriptures and the Christ accessible to us through the Church. Francis' spirituality was thus sacramental, scriptural, and ecclesial.

Christ was for Francis the way to the Father. There is in all his writings a profound veneration for the power of God, for the divine Providence which cares for creation, and for the Father as the source of all goodness. His favourite invocation was "My God and my all!" and a paragraph from his draft of the Rule in 1221 sums up his attitude: "With all our hearts and all our souls, all our minds and all our strength, all our power and all our understanding, with every faculty and every effort, with every affection and all our emotions, with every wish and desire, we should love our Lord and God who has given and gives us everything, body and soul and all our life. It was he who created and redeemed us, and of his mercy alone he will save us; wretched and pitiable as we are, ungrateful and evil, rotten through and through, he has provided us with every good and does not cease to provide for us . . . we must love, honour, adore, serve, praise and bless, glory and acclaim, magnify and thank, the most high, supreme and eternal God, Three and One . . . [who] is sublime, most high, kind, lovable, delightful and utterly desirable beyond all else, for ever and ever" (quoted in Moorman). It is important to grasp the power that even the name of God possessed for Francis and his desire to praise God in everything he did. While Christ was the principal manifestation of the Father's love, there was another one, and that was the created world. This brings us to another facet of Francis' outlook, his concern for and empathy with the whole of creation, animate and inanimate. It is the facet that endears him to many modern people, and there is no doubt that it struck his contemporaries as being out of the ordinary even in an age when people were much closer to the natural world. It must, however, be seen in the whole context of Francis' spirituality.

As John Moorman has pointed out in his perceptive study, Francis certainly preached to the birds on a number of occasions, but this was far less important than preaching to people to save them from sin. He rescued lambs from slaughter, but it was more important to him to save lepers from rotting to death unloved and uncared for. He tamed the wolf at Gubbio, but he was much more concerned with taming the quarrelsome inhabitants of the warring cities through which he passed. Francis loved and cared for the natural world for two basic reasons: it was the work of the Creator and therefore good in itself, and it carried reminders of that Creator and of Christ. To have venerated anything in the created world without directly linking it with the worship of God would have been for Francis the greatest blasphemy. And so his famous *Canticle of the Sun* calls on us to praise God who has given us what we need to live: sun, moon, wind, water, fire, and earth, and that is why it begins, "Most high, omnipotent, good Lord, all praise, glory, honour and blessing are yours; to you alone, Most High, do they belong, and no one is worthy to pronounce your name."

As has just been said, the created world was, in Francis' thinking, good in itself. This was a useful corrective to those heretical movements of his time that were tinged with a certain Manicheism and believed that the material world was evil, the work of the devil, and that Christ therefore had not had a physical body and so could not have suffered and died. As well as being good in itself, the created world reminded Francis of Christ in ways that may sound exaggerated to us: he saved a worm from being trodden on because scripture had applied to Christ the words, "I am a worm and no man"; he objected when a tree was being cut down because Christ was a branch of the tree of Jesse; when he saw a lamb being killed he immediately thought of the death of the Lamb of God; a rock reminded him of Christ the cornerstone. Was this what Francis had in mind when he said, "We are all blind and the Lord opens our eyes by means of his creatures," or when he exclaimed, "Every creature proclaims 'God made me for your sake, O man'"?

Francis was totally dedicated to poverty and humility; the four other virtues he espoused and urged on his friars were wisdom (he called it "the queen of virtues"), simplicity, charity (he called this the "holy mistress"), and obedience. The love of his friars for God, for people, and among themselves, he believed, must be greater than the love of a mother for her child. Obedience must be blind, "as of a corpse," without a will of its own and exercised toward every superior and the Rule; it would "put to shame all natural and selfish desires, and mortify our lower nature to make it obey the spirit and our fellow human beings." Obedience was the way the friars would become available to seek and do only the will of God. One might, perhaps, add a seventh virtue—joy. On one level this was straightforward enough: "Always do your best," he advised, "to be cheerful when you are with me and the other brethren; it is not right for a servant of God to show a sad or gloomy face to his brother or to anyone else." On another level this joy was far removed from jollity and external happiness. Francis himself was always far more likely to be found crying than laughing, yet the inner joy was always there, the joy that conquers weariness and sickness, that overcomes the mockery and hostility of others and betrayal by friends (Moorman).

There was a close link between these virtues and Francis' attitude to learning. He had had little formal education himself, and his view of it was somewhat ambiguous, which has led later writers to differ substantially on the issue. In no sense did he despise learning, but he feared it for his followers: it was good if they studied, especially the scriptures, to improve themselves ("to preach to themselves rather than to speak learnedly to others"), but study could easily feed vanity and destroy charity and devotion. But above all, he feared Lady Learning as a rival to Lady Poverty, for she would lead his friars to want libraries and schools—as of course happened as they joined in the theological revival in the universities, an apostolate of immense value at the time. Francis did not include study among the useful work his friars might engage in, though it could be seen to be in the Rule implicitly; but he received many learned people into the Order and approved of their continuing their theological studies, and he praised theologians in general, as they could explain the scriptures to the people. Before the end of his life, and despite his earlier condemnation, he approved the establishment of a theological school in Bologna, with St Antony of Padua (13 June) as its first lecturer.

Francis' own writings number about twenty and may be divided into four categories: legislative texts such as the *Rules* of 1209 and 1223; admonitions and other pieces written to the friars, such as the *Testament* of 1226; his letters, of which six are certainly authentic and which comprise three addressed to "all the faithful" or "all the clergy," one to Brother Leo, one to St Antony of Padua on his appointment as lecturer, and one to Brother Elias the minister general; the authenticity of other letters is disputed. The fourth category comprises various hymns, prayers and liturgical compositions, including the *Canticle of the Sun* (the only piece written in the Umbrian vernacular), an office of the passion of Our Lord, the *Laudes Dei* (Praises of God) to be recited before the divine office, and the two salutations, "In Praise of the Virtues" and "In Praise of Our Lady." The popular "Prayer of St Francis" ("Lord, make me an instrument of thy peace") is a modern compilation with no direct connection with the saint. There exist three genuine fragments in Francis' own hand.

Two quotations from these writings may be used in conclusion. From the *Rule*: "In that love which is God, I entreat all my friars, ministers and subjects, to put away every attachment, all care and solicitude, and serve, love, honour and adore our Lord and God with a pure heart and mind. This is what he seeks above all else. We should make a dwelling-place within ourselves where he can stay, he who is the Lord God Almighty, Father, Son and Holy Spirit." And from Francis' *Testament*: "We adore you, Lord Jesus Christ, here and in all your churches throughout the world, and we bless you, for by your holy cross you have redeemed the world."

The literature associated with the life of St Francis is so vast and ever-increasing that no more than a brief indication can be given here. There are problems of interpretation and chronology in dealing with the principal sources, especially in fixing the exact order of events connected with Francis' conversion. The key early biographical writings are Thomas of Celano's *Vita prima* (1228-9); his *Vita secunda* (1246-7), which added material from the saint's three intimate companions and other friars; his brief *Legends of St Francis for Use in Choir* (1230) and his *Tractatus de miraculis S. Francisci* (or Celano III), written *c.* 1250; Giuliano da Spira's *Vita s. F.* (1232-5); and St Bonaventure's *Legenda Major s. F.* (1261-2). See *AA.SS.*, Oct., 2, pp. 545-1004; R. Brown and M. A. Habig, *St Francis of Assisi: Writings and Early Biographies*. For the *Little Flowers of St Francis*, see the Everyman Edition (1975). For full bibliographies, see *O.D.C.C.*, pp. 530-1; *Bibl.SS.*, 5, 1052-1150; *Dict.Sp.*, 5, 1271-1303. The following have been selected from the multitude of modern Lives and studies: John R. H. Moorman, *Richest of Poor Men: The Spirituality of St Francis of Assisi* (1977); R. Manselli, *San Francesco* (1980); J. Lortz, *The Incomparable Saint* (1986); R. D. Sorrell, *St Francis of Assisi and Nature* (1988); E. Atanassiu *et al.*, *Saint François et ses Frères* (1991); G. Miccoli, *Francesco d'Assisi* (1991); A. Sicari, *Nuovi ritratti di santi* (1992), pp. 25-33. On the general historical context, see D. Knowles and D. Obolensky, *The Christian Centuries, 2 : The Middle Ages* (1969). One can only agree with the previous edition of this work when it said, "It is hard to keep pace with Franciscan literature."

It is equally difficult to deal with the iconography of St Francis; every generation has sought to portray and interpret him, from the earliest portrait by Cimabue of an intense, ascetic but human figure, to Giotto's frescoes of Francis preaching to the birds, to sixteenth- and seventeenth-century idealized and romanticized portraits by such as Murillo, and El Greco's elongated ascetic holding a skull. The entry in *Bibl.SS.* mentioned above is well illustrated; see also E. Atanassiu, above.

St Ammon (*c. 350*)

Ammon, or Amoun, was one of the most famous of the monks who lived in the Egyptian region of Nitria. As a young man he had been forced to marry by his wealthy relatives, but he and his wife were inspired by St Paul's praise of virginity to live celibate lives. After eighteen years, on the death of his relatives, he retired to the desert to live as a hermit, a way of life for which he had been preparing himself for many years; meanwhile his wife used their house as a centre for a number of religious women. They continued to meet twice a year.

Nitria (the modern Wadi Natroun) is about seventy miles south-east of Alexandria, and at the time when Ammon went there it was an extremely unhealthy and unpleasant place. A number of hermits lived there in separate cells, seeking holiness through an extreme asceticism and each following his own inclinations. At the suggestion of St Antony (17 Jan.), Ammon established a new centre for those who wished to live in greater solitude; this was about eleven miles south of Nitria at the entrance to the Libyan desert and became known as the Kellia. The monks lived in cells scattered about the area and came together on Saturdays and Sundays to celebrate the liturgy and take a meal in common. There was a priest-monk who officiated at the liturgy: he exercised some sort of authority over the hermits and was assisted by a council of the more senior monks. As well as this overall, rather loose, organization, groups of monks formed themselves into brotherhoods or fraternities. According to Palladius, nearly six hundred monks were living in the Kellia by the year 400. While it would be inaccurate to call this a monastery in the later Western sense, it was, perhaps, the beginning of groups of holy people living according to a commonly accepted rule.

Ammon himself was famous for his austerity in a world where austerity was the order of the day. It was said that he lived almost entirely on bread and water and even then ate only every few days. In advising his disciples about prayer he said, "It is indeed essential for a man to take up the struggle against his thoughts if the veils woven from his thoughts and covering up his intellect are to be removed, thus enabling him to turn his gaze without difficulty toward God and to avoid following the will of his wandering thoughts." He is reported to have worked many miracles before his death at the age of sixty-two about the year 350. St Antony, then living a long way away, was said to have had a vision of Ammon's soul ascending to heaven. Ammon is mentioned in St Athanasius' Life of St Antony, and his feast is celebrated in the Greek church; he is not mentioned in the Roman Martyrology.

Most of our information comes from Palladius' *Lausiac History*, vol.1, pp. 35-8, vol. 2, pp. 26-9; see also, *Historia Monachorum*, ch. 29; *AA.SS.*, Oct., 11, pp. 413-21; B. Ward, *The Sayings of the Desert Fathers* (1975). *The Coptic Encyclopedia*, 5 (1991), pp. 1397-1409, has an excellent account of the Kellia based on recent archaeology.

St Petronius of Bologna, *Bishop* (*c.* 445)

Petronius may have been the son of a Roman army officer in Gaul at the beginning of the fifth century and may have held an important civil office before entering the service of the Church in Italy. A twelfth-century *Life* says that he went to Palestine to collect relics of early Christianity, but this seems to be doubtful. He became bishop of Bologna about the year 432 and devoted his time to repairing the churches that had been ruined by the Goths during their invasion. He had a very high reputation among his contemporaries; the bishop of Lyons put him on the same level as SS Ambrose (7 Dec.), Hilary of Arles (5 May), and Paulinus of Nola (22 June).

He is said to have built a large monastery outside the city to the east and dedicated it to St Stephen. He put the knowledge he had gained in Palestine to good use by incorporating in its plan several features of the Holy Places. He made this church of St Stephen his cathedral, and in the Middle Ages it became a place of pilgrimage for those who could not get to the Holy Land itself. The relics of St Petronius were discovered in the early twelfth century, and a *Life* of the saint was written "in which fables and nonsense make up for a lack of precise information" (former edition of this work). Both the discovery and the *Life*, however, caused a flowering of his cult outside the monastery, and he became the patron of Bologna: it was felt that the restorer of the city after the devastations of the Gothic invaders would be an effective defender of it in the wars with the emperor Frederick Barbarossa.

The *Nuova Gerusalemme* (*New Jerusalem*) of Bologna still exists, though it has been greatly modified over the centuries. The present church of St Petronius is a gothic building begun in 1390. A reliquary said to contain the head of the saint was deposited here in the early eighteenth century. The saint is usually portrayed holding the city of Bologna in his hand; there is a statue of him by Michelangelo in the church of St Dominic in Bologna.

AA.SS., Oct., 2, pp. 422-70, gives the historically worthless *Life*; an Italian translation with other documents was edited by M. Corti (1962); *Anal.Boll.* 27 (1908), pp. 104-6; *D.H.G.E.*, 9, 651-2, 655; *N.C.E.*, 2 (1967), pp. 649-51; *Bibl.SS.*, 10, 521-32; *O.D.C.C.*, pp. 1076-7.

5

St Apollinaris of Valence, *Bishop* (*c.* 520)

Apollinaris was the elder of the two sons of Hesychius, bishop of Vienne in France, the younger being St Avitus (5 Feb.), who succeeded his father as bishop. Apollinaris was born about the year 453, educated under St Mamertus (11 May), and consecrated by his brother Avitus as bishop of Valence. The diocese had been neglected for some years and was in need of substantial reform, which the new bishop attempted to introduce. He fell foul of the king, however, when a synod condemned an official of the court for an incestuous marriage, and Apollinaris had to go into exile in Sardinia. The king is said to have repented of his actions when he was cured from a serious illness by the laying on of the exiled bishop's cloak.

Some letters between Apollinaris and his brother Avitus are extant. In one of these Apollinaris reproves himself for not having observed the anniversary of his sister's death; in another Avitus hopes that the occasion of the dedication of a church will not be the excuse for too much revelry. Apollinaris is said to have been forewarned of his death and to have made a journey to visit his friend St Caesarius of Arles (27 Aug.), a journey marked by many miracles; it is doubtful, however, if the journey took place. He died at Valence about the year 520 and is venerated as the principal patron of the diocese under the local name of St Aplonay. His relics were enshrined there in 1060 but were destroyed at the time of the Reformation.

AA.SS., Oct., 3, pp. 45-65, gives what is said to be a contemporary Life but is almost certainly much later; B. Krusch, *M.G.H.*, *Scriptores rerum merov.*, 3, pp. 194-203; *D.H.G.E.*, 3, 982-6; *Catholicisme*, 1, 704; *Bibl.SS.*, 2, 249-50.

St Galla (*c.* 550)

Among those executed by Theodoric the Goth was Quintus Aurelius Symmachus, a Roman patrician who had been consul in 485. He left three daughters, Rusticiana, the wife of the philosopher Boethius, Proba, and Galla, who is mentioned in the Roman Martyrology under 5 October. St Gregory the Great (3 Sept.) gives a short account of her life in his *Dialogues*. She was left a widow after a year of marriage, and instead of remarrying as her family urged, devoted herself to God and the relief of the poor, living in a community of consecrated women near St Peter's "in simplicity of heart, dedicated to prayer and giving many alms to the poor."

After many years she contracted cancer of the breast. St Peter appeared to her in a vision and after assuring her that her sins were forgiven foretold her imminent death, which occurred three days later. The death of her friend, Benedicta, was also foretold as following in thirty days, and this also happened. St Gregory, writing about fifty years later, said, "the nuns now in that monastery, receiving them by tradition from their predecessors, can tell every little detail as though they had been present when the miracle happened."

The letter of St Fulgentius of Ruspe (1 Jan.) on widowhood is said to have been written to Galla. Her relics are claimed by the Roman church of Santa Maria in Portico. A hospital in her name was opened in the seventeenth century. It is likely that the church known as San Salvatore de Gallia in Rome commemorates this saint, as when the French moved their hospice close to this church the original Galla was changed to Gallia by mistake.

AA.SS., Oct., 3, pp. 147-63; *Bibl.SS.*, 6, 8-9; letter of St Fulgentius in *P.L.*, 65, 311; G. B. Proja, "S. Galla patrizia romana," *Rivista storica benedettina* (1954).

St Magenulf (c. 857)

Magenulf, or Meinulf, was born in Westphalia in Germany of a noble family. The death of his father forced his mother to flee to the court of the emperor Charlemagne for protection, and Magenulf was adopted by the emperor as his godchild and sent for his eduaction to the cathedral school at Paderborn. He heard a sermon on the text, "The foxes have holes and the birds of the air nests, but the Son of Man has nowhere to lay his head," and decided to become a priest. When he had received minor orders he was presented to a canonry in Paderborn; his ordination as a deacon was followed by promotion to the office of archdeacon.

He wanted to use his wealth to establish a monastery for women on his estates. Like St Eustace (2 Nov.) and St Hubert (3 Nov.) he had a vision of a stag with a cross between its antlers, and this decided where the foundation should be, at Bodeken. The nuns for it initially came from Aachen, and Magenulf drew up a Rule of life for them. The monastery became a base for his preaching throughout Westphalia, and he is venerated as one of the region's principal apostles. He died at Bodeken about the year 857. He was remembered for his humility and generosity; miracles were reported to have taken place at his tomb, and his cult was established in the region. A Life of the saint was written about forty years after his death on the occasion of the exhumation of his remains for veneration.

AA.SS., Oct., 3, pp. 171-225, gives a Life of c. 1035 and one of c. 1410, both based to some extent on the early Life; *Bibl.SS.*, 9, 277-9.

St Flora of Beaulieu (c. 1300-47)

The Sisters of the Order of St John of Jerusalem had a priory at Beaulieu on the road to the famous shrine of Rocamadour in France, which served as a hostel (or hospital, as such hostels were called) for the care of pilgrims. Flora, or Fleur, the daughter of a noble family, entered this priory about 1320, having resisted the attempts of her parents to get her to marry. She suffered severe spiritual trials and was comforted only by regular visions of Our Lord, who persuaded her that these, along with strong temptations against chastity and the bad treatment she was receiving from her religious Sisters, were all part of her sharing in his passion. She underwent many mystical experiences such as ecstasy and levitation and was said to have the gifts of discerning spirits and prophecy. Such was her devotion to the passion of Our Lord that she seemed to be carrying his cross inside her body; this caused her intense pain and led to frequent hemorrhages. She also had a strong devotion to Our Lady, especially to the Annunciation, and to St John the Baptist, the patron of her Order, and she led a life devoted to prayer and to the recitation of the divine office.

On one occasion Flora was so moved by the sufferings of the poor during a famine that she tried to give them the community's bread, against the express wishes of the prioress. When challenged she opened her cloak, and the bread which she had been hiding changed into flowers. Another story tells how an angel brought her a piece of the consecrated host from a church about eight miles away; the priest was distressed about the loss and consulted Flora about what he should do, and she was able to convince him that she had received the missing piece. Little credence should be given to these and other miracles associated with the saint. Our only source is a fifteenth-century Life in very coarse vernacular French and a list of miracles from the same hand. The Life is thought to be a translation of a Latin Life written by the saint's confessor. While it is full of detail, much of it reads like standard hagiography of the time, and its stories are common to several medieval Lives of saints.

Flora died in 1347, perhaps of the hemorrhages already mentioned. Miracles were soon being attributed to her intercession, and her body was translated on 11 June 1360, which became her feast-day. Her aid was invoked against bodily ills and moral problems, and in those western parts of France where her cult was strong, she and St Barbara were called on for protection against violent storms. The local diocesan Breviary changed her feast-day to 5 October in the eighteenth century, and a decree of the Holy See recognized her office in 1852.

AA.SS., June, 2, pp. 36-54, has a late Latin version of the Life; the vernacular French version was edited by C. Brunel, *Anal. Boll.* 64 (1946), pp. 5-49; C. Lacarrière, *Vie de Ste Flore ou Fleur* (1866); *Analecta juris pontificii* 18 (1879), pp. 1-27; J. Amadieu, *Ste Fleur de l'hôpital Beaulieu* (1923); M. Even, *La vie de la chère Ste Fleur* (1943); *Bibl.SS.*, 5, 929-30.

Bd Raymund of Capua (1330-99)

Raymund was born in 1330 in Capua, a town north of Naples. He came from the noble delle Vigne family, and his forebears had been officials in the imperial service. He became a student at the university of Bologna and while there joined the Dominicans. At the age of thirty-seven he was appointed prior of the Minerva in Rome, was later lector at Santa Maria Novella in Florence, and then, in 1374, in Siena. Here he met the great St Catherine (29 Apr.), who attended his Mass and heard a voice saying, "This is my beloved servant; this is he to whom I shall entrust you." He became her spiritual director and at first found her a difficult subject, but as the previous edition of this work puts it, "he was a cautious, deliberate man, and did not allow himself either to be carried away by her vehemence or put off by her unusualness; he did not at once recognize her mission, but he did recognize her goodness." As her confessor he allowed her to receive Communion as often as she wished, and for the last six years of her life, which in many ways were also the most important, he guided and encouraged her.

Their first work together was to care for the people of Siena who were suffering from an outbreak of plague. Raymund himself was taken ill and was thought to be dying; Catherine prayed by his bedside for an hour and a half, and the next day Raymund was completely better. This led him to believe in her miraculous powers and to become totally dedicated to helping her achieve her mission. This lay outside the confines of Siena and involved them in ecclesiastical politics of the highest order. She wanted to launch a new crusade against the Turks in the Holy Land, and so Raymund preached about it at Pisa and personally delivered her famous letter to the English pirate, John Hawkwood, asking him to help the enterprise. Their work for the crusade was interrupted by a revolt of some of the Italian city-states against the pope, who was living in Avignon in France at the time. Catherine and Raymund tried to act as peacemakers and to persuade the pope to return to Rome; it is probable that the importance of their actions has been exaggerated and that they had little practical effect on the parties concerned.

In 1378 the Great Western Schism began, with the election of an antipope, Clement VII, against Urban VI. There was considerable confusion and much lobbying of princes and bishops by the rival factions. Raymund was sent by Urban to preach against Clement in France but was stopped at the frontier and threatened with execution by soldiers loyal to Clement. He returned to Italy, to face stinging rebukes from Catherine for what she claimed to be his faint-heartedness. But he stayed in Genoa, preaching against Clement and studying theology. Catherine died soon afterwards, in 1380, promising that she would be with Raymund in every danger: "If he fails, I will help him up again." He took charge of the group of faithful disciples who had been her companions for some years and worked tirelessly for the rest of his life to achieve what had been her greatest wish, to end the schism in the Church.

Raymund also had other work to do. At the time of Catherine's death he was elected master general of that part of the Dominican Order that supported Pope Urban. He saw it as his duty to restore the fervour of the Order, damaged by the effects of the Black Death and the schism. He thought that the answer lay in concentrating on the monastic side of Dominican life, so he established a number of houses of strict observance in several provinces. These reforms were controversial, and Raymund has been blamed for reducing the importance attached to the studies carried on by the friars outside their houses in universities and elsewhere and for trying to turn the friars into cloistered monks. Yet the reforms were effective in producing many holy friars, and Raymund has been called by some the second founder of the Dominicans. He was also very interested in spreading the Third

Order of St Dominic in as many parts of the world as he could, no doubt influenced here by the example of St Catherine and all that she achieved as a tertiary. After nineteen years as master general, Raymund died on 5 October 1399 at Nuremberg, where he was working for the reform of the German Dominicans. He was beatified in 1899.

He wrote a very influential Life of St Catherine, which has been critized by some modern scholars for exaggerating the saint's influence, and a volume of his other writings and letters, *Opuscula et Litterae*, was published at the time of his beatification. Whatever may be said about particular initiatives he introduced, he was a man of peace, eager to heal divisions and keen to reform and renew the religious life of the Dominican Order.

No early Life of Raymund exists, but a great deal about him can be learned from the sources for St Catherine's Life and biographies of her. His generalship of the Domincans is covered by the *Registrum Litterarum*, edited by Fr Reichert, but this is not complete. See also *Vies des Saints*, 10, pp. 132-7; *Bibl.SS.*, 11, 8-11; Mortier, *Histoire des Maîtres Generaux*, 3 (1907), pp. 491-686.

Bd Bartholomew Longo, *Founder* (1841-1926)

Bartolo Longo was born on 10 February 1841 in Latiano, near Brindisi in Italy. After finishing his secondary schooling he thought about going to the university of Naples to study law, but it was in so much turmoil at the time because of political upheavals that he decided instead to pursue his legal studies privately. He had a very extrovert personality and such a passion for music that in order to get the money for a piano and a flute he lived on a diet of potatoes for a year, damaging his health in the process. He also took up fencing and dancing. In 1863, as a result of the union of Naples with the rest of Italy, his private legal studies were no longer recognized, and he went to the university. There he was gradually won over by the strong anti-clericalism of the staff and took part in demonstrations against the pope and the clergy.

At the same time he was troubled by doubts about the truth of his religious beliefs and became interested in spiritualism. There was a well-developed spiritualist movement in Naples, which organized itself almost as a religious sect, appointing its own priests and imitating some of the rites of the Church. Its adherents claimed frequent communication with the devil, who was said to appear under the guise of the archangel Michael. Bartholomew was saved from the worst excesses of the movement through his friendship with Vincenzo Pepe, a professor from Bartholomew's hometown, who had a strong religious faith and who gradually got him to confide in a holy and learned Dominican friar. Under this dual influence Bartholomew returned to the practice of the faith and became a Dominican tertiary. After graduating in law at the end of 1864 he returned home and began to practise as a solicitor. He lived with his family and became involved in its life of piety and charitable work.

Bartholomew was twice on the point of marrying but eventually gave up the idea, influenced mainly, it seems, by the words of a Redemptorist priest, the Venerable

Emanuele Ribera, who said to him, "The Lord wishes great things from you; you are destined to fulfill a high mission." Bartholomew decided to give up his work as a solicitor, took a vow of lifelong chastity, and thought of returning to Naples to devote himself to a life of good works. He began a close friendship with the Countess Maria Anna De Fusco, which was to determine his whole future, as he became the teacher of her children and the administrator of her properties, at the same time joining in her many and varied charitable activities. Their friendship was so close that it caused considerable unpleasant gossip, which they ignored at first, but then found it was interfering with the work they wished to do. Eventually, after being counselled by Leo XIII to do so, they married in 1885, although they vowed to live together as brother and sister.

The countess had properties in the area around Pompeii which Bartholomew had to visit. In the course of these visits he found out how ignorant the country people were about their religion and began to teach them the catechism and how to say the rosary. He set up a large figure of Our Lady of the Rosary on an altar in the tiny parish church, and a number of miracles were recorded in answer to the prayers of the local people. The shrine soon became famous, and it was felt that a more fitting church was needed. The local bishop encouraged Bartholomew, and in 1876 the foundation stone of a new shrine was laid. This was finished in 1887 and the famous image of Our Lady was placed on a splendid throne and crowned with a precious diadem blessed by the pope, Leo XIII. Bartholomew founded a periodical, *The Rosary and the New Pompeii*, which he used to spread devotion to Our Lady and give accounts of the graces and favours gained at the new shrine; he distributed it to subscribers and non-subscribers alike. He set up a printing press and published a large number of pamphlets and books on the same themes, and he was especially keen to encourage people to say the rosary.

During this time he was still involved in works of charity. He established an orphanage for girls and handed over its running to the Daughters of the Rosary of Pompeii, a religious Congregation he had founded. Not content with this, he set up an "Institute for the Sons of the Imprisoned"; his aim was to help those who were suffering through no fault of their own and also to disprove current theories that criminals were incorrigible and destined to a life of crime because of a natural inherited instinct. He wrote, "Christ is my teacher, my guide, my light. . . . Now Christ took pity on the little children, and said, 'Allow the little children to come to me.' And believe me, when he received them he did not differentiate between those born of criminals and those born criminals; still less did he set out to study their skulls or their faces to find . . . the fatal signs of innate criminality. No; he embraced them all. . . . And that's what I do: when I receive my little children, the sons of the condemned, I don't look at their skulls or faces; I just find out if they are rejected and abandoned innocents, and that's enough for me: I take them to my heart and start to educate them" (Mondrone). He called on the Brothers of the Christian Schools to run the Institute, and they launched very successful educational and vocational programmes. The work was extended in 1922 with the building of a similar school for the daughters of prisoners. Bartholomew's work and ideas in this area won him praise from penal reformers around the world.

In 1893 he presented the pope with the new shrine and the land around it, along with the other works he had undertaken in Pompeii. He remained as administrator, but eventually gave this up at the request of Pope St Pius X (26 Aug.) and retired in 1906. While he had achieved so much, he had also had his trials and had met with opposition: some of this arose from envy at his success, some of it from those who were opposed to the religious influences he was helping to advance. At different times he was accused of being mad, of profiteering, and of lining his own pockets with money given to the shrine and other good causes. He also suffered from ill health for much of his life.

In May 1925 he was made a Knight of the Grand Cross of the Holy Sepulcre. He used the occasion to announce publicly his will: he had no money or property left of his own, he said, but wished to distribute to his various foundations the insignia of the awards and orders he had received, and he asked that he might be buried in the shrine he had established. He died in October 1926, with his rosary beads wound around his fingers and holding a crucifix. He was buried as he had wished, beneath the throne in Our Lady's shrine, and he was beatified in 1980. The prayer approved for use in the liturgy speaks of him as the "Herald of the Blessed Virgin Mary's Rosary, and father of needy children and orphans, a man of wonderful piety and an example of charity."

His New Pompeii comprises orphanages, two hostels for educating the sons and daughters of criminals, a printing house, an observatory, a museum of Mount Vesuvius, a hotel for pilgrims, a very modern House of the Rosary, and a seminary—all in addition to the shrine itself, which attracts hundreds of thousands of pilgrims. Not all of this existed by the time Bartholomew died, but in it one can see the flowering of his vision and energy.

Notitiae, 16 (1980), pp. 576-7; A. L'Arco, *Bartolo Longo* (1966); D. Mondrone, "B. L. Scrittore" in *Civiltà Cattolica*, anno 103, pt. 2 (1952), pp. 490-501; *Bibl.SS.*, 8, 96-9.

ST FAITH (p. 39)
The symbol of the Faith, the Holy Trinity.
Gold emblem with black lettering on blue field.

6

ST BRUNO, *Founder* (*c.* 1035-1101)

Bruno was born in Cologne about the year 1035. He began his studies at Reims and then moved to Tours to study philosophy, where he built up a reputation as a brilliant scholar in all branches of knowledge. He returned to Cologne for his theological studies and obtained a canonry at the cathedral before his ordination about the year 1055. He seemed to be destined for a distinguished academic career when he was appointed director of the famous school at Reims which he had attended as a pupil. He maintained its reputation for about twenty years and taught a number of scholars who were to hold important positions in later life, including Pope Urban II.

This peaceful and successful life was interrupted when he became chancellor of the diocese of Reims. The bishop had obtained his position by simony and led a life that showed how unsuitable he was for the post. Bruno and some other priests denounced him at a council but were forced to leave the city. Despite the intervention of the pope, St Gregory VII (25 May), the bishop was able to maintain his position, and so Bruno went back to Cologne. It seems to have been about this time that he began to think of retiring from the world. There is a Carthusian tradition that this conversion to a life of solitude occurred when Bruno attended the funeral of a famous professor who from his coffin warned the mourners of the dangers of an evil life such as he himself had led. The truth appears to be more ordinary: after a life of public esteem and ecclesiastical preferment, the quarrel with the bishop showed him how insubstantial such achievements were. He was able to return to Reims, and there was talk of choosing him as the next bishop; instead, he resigned his various offices, gave up his wealth, and retired with a few companions to Molesmes to put himself under the direction of St Robert (29 Apr.), the founder of the Cistercians.

Although he and his companions lived in a hermitage away from the main monastery, Bruno believed that their solitude was not severe enough. They applied to a former pupil of his, St Hugh, bishop of Grenoble (1 Apr.), for permission to settle in his diocese, and arrived there about the year 1084. Hugh gave them a remote valley, variously called Cartusia or La Chartreuse, and in 1085 they built an oratory and some small cells there. This was the origin of the great Carthusian Order and its motherhouse, La Grande Chartreuse. Their life was one of solitude and extreme severity: they met together only for Matins and Vespers and, on the great festivals, for their main meal. Some twenty-five years later an abbot of Cluny described their way of life: "Their dress is poorer than that of other monks, so short and thin and rough that the very sight frightens me. They wear hair shirts next their skin and fast almost perpetually; eat only bran-bread; never touch meat, either sick or well; never buy fish, but eat it if given to them as alms. . . . Their constant occupation is praying, reading and manual work, which consists chiefly in transcribing books. They celebrate Mass only on Sundays and festivals." Their inspiration was drawn partly from the ancient monk-hermits of the early Church in places such as Egypt. Bruno had not intended to found a new Order. As with other monastic reformers of the time, he wanted to return to a more ascetic and simpler way of life while taking St Benedict (11 July) as his general model.

Bruno was not left in peace for very long. His former pupil, now Pope Urban II (bd; 31 July), ordered him to Rome to act as his counsellor. Although he was allowed to live in a cell in the ruins of the baths of Diocletian, Bruno was inevitably drawn into public life. The details of his work are not clear, but he was probably engaged in preparing a number of synods to reform the clergy, and in Urban's controversies with the antipope Gilbert of Ravenna. When the pope had to flee from Rome because of Gilbert's active hostility, Bruno accompanied him to Calabria and, after refusing Urban's demands that he should become bishop of Reggio, was able to found a second monastery on the Carthusian model at La Torre in 1094. Five years later the number of his disciples had grown enough to warrant another foundation in southern Italy, dedicated to St Stephen. When he was consulted by the monks at Grande Chartreuse, he wrote them a letter, which is still extant, explaining his ideals and instructing them in the practice of the solitary life, solving their problems and encouraging them to persevere. From another letter we can see clearly the joy he found in his way of life; he had a balanced outlook that scorned anything resembling morbid introspection or harshness in the approach of the solitary monk or nun to religion. He remained the friend and spiritual counsellor of the powerful as well as of his monks; the Norman count Roger was a particularly generous patron.

It is said that before he died Bruno gathered his monks together and made a solemn profession of faith, stressing most strongly his belief in the Trinity and in the Eucharist, perhaps because one of his teachers at Tours had been Berengarius, whose theories on the Eucharist had been condemned by a number of councils. Some doubts remain about the authenticity of this testament. Bruno died at La Torre on 6 October 1101 and was buried at St Stephen's; his body was found to be incorrupt when it was transferred to La Torre in 1513. He was never formally canonized, though a popular cult developed quickly in Calabria; in 1514 Pope Leo X granted the Carthusians a special office in his honour, and in 1623 his feast was extended to the Universal Church. Popular cults in southern Italy and around La Grande Chartreuse reflect a belief in Bruno's power to free people from possession by the devil and, in Calabria, in the curative powers of a small lake near a grotto claimed to have been a favourite place of prayer of the saint.

All later Carthusian houses (or charterhouses, as they were known in England) modelled themselves closely on La Grande Chartreuse and the two houses in southern Italy, combining the cenobitical and eremitical traditions. Bruno did not leave a written rule for his disciples, and the first formal constitution was issued by Guigo I, prior of La Grande Chartreuse from 1109 to 1136. There is a continuing debate about how much of this key document was due to Bruno's inspiration; what is clear is that the basic themes of Carthusian spirituality and way of life can be found in the saint's letters. As he wrote to his friend the provost of Reims, "Here we strive for that vision by whose clear gaze the bridegroom is wounded with love, and by whose cleanness and purity God is discerned. Here we practise a working leisure and are stilled in quiet activity. Here God provides his athletes with the desired reward for the labour of combat—a peace that the world does not know, and joy in the Holy Spirit." It was typical of him that he should try to draw his friend to join the community by stressing the love and joy to be found there.

His legacy is a religious Order which, alone of all the Orders, has never had to be reformed, so strictly have his followers stuck to his ideals. He played an important role in the Gregorian reform of the Church in the eleventh century and provided the basis of a spiritual theology that has been of universal value, with its stress on love, self-knowledge, and the true vision that comes to the believer who delights in the world as God's creation but sees beyond its attractions through study, prayer, humility, and asceticism. With that vision, Carthusians could become involved in secular affairs, as Bruno himself had been, without being distracted by them.

A number of Bruno's writings survive. There is an *Exposition of the Psalms*, an *Exposition of the Epistles of St Paul*, his final testament, and two letters about the Carthusian way of life. There is also a youthful Latin piece on the worthlessness of the world. Bruno features perhaps surprisingly often in religious art. The extension of his cult in the sixteenth century inspired a range of artists, perhaps the most famous of them being the Spanish painter Zurbarán, noted for his ascetic portraits of saintly monks. He painted Bruno at the papal court with his pupil Bd Urban II; Bruno seems to sit a little uneasily in such surroundings. There are frescoes in Spanish and Italian churches. His iconographic features include a skull, the rejected mitre and crozier, and a star—the last a reference to St Hugh's vision of the first Carthusians as seven stars. The Louvre has a series of twenty-two scenes from the saint's life by Eustache le Sueur (1649).

There is no early Life of St Bruno; *AA.SS.*, Oct., 3, pp. 491-777, prints a thirteenth-century Life along with later sixteenth-century ones; these latter coincided with the extension of the cult to the Universal Church. His writings are in *P.L.*, 152-3; there is a French trans. of three letters, with an introduction, in *S.C.*, 88 (1962), pp. 9-93. See also *D.T.C.*, 2 (1905), 2279-82; *Dict.Sp.*, 2 (1953), 705-76; *Bibl.SS.*, 3, 561-77; *O.D.C.C.*, p. 205; B. Bligny, *Saint Bruno* (1984). *Cartusiana*, 1 (1976), pp. 54-8, gives a definitive bibliography. See also *La Grande Chartreuse par un Chartreux* (1984); G. Mursell, *The Theology of the Carthusian Life in the Writings of St Bruno and Guigo I*, vol. 127 of *Anal. Cartusiana* (1988).

St Faith, *Martyr* (? Third Century)

The young martyr Faith is listed in St Jerome's martyrology as having suffered death at Agen in Gaul, and this is all that can stated about her with any degree of certainty; she may have suffered under the procurator Dacian in the third century along with St Caprasius (20 Oct.). Her *passio*, which dates from the eleventh century at the earliest, says that she was born of noble parents; at the age of twelve she was called before Dacian and ordered to offer sacrifice to idols. She refused, was roasted on a gridiron, and then beheaded along with Caprasius.

What is remarkable is the very widespread popularity of her cult in the Middle Ages. In the fifth century her relics were translated to a basilica built in her honour at Agen, and many miracles were recorded at her shrine. Sometime in the ninth century her relics were stolen by a monk from the monastery at Conques-en-Rouergue, in Limousin; he had been deliberately sent on this mission and after spending ten years as an apparently *bona fide* canon at Agen, was put in charge of the shrine and so was able to effect the theft. His story was told openly by the monks at Conques in order to prove the authenticity of the relics; no blame was attached to him for what he had done. The saint's new resting place was on the great pilgrim route to Compostela in Spain, and this made her shrine even more famous. France has many place names and churches that reflect her cult, and in England twenty-three churches were dedicated to her, as were chapels in both St Paul's and Westminster Abbey; she was one of the patrons of medieval London. Her fame spread outside Europe, and places such as Santa Fe in New Mexico reflect her popularity. She was prayed to particularly by pilgrims, prisoners, and knights from the area around the monastery.

Most of the representations of the saint show her with the instruments of her torture, the gridiron and sword, and she usually carries the martyr's palm. Surprisingly, given her legend, she is rarely shown as a young girl but usually as a mature figure, although medieval accounts of apparitions, of which there are many, depict her as youthful and often demanding gifts of jewellery in return for protection. She features in windows at Chartres and Winchester, and there is a fresco of her in Westminster Abbey. Most striking is the magnificent reliquary from the monastery at Conques in the shape of a seated figure, dressed in royal or priestly robes and wearing a crown, and covered in gold leaf and jewels; this dates from about 980 and is the oldest surviving large (27 inches high) Christian sculpture in Europe. The relics of the saint were kept in the head of this forbidding figure, which was carried in procession to protect the monastic lands, taken to disaster areas to bless those afflicted, and even presided at meetings where important business of the community was being discussed. It is clear that the saint was regarded as "the living, present, and powerful patron of the monks" (Ward).

AA.SS., Oct., 3, pp. 263-329, and 8, pp. 823-5; H. Leclerq in *D.A.C.L.*, 3 (1914), 2563-79; *Anal.Boll.* 72 (1954), p. 395; J. Angely, *La Passion de Ste Foy* (1956); *Bibl.SS.*, 5, 511-6; *O.D.S.*, p. 174; J. Daoust in *D.H.G.E.*, 17 (1971), 1358-64; *O.D.C.C.*, p. 500; B. Ward, *Miracles and the Medieval Mind* (1982), pp. 36-42.

St Nicetas of Constantinople (*c.* 763-838)

Nicetas was a courtier who supported the empress Irene (780-802), to whom he was related, in her efforts to uphold the practice of venerating images of Our Lord and the saints against those (the Iconoclasts) who held that such veneration was a form of idolatry and wanted to destroy all images. There is a tradition that he attended the Second Council of Nicaea in 787, which upheld and explained the doctrine behind the practice of veneration; it is more likely that he was in Sicily as prefect at the time. He survived a palace revolution, which deposed Irene, and seems to have sided with the victorious Nicephorus for a time on the side of the Iconoclasts. He then retired to a monastery, but when a new emperor, Leo V, began a campaign against images, Nicetas tried to hide a famous icon of Our Lord; the emperor sent soldiers to take it away by force and Nicetas was put under house arrest. He was driven into exile during another bout of Iconoclasm and eventually found security on a farm in his native region of Paphlagonia; here he lived until his death in a monastery about the year 838.

AA.SS., Oct., 3, pp. 444-50; *Bibl.SS.*, 9, 892-3; *Vies des Saints*, 10, pp. 160-1; on Iconoclasm, *N.C.E.*, 7, pp. 327-9, and *O.D.C.C.*, pp. 687-8.

St Mary Frances of Naples (1715-91)

Anna Maria Rosa Gallo was born in Naples in 1715. As a child she showed signs of outstanding piety. When she was sixteen her father tried to force her to marry a well-to-do young man; on her refusal he beat her and treated her very roughly, as he had treated her mother before the girl was born. Eventually he was persuaded to allow her to join the Third Order of St Francis, which she did in September 1731. She took the name Mary Frances of the Five Wounds because of her special devotion to the passion of Our Lord. She also had a strong devotion to Our Lady, whom she called the "divine shepherdess." She continued to live at home and to suffer ill-treatment from her father and other members of her family. For a time, in order to try her faith, she was put under the spiritual direction of a local priest who had Jansenist tendencies, which caused her severe trials. She spent the last thirty-eight years of her life as a priest's housekeeper.

Mary Frances exhibited some of the more extreme physical signs of a deep mystical life of prayer and complete devotion to God. While making the Stations of the Cross, for example, she suffered the pains of Our Lord's passion; she is said also to have received the stigmata. She was allowed to receive Holy Communion every day and various miracles were associated with this practice, especially her reception of the host straight from the altar without the agency of the priest; St Francis Xavier Bianchi (31 Jan.) testified to similar occurrences with the consecrated wine during Mass. While she was praying at the crib at Christmas 1741, Mary Frances had a vision of Jesus stretching out his hand and saying, "This night you shall be my bride." She had frequent visions and often seemed to be in bodily ecstasy.

Although she suffered very much from ill health, she practised severe bodily mortifications and asked God to allow her to take on the sufferings of the souls in purgatory and of her sick and sinful neighbours. She claimed to Father Laviosa, the Theatine provincial who was to write her *Life*, that she had endured all that could be endured. She gave spiritual counsel to many priests and laypeople and was particularly skilled in advising confessors on how to deal with their penitents. She died on 6 October 1791, apparently foretelling some of the horrors of the French Revolution, and was canonized in 1867. Her cult is particularly strong in Naples, where her house has become a shrine and the base for an Institute of Franciscan tertiary Sisters.

Father Laviosa's *Vita di Santa Maria Francesca delle Cinque Piaghe di Gesù Cristo* was revised in 1866 and later translated into French; another *Life* by L. Montella was published in 1866; *Bibl.SS.*, 8, pp. 1065-7; M. P. Adami, *S. Maria delle Piaghe di N.S.* (1957).

Bd Mary-Rose Durocher, *Foundress* (1811-49)

Eulalie Mélanie Durocher was born on 6 October 1811 in the village of Saint-Antoine-sur-Richelieu in Quebec. She was the youngest of ten children; three of her brothers became priests and two of her sisters nuns. She had a pious upbringing under the care of her mother and was educated by the Sisters of Notre Dame, although her ill health made her attendance at school spasmodic. Her ill health also prevented her from joining a religious Order, which she tried to do several times. For twelve years or so she helped her brother, who was a priest, in various tasks in his parish, organizing works of mercy and becoming so involved in helping him and another Oblate priest that she was known as "the third missioner." She established the first Confraternity of Mary in Canada and during this time pledged herself to Our Lady and bound herself privately to observe the three religious vows.

She became aware of the severe lack of schools in Canada outside Quebec and Montreal, a lack that was already causing concern to the church authorities. When a project to bring a teaching Congregation from France fell through, the bishop gave his approval in 1843 for her to found a Congregation dedicated to the work of educating the poor. This became known as the Congregation of the Sisters of the Most Holy Names of Jesus and Mary and was given canonical approval in December 1844. Taking the name of Mary-Rose, she made her own religious profession in the new Congregation. Her spirituality was based on devotion to Jesus in the Blessed Sacrament and on imitation of Our Lady.

The bishop appointed her superior, and she ruled the new Congregation until her death in 1849. Although she was in charge for so short a time, she gave it a secure foundation, despite severe trials caused largely by an apostate nun. Today the Sisters of her Congregation work in a number of countries outside Canada—the United States, Lesotho, Peru, Brazil, and Haiti. She was beatified in 1982.

A.A.S., 74:2 (1982), pp. 824-5, 1208-10; *Notitiae*, 18 (1982), pp. 381-2; *Bibl.SS.*, Suppl. 1 (1987), 435-6; P. Duchaussois, *Rose du Canada* (1932; Eng. trans. 1934); Eulalia Teresa, *So Short a Day: The Life of Mother Marie-Rose, Foundress . . . Jesus and Mary* (1954).

Bd Isidore De Loor (1881-1916)

Isidore was born at Vrasene in the diocese of Ghent in Belgium in 1881, the eldest child of Aloysius De Loor and Camilla Hutsebaut, who were farmers. He showed early signs of an unusually strong devotion, going to Mass on weekdays and saying the rosary each evening with his parents; once he had made his first Confession and received Holy Communion at the age of eleven, he became a regular communicant even though this was not customary at that time. He taught catechism classes in his own village and also in Saint-Gilles, and he joined the Pious Union of St Francis Xavier. When he was twenty-six he was counselled by the famous Redemptorist missionary, Fr Bouckaert, to join the Passionists as a brother; he did so at the Retreat in Tournai, making his religious vows in September 1908.

In 1910 he was moved to a new Retreat at Wezembeek-Oppem near Brussels, where he was given the jobs of cook, porter, and gardener. He tried to please Christ through serving his brethren in the community and dedicated himself to this service to make it easier for them to perform their missionary apostolate, something he was not himself called to take a direct part in. His private motto was *Omnia pro pulchro caelo*, or, "Everything for the beauty of heaven," which he used to whisper to himself when engaged in boring or apparently unrewarding jobs. He was always cheerful and calm, doing things for everyone and in general looking after the community with an almost parental care. He was so obedient to the Rule and to his superiors that he was regarded as an incarnation of the Congregation's Constitution.

He developed eye trouble and had to undergo a painful operation; this failed to save his eye and caused him great suffering, which he bore with exemplary fortitude. He was moved to Kortrijk (in the diocese of Bruges) in 1912, but his health began to deteriorate. His eye trouble had been caused by cancer, and in 1916 he was diagnosed as having cancer of the bowel; later that year he contracted pleurisy, and he died on 6 October after a very painful illness, during which he used to comfort himself by saying, "Paradise, once gained, is gained for ever." He was only thirty-five years old. He was buried in the cemetery at Kortrijk, but in 1952 his remains were moved to a tomb in the Passionist church. He was beatified in 1984. The prayer approved for liturgical use on his feast-day speaks of his spirit of humility and hard work, and the example he provides of a life "hidden in the shadow of the Cross."

Notitiae, 20 (1984), pp. 979-82; *Bibl.SS.*, 7, 972, has a photograph. Some of his letters were edited by R. P. Ange, C.P., in 1955. See also L. Zaman, *Broeder Isidor* (1961).

7

OUR LADY OF THE ROSARY

It was customary for the members of Rosary confraternities, established in the fifteenth century, to celebrate a feast in honour of Our Lady of the Rosary; the practice was also common among members of the Dominican Order. The first Sunday in October was the usual day for these celebrations, and when the Christian forces won the decisive naval battle of Lepanto against the Turks on 7 October 1571, which happened to be the first Sunday of the month, the victory was naturally attributed to Our Lady of the Rosary, especially as the Roman confraternities had been saying the rosary in street processions as the battle was being fought. In the following year Pope St Pius V (30 Apr.) granted a Spanish confraternity the right to celebrate a feast-day in honour of Our Lady of Victory on the first Sunday in October, and in 1573 Gregory XIII changed its name to Our Lady of the Rosary and allowed any church with a Rosary confraternity to celebrate it. In 1716 the feast was extended to the Universal Church in thanksgiving for another Christian victory over the Turks. Finally, in 1913 the date was fixed as 7 October.

There is an old and strongly-held Dominican tradition that the rosary in the form we know it was devised by St Dominic (8 Aug.) himself after Our Lady revealed it to him in a vision and that the saint then used it in his missionary work among the Albigensian heretics. This tradition has been the subject of intensive and heated debate for the last 250 years, since the Bollandists first attacked its authenticity. Certainly the use of praying beads is much older than St Dominic, and the practice of saying a number of Our Fathers or Hail Marys and keeping count by using beads goes back at least to the twelfth century, replacing in popular use the recitation of the 150 Psalms. The famous Lady Godiva of Coventry, who died about 1075, bequeathed "the circlet of precious stones which she had threaded on a cord in order that by fingering them one after another she might count her prayers exactly" (William of Malmesbury). Such strings of beads were used initially for saying the Our Father—hence their name "Paters" and Paternoster Row in London, where they were made. Meditating while saying a number of Hail Marys may have started in some Carthusian houses in the fourteenth century, although a Dominican writer in the previous century talked of the "Psalter of St Mary" and referred to its earlier use. The rosary was used in some monastic communities by illiterate lay brothers as a substitute for the divine office. It seems that the devotion developed principally in the Rhineland and that it was there that it was given the name "rosary" to signify a garland of roses.

Whatever the origins of the devotion, its spread since the fifteenth century in its present form has owed most to the Dominicans and to the lay confraternities they established. Such confraternities imposed the saying of certain prayers on their members, and this imposition increasingly became the saying of the rosary; special indulgences were attached to the practice, and Dominican friars were licenced to grant them wherever they worked. While the themes, or "mysteries," for meditation during the recitation of the prayers were not at first fixed, by the end of the fifteenth century the present division into the Joyful, Sorrowful, and Glorious Mysteries had become the commonest pattern.

The present-day complete rosary consists of 150 Hail Marys divided into "decades" of ten; each decade is begun by an Our Father and ends with the doxology "Glory be to the Father. . . ." A set of rosary beads covers five decades, and each decade is devoted to meditation on one of the sets of mysteries: Joyful, covering the birth and early life of Our Lord; Sorrowful, covering his sufferings and death; and Glorious, covering the resurrection and ascension, the sending of the Holy Spirit, and the Assumption and Coronation of Our Lady. It is customary to allocate the mysteries to set days in the week. Manuals of devotion include introductions to the theme of each mystery to aid the mental concentration necessary for the correct saying of the rosary so that it does not become a mechanical recitation.

The devotion was given a new boost in the nineteenth century through the apparition at Lourdes of Our Lady carrying a rosary, the establishment of the Living Rosary Association, and the writings of Pope Leo XIII, who published several encyclicals about it and was sometimes known as "the pope of the rosary." In the twentieth century there have been a worldwide Rosary Crusade and the introduction of the Month of the Rosary, and both witness to the enduring popularity of the devotion. The Dominicans continue to spread the devotion as a major part of their apostolate. Since the liturgical changes following the Second Vatican Council, however, the public recitation of the rosary in various para-liturgical forms has declined, and it has tended to revert to being a private or small-group activity. Recent popes have continued to stress the value of the devotion, and Paul VI in his Apostolic Exhortation on the cult of Our Lady devotes ten pages to it, calling it "a summary of the whole gospel." He underlines the council's distinction between such devotional practices and the sacred liturgy and forbids the recitation of the rosary during Mass, but stresses most strongly its value as a form of family prayer. He argues that it is a "most excellent and efficacious" prayer, containing as it does the three essential elements of praise, contemplation, and adoration. The involvement of the mind in the contemplation of the mysteries is, according to the pope, most important, for without it there is a danger of a merely mechanical repetition of words. By its nature the rosary requires "calm and thoughtful slowness" in its recitation so that the person praying becomes involved in the meditation on the mysteries of Our Lord's life and their riches.

A.A.SS., Aug., 1, pp. 422ff.; on the historical aspects, H. Thurston, S.J., several articles in *The Month* 96 (1900), and 97 (1901); M. M. Gorce, O.P., in *D.T.C.,* 13 (pt. 2, 1937), 2902-11; *Dict.Sp.,* 13 (1988), 937-80; *N.C.E.,* 12, pp. 667-70; M. Walsh, *A Dictionary of Devotions* (1993), pp. 219-24; Pope Paul VI, *Marialis cultus,* in *A.A.S.,* 66 (1974), pp. 113-68, Eng. trans., *To Honour Mary* (1974).

St Justina, *Martyr* (date unknown)

A church was built in honour of St Justina in Padua in the sixth century, and in the twelfth century relics were discovered there, which were claimed to be hers. A forged account of her death appeared about the same time, in which the saint was said to have been instructed by St Prosdocimus, a disciple of St Peter the apostle and first bishop of Padua, and to have died by the sword for her faith. No historical facts can be gleaned from this source, but St Venantius Fortunatus, bishop of Poitiers in the seventh century (14 Dec.), ranked her among the most illustrious of those virgins whose sanctity and martyrdom adorned the Church; he bade those who visited Padua to kiss her shrine. At Rimini she was placed alongside St Andrew (30 Nov.) as protector of the city, and a church was dedicated to her in 617 at Como in northern Italy. She features in the beautiful mosaics in San Apollinare Nuovo in Ravenna, which date from the second half of the sixth century.

In the tenth century the monastery at Padua was very well endowed with property and privileges; in the following century it was reformed and acquired various sets of relics, including some which were said to be of St Luke the Evangelist (18 Oct.) and those of St Justina—these were translated after an earthquake in 1117. In the fifteenth century it was again reformed and this time became the home of the Benedictine Cassinese Congregation, which took St Justina as its patron. Her church was rebuilt on a grand scale between 1521 and 1587, and her relics were enshrined under the high altar in 1627. The patronage of the monks was very important for the spread of her cult, and she features in paintings by many of the great Italian artists, including Bellini, Mantegna, Tiepolo, Tintoretto, and Veronese. Venice adopted her as a patron after the battle of Lepanto against the Turks was won on her feast-day. The cult fell into abeyance to some extent when the monastery in Padua was closed in 1810 but revived when it was reopened in 1919.

AA.SS., Oct., 3, pp. 790–826; *Anal.Boll.* 10 (1891), pp. 467–70, and 11 (1892), pp. 354–8; H. Leclerq, *D.A.C.L.*, 13, 237–8; *Bibl.SS.*, 6, 1345–9; *O.D.S.*, p. 276.

St Mark, *Pope* (336)

Mark was Roman by birth and may have held ecclesiastical office under Pope St Sylvester (31 Dec.). When the latter died in 335, Mark was chosen as his successor on 18 January 336, and ruled as pope for just over eight months, dying on 7 October. The *Liber Pontificalis* says he was responsible for promulgating a document called the *Constitutum de omni Ecclesia*, but other sources do not mention the document, and its contents are unknown. According to Duchesne, Mark's pontificate saw the start of two important lists, the *Depositio episcoporum* and the *Depositio martyrum*. The first of these gave the dates and place of burial of the bishops of Rome who had not been martyred, the second listed all the martyrs who were venerated in Rome, ending with those who had died during Diocletian's persecution. They were begun in the year of Mark's reign and were then continued down to the year 354; together they formed the basis of the Roman Calendar and were part of an almanac drawn up for the use of Christians in Rome by the so-called Chronographer of 354.

It is likely that he built the church of San Marco in Rome and another at the cemetery of St Balbina on the Ardeatine Way. He may have granted or confirmed the right of the bishop of Ostia to consecrate the Bishop of Rome. The church was troubled by Arian disputes at that time, and he probably was involved in these, but no details are known to us; a letter to St Athanasius about the Council of Nicaea is now thought not to be his. He was buried in the cemetery of San Callisto. His main relics are in San Marco's, with part in Florence.

Mark is commemorated on 17 October in the Gregorian and Gelasian Sacramentaries, while the *Hieronymianum* gives the date 4 October.

Liber Pontificalis, 1, pp. 202-4; *AA.SS.,* Oct., 3, pp. 886-903; H. Leclerq in *D.A.C.L.,* 10:ii, 1741-9; *Bibl.SS.,* 8, 699-700; *Diz. dei Papi,* p. 35. On San Marco, see S. G. A. Luff, *The Christian's Guide to Rome* (n.e., 1990), pp. 122-3. On the lists of saints, see *O.D.C.C.,* p. 284.

St Helan of Cornwall (date unknown)

Helan, or Helen, was an Irish priest who visited Cornwall probably with a group of Irish missionaries such as Germoe and Breage who were his brothers and sisters. They moved on to Brittany and founded a number of churches before going to Reims, where they were well received. Helan then settled at Bisseuil on the river Marne and spent many years preaching to the local people before his death and burial there; the church is dedicated to him. He is probably the St Helen of Cornish church names; there are several dedications to him in west Cornwall. Nothing certain has been found out about his dates or the details of his ministry, but he features in a number of early Reims and Irish lists of saints and in the Reims Breviary for 7 October.

AA.SS., Oct., 3, pp. 903-5, discusses critically the Reims office and the Life that it contains; a seventh-century Life of St Tressian (7 Feb.), *AA.SS.,* Feb., 2, p. 53, says Helan was his brother; Baring-Gould and Fisher, 3, pp. 253-4; *O.D.S.,* p. 226; *Bibl.SS.,* 4, 981-2.

St Osyth, *Martyr* (*c.* 675)

According to legend Osyth, or Osith, was the daughter of Frithwald, a Mercian chieftain, and his wife, Wilburga, the daughter of Penda of Mercia. She was brought up in a nunnery, perhaps at Aylesbury, and wished to take the habit herself; her parents, however, married her to Sighere, king of the East Saxons. When he wished to consummate the marriage she refused, and the king was miraculously distracted by the appearance of a white stag, which he went off to hunt. While he was away, Osyth persuaded two local bishops to allow her to take the veil. On the king's return, he reluctantly agreed to his wife's decision and gave her some land at Crich near Colchester in Essex for the foundation of a convent. She was later beheaded by a group of pagan pirates because she refused to join in pagan worship, or perhaps because she resisted their attempts to carry her off. She then carried her head to a nearby church and placed it on the altar. She was buried there but her parents recovered her body and had it re-buried in Aylesbury. At some later date her body was returned to Crich and became the focus of pilgrimage when a priory of Austin canons was established there in the twelfth century.

It is difficult to discover the historical truth behind these legends. St Bede (25 May) does not mention Osyth at all, though he does deal with Sighere. Despite the story of her virginity, she and Sighere had a son, Offa, who became king of the East Saxons and then a monk and who is venerated as a saint (15 Dec.). There were two distinct feast-days, 3 June in the west of England and 7 October in the south-east. It is likely that there were two saints with the same name, one with her origins in Essex, the other in Buckinghamshire—the latter would explain the Mercian parentage. Some time in the Middle Ages the two stories were conflated, hence the need to create the story of the moving of the body back and forth. The cult of St Osyth was weak before the Norman Conquest, though her Essex shrine is mentioned in a treatise of c.1000; it seems to have flourished with the establishment of the later priory at Crich. Her cult also existed in Hereford, Worcester, and Evesham, because she was said to have been a princess of the Hwiccas tribe. Just before the Reformation the bishops of Lincoln and London tried to suppress the Aylesbury cult in favour of the Essex one. There are four ancient churches dedicated to her.

AA.SS., Oct., 3, pp. 942-3; *D.N.B.*, 42, p. 337; *Bibl.SS.*, 9, 1281-3; A. T. Baker, "An Anglo-French Life of St Osith," *Modern Languages Review* 6 (1911), pp. 476-502; D. Bethell, "The Lives of St Osyth of Essex and St Osyth of Aylesbury," *Anal.Boll.* 88 (1970), pp. 75-127; C. Hohler, "St Osyth and Aylesbury," *Records of Buckinghamshire* 18 (1966), pp. 61-72.

St Artaldus, *Bishop* (*c.* 1101-1206)

Artaldus, or Arthaud, was born in Savoy and joined the Carthusians at Portes in his early twenties. After several years there he was sent, about 1132, to become prior of a new foundation established by the bishop of Geneva and the count of Savoy in Val Romey, about twenty-five miles south-west of Geneva. The first house was destroyed by fire and so a second was established on the Arvières River; although this was always a small, poor house, Arthaud's fame spread widely. Among his correspondents, for example, was Pope Alexander III, a strong supporter of the Carthusians in general, who exempted them from local episcopal jurisdiction. Such was the prior's reputation for holiness that when he was over eighty years old he was commanded by the pope to become bishop of the nearby town of Belley, despite his vehement objections. After two years as bishop his resignation was accepted and he returned to Arvières, where he died in 1206 at the age of 105. During his last years he was visited by St Hugh of Lincoln (17 Nov.), himself a former prior of a charterhouse, who persuaded King Henry II to become a benefactor of Arvières.

The cult of Arthaud was largely a Carthusian one, although it existed also in the diocese of Belley, where he had been bishop. His remains were removed to a parish cemetery to avoid desecration at the time of the French Revolution; they were enshrined in the parish church in 1830, and his cult was officially confirmed for the diocese of Belley in 1834.

AA.SS., Oct., 3, pp. 778–86, gives a short medieval Life; *D.H.G.E.*, 4, 774–5; *Bibl.SS.*, 2, 482.

ST DENIS (p. 54)
Silver cross and lions on red field
(also used of St Dionysius the Areopagite, p. 53).

8

St Pelagia the Penitent (date unknown)

Perhaps the main interest in the story of St Pelagia is seeing how a traditional cult has been altered out of all recognition by legends. The genuine St Pelagia, so to speak, was a young virgin martyr of Antioch who was venerated there on 8 October at least as early as the fourth century; she is mentioned by both St John Chrysostom (13 Sept.), who lived from c. 347 to 407, and St Ambrose (7 Dec.), who lived from c. 340 to 397. She is commemorated on this day in the Syriac Breviary of the early fifth century.

Her name was taken over by a later writer and attached to a story told by St John Chrysostom in another context altogether: in a homily on St Matthew's Gospel he relates how an actress from Antioch, infamous for her evil ways, underwent a sudden conversion and after her baptism lived a life of extreme austerity as a recluse. Chrysostom does not give this penitent a name, nor does he suggest that she was the object of any cult. The later writer took this moral tale, attached the name of Pelagia to the actress, and called her St Pelagia the Penitent, the name by which she has been subsequently known. This later writer also gave himself a false name, claiming to be a deacon called James who worked for St Nonnus, a bishop of Edessa. He elaborated his story still further by saying that Pelagia's conversion was due to Nonnus' preaching and that the bishop had baptized her. After this, he went on, she put on men's clothes, went to Jerusalem, and lived as a recluse. She was reverenced by the local people, who referred to her as "the beardless monk"; it was only on her death that her identity was revealed.

The previous edition of this work, quoting the work of Fr Delehaye, said that this "popular romance" of the "Repentance of Pelagia" was the starting point for the tales of a whole group of imaginary saints, of whom a good example would be St Marina (formerly 12 Feb., whose name is the Latin version of Pelagia). The legend of the saint of Antioch "lost by degrees every vestige of historical fact . . . and the purely legendary *residuum* passed under various names . . . thanks to which we have the saints Mary and Marina, Apollinaria, Euphrosyne and Theodora, who are simply literary replicas of the Pelagia of the self-styled James."

An account of the genuine Pelagia appeared under 9 June in the previous edition; Alban Butler had ignored her and given only the legendary story, following the example of the then current Roman Martyrology. Marina has been dropped from the new Roman Martyrology.

AA.SS., Oct., 4, pp. 248-68, gives the fictitious *acta*. The unravelling of the true from the false was done by Delehaye, *Legends of the Saints* (1927). Deacon James' story features in H. Waddell, *The Desert Fathers* (1936), pp. 285-302.

St Demetrius, *Martyr* (date unknown)

Demetrius was probably a deacon who was martyred sometime before the fifth century at Sirmium (Mitrovic in former Yugoslavia). During that century two churches were built in his honour, one at Sirmium and the other at Thessalonika. It may be that the cult of the saint migrated from Sirmium when Leontius, the prefect of Illyricum, moved the seat of civil authority to Thessalonika—he is reputed to have built both churches. Certainly Demetrius was honoured as a saint at Sirmium before the church at Thessalonika was built. Sirmium, however, was destroyed by the invading Huns in 441, and it was the second church that became the principal centre for the cult of the martyr and attracted very large numbers of pilgrims. The church was destroyed by fire in 1917 but has since been rebuilt; it was obviously meant to hold a great number of people. The previous edition of this work says that the bones of the saint may have been transferred to this church about the year 418, but there is no archaeological evidence of such a shrine.

In time Demetrius became known as "the Great Martyr," and a legend grew up about his life. According to this he had been a citizen of Thessalonika who had been arrested for preaching the gospel and executed without trial in the local baths. The church was built over the baths and incorporated part of them as a kind of crypt. At a later date relics of the saint were said to exude a miraculous oil, but the arrangements whereby the pilgrims could collect some of this seem to have been quite fraudulent.

The earliest written account we have dates from the ninth century and says that the order for his execution came from the emperor Maximian himself. Later accounts make out that he was a proconsul (this is how the Roman Martyrology described him) or a warrior-saint similar to St George (23 Apr.) and second only to him in popularity. He was one of the saints adopted by the Crusaders as their patrons in battle. None of these later accounts can be trusted, though we can be sure of the existence of a martyr of that name. His feast-day is kept with great solemnity throughout the Eastern Church on 26 October, and he is named in the preparation of the Byzantine liturgy. The popular Slav name, Dmitry, comes from him. His cult was popular also in Ravenna in Italy, where the earliest chapel was dedicated in his honour.

The original basilica, destroyed in 1917, had important mosaics from the sixth to the ninth century; in these Demetrius was portrayed as a deacon. More often he was depicted as a soldier, and he appears in military garb in the painting of the martyrdom of St Sebastian by Ortolano in the National Gallery in London.

AA.SS., Oct., 4, pp. 50-209, gives an excellent account of the martyr, including Greek texts of the two main forms of his *passio*; Delehaye has shown that Demetrius was venerated at Sirmium before the building of the basilica at Thessalonika: see his *Légendes grecques des saints militaires* (1909). See also C. Mango, *Byzantine Architecture* (1986), pp. 44-8, for the archaeological evidence, and *Bibl.SS.*, 4, 556-65, for a balanced critical account.

St Keyne (? Sixth Century)

St Keyne was very well known in parts of south Wales and Cornwall, and may have been active in Herefordshire and Somerset, though there is no trustworthy evidence of an ancient cult of the saint in the latter county. Very little of her *vita*, edited by John of Tynemouth in the fourteenth century, can be trusted. It says that she was the daughter of the Welsh king Brychan of Brycheiniog, who had twelve sons and twelve daughters. Keyne grew up to be very beautiful but refused to marry; she took a vow of virginity (hence her Welsh name Cain Wyry, Keyne the Maiden), crossed the Severn, and lived as a solitary. She travelled a great deal and founded several oratories; at St Michael's Mount in Cornwall her nephew persuaded her to return to Wales, and a healing spring marked the spot where she settled and later died.

Much effort has gone into trying to identify her resting place, and Llangeinor in Glamorgan probably has the best claim to be it; nearby is an ancient well which is still said to have healing properties. Keyne may have been one of a band of missionaries who moved into Herefordshire from Brecknock in south Wales and then moved about the south-west of England—she can be identified in place names of two parishes in Cornwall and three in south Wales and is listed in several martyrologies. It has been suggested by Doble that Keyne might have been a man, as the journeyings are more in character with male saints of that period.

One of the legends associated with St Keyne is that whichever partner of a marriage was the first to drink from the well would be able to rule the other. This story has been preserved by the ballad written by the poet Robert Southey in honour of the well that bears her name in Liskeard, Cornwall. The story was known in the Middle Ages.

AA.SS., Oct., 4 , pp. 275-7; G. H. Doble in *Downside Review* (1931), pp. 156-72; *ibid.* "St Nectan, St Keyne and the Children of Brychan in Cornwall," in *Cornish Saints* no. 25 (1930), which gives a translation of the Tynemouth *vita*, and Southey's ballad.

9

ST JOHN LEONARDI, *Founder* (*c.* 1542-1609)

John Leonardi was brought up in the Italian city of Lucca, where he became apprentice to an apothecary. He joined a lay confraternity and then studied for the priesthood. He wanted to join the Franciscans but failed to be accepted. After his ordination in about 1572 he was active in the hospitals and prisons of the city, and gathered round him a group of young laypeople to help in this work; they lived in common and shared a life of prayer as well as active ministry. John developed a special interest in education and preaching, to increase people's knowledge of Christian doctrine as defined by the Council of Trent and to implement the latter's reforms. He believed that the Church at the time was going through a period of great crisis and that only a return to Christian essentials could save it. As a result, the local bishop gave him the task of preaching in all the churches of Lucca. His efforts in this regard were especially important because some of the leading families of the city had been influenced by the early Italian reformers such as Peter Martyr Vermigli and Bernardino Ochino, whose preaching on the Trinity, the Eucharist, and the nature of the Church had been highly unorthodox.

He wrote to Pope Paul V that those who would be reformers of people's morals should "place themselves in the sight of the people as mirrors of all the virtues, like lamps set on a stand to give light by their integrity of life and example . . . thus they will draw them gently to reform rather than compel them, and there will not be required of the body what is not found in the head." He believed that it was essential to start with the young: "We should not overlook those in whom all renewal must begin. It would not be right to leave anything untried to educate boys from their tender years in a sincere Christian faith and holy life."

Several of his helpers wanted to become priests, and John thought of founding a new religious Congregation dedicated to the work of education, clerical reform, and the works of mercy. He met with strong and even violent opposition, however, the full reason for which is not clear. It seems to have been partly political and partly inspired by the self-interest of those opposed to reform, and it may also have been due to the earlier unorthodox leanings of some of the leading families. Whatever the reason, the opposition was so powerful that John spent the rest of his life away from the city and needed special papal protection even to visit it.

In 1583 his followers were officially recognized by the bishop of Lucca, with the approval of Pope Gregory XIII, and became an association of secular priests with simple religious vows. John was encouraged and helped by St Philip Neri (26 May), who gave him his premises of S. Girolamo della Carità (along with the care of his cat), and by St Joseph Calasanctius (25 Aug.), with whose Congregation John's association was joined for a short time. John and his followers built up such a reputation throughout Italy that in 1595 Pope Clement VIII recognized them formally as a religious Congregation. At the same time John was commissioned to reform a number of monasteries and was involved in the planning of a special Roman seminary for the foreign missions, another of his principal interests; he thought at one stage of developing a missionary wing to his Congregation. (The seminary was later fully established by Pope Urban VIII as the *Collegium de Propaganda Fide*.) He became a noted devotee and propounder of the Forty Hours' Devotion, and urged the practice of frequent Communion. In addition to a practical manual on preaching, published in 1574, he wrote a fairly large number of works on various branches of theology and educational treatises on the duties of parents and children, but very little of this output was published. Overall, his work was an important part of the Catholic reform movement that followed the Council of Trent.

On 9 October 1609 John died of plague caught while visiting the sick. In 1621 the members of his Congregation were allowed to take solemn religious vows and adopted their present name of Clerks Regular of the Mother of God. They remained by design a small Congregation, with never more than fifteen churches in Italy and only one foundation elsewhere. John was beatified in 1861 and canonized in 1938; his feast was added to the universal Calendar in 1941.

A.A.S., 30 (1938), 369-80, 441; *Propylaeum*, p. 446; *Bibl.SS.*, 6, 1033-39; *Vies des Saints*, 10, pp. 302-5; *Catholicisme*, 6, 464-5.

St Dionysius the Areopagite (First Century)

While St Paul was waiting in Athens for his companions Silas and Timothy he was invited to address the city's council in its meeting place on the Areopagus. He gave his famous discourse on the Unknown God and spoke about the resurrection of the body; at this most of his hearers listened to him no longer, and some were openly derisive. There were, however, some who became his disciples—among them a woman named Damaris and a man called Dionysius the Areopagite, so called because he was a member of the council.

The account in Acts (17:13-34) of St Paul's stay in Athens is all we know for certain about Dionysius. The historian Eusebius (*c.*260-340) accepted an early tradition that he had become the first bishop of Athens; others referred to him as a martyr. The Menology of Basil adds that he was burned alive at Athens during the persecution under Domitian. The ancient calendars give his feast-day as 3 October, and it is still celebrated on that date in the Byzantine and Syrian churches.

From the seventh century onward his name was connected with places outside Greece, such as Calabria in southern Italy and Paris. This last was the result of confusing him with St Denis or Dionysius, the first bishop of Paris, presumably to give the city a direct link with apostolic times. The bishop's Life was deliberately falsified in this way by the ninth-century abbot Hilduin (see under St Denis, below). But this was only part of the confusion, for Hilduin also made out that this conflated Dionysius was the author of a number of spiritual and theological treatises and letters, which in fact had been written about the year 500. These were the work of an unknown writer who, in order to give his writings a spurious apostolic respectability, had attributed them to Dionysius the Areopagite. The writings were extremely highly regarded during the Middle Ages and are still recognized as valuable in their own right. The original Roman Martyrology and the Roman Breviary both accepted the false attribution of them to Dionysius, which was not questioned until the sixteenth century, although it is worth noting that as early as the Council of Constantinople in 533 they were rejected as forgeries by the bishop of Ephesus. Their unknown author is now referred to as the Pseudo-Dionysius.

Where does this leave the genuine Dionysius the Areopagite? In some obscurity, it must be said, but content, no doubt, to have been converted by St Paul and to have been his disciple.

AA.SS., Oct., 4, pp. 696-767; *Bibl.SS.*, 4, 634-7; *O.D.C.C.*, pp. 404-7.

St Denis, *Bishop*, and Companions, *Martyrs* (? 258)

We learn from St Gregory of Tours (17 Nov.), writing in the sixth century, that St Denis, or Dionysius or Denys, of Paris was Italian by birth. He and six other missionary bishops were sent by the pope about the year 250 to evangelize Gaul, and Denis established a Christian presence on an island in the Seine. He was helped by Rusticus, a priest, and Eleutherius, a deacon. They were so effective in spreading the Christian message that they were arrested, and after a long imprisonment all three were beheaded. Their bodies were thrown into the river but were recovered, and a chapel was built over their graves; later the great abbey of Saint-Denis, the burial place of French kings, was built around this chapel by King Dagobert in the seventh century. Denis was honoured as the first bishop of Paris and became the pricipal patron of France.

Later accounts falsely identified Denis with the famous Dionysius the Areopagite, the Athenian disciple of St Paul, and claimed that he had been sent to Gaul by Pope Clement I in the first century. This Dionysius was supposed to be the author of the writings of the so-called Pseudo-Dionysius (see previous entry). This false conflation of three different people was deliberately fostered by an abbot of Saint-Denis, Hilduin, in the ninth century and was responsible for a growth in the importance of the original cult. According to Hilduin's *Areopagitica*, the three martyrs were finally beheaded on Montmartre after various methods to kill them had failed; Denis then walked two miles to the site of the future abbey, carrying his head and led by a choir of angels. The previous edition of this work said that Hilduin's account made use of "spurious and worthless materials, and it is difficult to believe in his complete good faith: the life is a tissue of fables." But it served his purpose and was accepted as genuine for many centuries.

The cult of St Denis was very popular in the Middle Ages. In England over forty churches were dedicated to him, and four Benedictine monasteries kept the feast of the translation of his relics to the abbey of Saint-Denis in 626 (21 Apr.).

AA.SS., Oct., 4, pp. 865-987; H. Leclerq in *D.A.C.L.*, 4 (1920), 588-606; *Vies des Saints*, 10 (1952), pp. 270-88; *O.D.C.C.*, p. 405; *Bibl.SS.*, 4, 650-61; S. McK. Crosby, *The Abbey of St-Denis 475-1122*, 1 (1942), pp. 24-52; R. J. Loenertz in *Anal.Boll.* 69 (1951), pp. 217-37; *D.H.G.E.*, 14 (1960), 263-5.

St Demetrius of Alexandria, *Bishop* (231)

Alexandria in Egypt was the second city of the Roman Empire, and the Christian church there was said to have been founded by St Mark the Evangelist (25 Apr.). Nothing is known of its early bishops before Demetrius, who was reputed to be the eleventh successor of St Mark. According to the *History of the Patriarchs*, which mixes historical fact with legendary and miraculous elements, he was from a Coptic farming background, almost certainly illiterate, and married. He was appointed patriarch against his will, claiming that his marriage made him ineligible; however, he proved to be very active in developing Christianity in Egypt and in meeting pastoral needs by ordaining a large number of priests and sending them out into the remoter parts of the country, despite the Roman persecutions. He also turned out to be inflexible in defending his own and the Church's rights.

He was a friend of Origen, one of the leading figures among the Alexandrian theologians, whom he appointed to head the city's famous catechetical school and whom he had to defend against those who condemned the mutilation which Origen underwent as a result of taking Our Lord's words too literally (see Matt. 19:10). The two friends fell out, however, when Origen accepted an invitation to preach before some bishops at Caesarea in Palestine, for he was still a layman. Some years later there was further trouble when Origen was ordained priest at Caesarea without the necessary canonical permission from Demetrius; the latter called a synod, had Origen condemned for this breach of discipline, and removed him from his teaching post. There were also doctrinal differences between the two, though these may well have been due to a failure on Demetrius' part to understand the subtleties of Origen's writings.

Demetrius is said to have set up the first three suffragan sees of Alexandria, and, according to Eusebius, was responsible for sending St Pantaenus (7 July) to preach the gospel in Ethiopia and the Yemen. He was bishop of Alexandria for forty-two years, and died in 231 at the age of 105. The reverence in which his people held him was, perhaps, mixed with a certain amount of fear, for he had the gift of reading people's minds and discovering their secret sins. Coptic liturgical texts rank Demetrius highly, especially with regard to liturgical matters, and attribute to him a correct method for determining the date of Easter. He wrote several letters to episcopal colleagues on this question.

AA.SS., Oct., 4, pp. 855-64; *D.A.C.L.*, 8, 2752-3, deals with Demetrius' letters; see also articles on Demetrius and Origen in *D.C.B.* and *The Coptic Encyclopedia*, 3 (1991), pp. 891-3. On Alexandria, see *N.C.E.*, 1, pp. 303-6; *D.H.G.E.*, 2, 289-369.

St Publia (*c.* 370)

The historian and theologian Theodoret, a native of Antioch writing in the first half of the fifth century, tells us that Publia was a well-to-do woman of the same city who, when she became a widow, either gathered together in her house a number of other women who wanted to live a common life of prayer and charity, or joined an existing convent of holy women and became its superioress. In the year 362 the emperor Julian the Apostate went to Antioch to prepare for his military campaign against the Persians. He had already gained a reputation for downgrading Christianity, the official religion of the empire, and doing all he could to restore the ancient pagan cults. He happened to be passing by Publia's house while she and her companions were singing the psalms, and heard the words, "The idols of the Gentiles are silver and gold, the works of the hands of men: they have mouths but never speak, eyes but never see. . . . Their makers will end up like them, and so will anyone who relies on them" (Ps. 115). Apparently Publia had deliberately chosen this psalm for the occasion. Julian took this as a personal insult and ordered the women to be silent and not to sing their songs ever again. They replied by singing a verse from Psalm 68: "Let God arise, let his enemies be scattered." In his anger the emperor had Publia ill treated by his guards, and apparently intended to execute all of the women on his return from Persia; since he died while away on the campaign the women were left in peace and continued their communal way of life. Publia died about the year 370. The Roman Martyrology used to refer to her as an abbess.

Theodoret's account in his *Church History* is quoted in *AA.SS.*, Oct., 4, pp. 995-6; see also *Bibl.SS.*, 10, 1235-6. On Julian and Theodoret, see *O.D.C.C.*, pp. 765-6, 1360, and *Anal.Boll.* 74 (1956), pp. 14-15.

St Savin (? Fifth Century)

This saint is venerated as the apostle of the Lavedan region in the Pyrenees, which includes the town of Lourdes. Almost nothing is known of him for certain, and even his dates are debatable. His legendary Life asserts that he was from Barcelona and was educated at Poitiers by an uncle. He then spent some years as a solitary near Tarbes, living first in a cell, then in a pit in the ground. When he was told that his austerities were too extreme, he replied that we all must do penance for our sins in the way that seems most appropriate to us. He preached to the local people, and was credited with many miracles. He foretold his death, and was surrounded by priests, monks, and local people on his death-bed. His body was venerated in a shrine in the monastic church, which was later renamed St Savin's, and the local village became known as Saint-Savin de Tarbes. He is venerated in a number of dioceses in southern France.

AA.SS., Oct., 4, pp. 1002-6, gives a short text of uncertain date; *AA.SS.*, July, 3, p. 189, says there is no doubt about his existence but adds "would that the account of his deeds and miracles was just a little fuller!" See also *Vies des Saints*, 7, pp. 250-2; *Bibl.SS.*, 11, 700-1. A note in *B.T.A.*

says that his Life shows how much can be made from very scanty records; one of the "Petits Bollandistes" wrote a biography of over 4,000 words with the same detail and certainty as he might have used in providing a summary of Napoleon's career!

Bd Gunther (*c.* 960–1045)

Gunther was a cousin of St Stephen of Hungary (16 Aug.) and related to St Henry the Emperor (13 July). For his first fifty years he lived a far from holy life as a nobleman, being worldly, ambitious, and unscrupulous. He then came under the influence of St Gothard of Hildesheim (4 May), who was engaged in reforming the ancient abbey of Hersfeld, and decided to become a monk. He gave most of his property to Hersfeld, using the remainder to endow an abbey in Thuringia; against the advice of Gothard he insisted on keeping this abbey as his own possession. On his return from a pilgrimage to Rome he did become a monk, but he had not overcome his ambition for power and insisted on being made abbot of his own monastery. He was, however, a failure as abbot and was finally persuaded to re- nounce his position and return to being a simple monk.

This second conversion was sincere and lasting. After a while he went to live as a hermit, and his reputation for holiness attracted a number of disciples. With these he moved to Bavaria, where he built cells and a church; the foundation later became a regular monastery. Gunther travelled about the countryside begging alms for the poor. He is said to have become a powerful preacher despite his lack of education: it is likely that he could neither read nor write. He encouraged his cousin St Stephen in his efforts to spread Christianity throughout his kingdom. He atoned for his former excesses by severe mortifications and was a rigid disciplinarian with his monks. He died in Bohemia in 1045 and was buried at Brevnov, near Prague. His reputation for holiness during the last thirty-five years of his life and the miracles that were reported at his tomb led to a popular cult; his feast-day is celebrated liturgically in parts of southern Germany.

The main facts in the Latin Life are probably reliable; it is based partly on the writings of a canon of Hildesheim who was a contemporary and is printed in *AA.SS.*, Oct., 4, pp. 1054–84. See also *M.G.H.*, *Scriptores*, 6, p. 672, and 9, pp. 276–9; *Bibl.SS.*, 7, 528–31.

St Louis Bertrán (1526–81)

Luis Bertrán was born in Valencia in Spain in 1526 and as a young man went on pilgrimage to the tomb of St James (25 July) to ask for guidance as to which religious Order he should join. His quest was in vain, but when he was eighteen he joined the Dominicans; he was ordained in 1547. He became novice-master at the remarkably young age of twenty-three, an office which he discharged on and off for thirty years. He was not a particularly gifted scholar and achieved what he did by sheer hard work and application; this was true also of his ability as a preacher. He was very severe with his charges and with himself and appears to have lacked any sense of humour. The dominant theme of his spirituality was the fear of God.

However, he gained a reputation for sanctity because of his work among the sick during an outbreak of plague in Valencia in 1557, and he was approached by St Teresa of Avila (15 Oct.) about her projected reform of the Carmelites. He encouraged her to undertake the work and foretold that in fifty years "Your Order will be one of the most famous in the Church."

In 1562 he undertook a new apostolate, to convert the people of Spanish America. He started work in present-day Colombia and received the gifts of tongues, miracle-working, and prophecy to help him. He converted many thousands, including all the inhabitants of Tubera and Cipacoa (he filled out the baptismal registers in his own hand). He then worked for a time in the Leeward, Virgin, and Windward Islands and finally returned to Spain after a ministry of six years. The previous edition of this work notes that such wholesale conversions were "tributes to the apostolic zeal rather than to the prudence" of the saint and were often a cause of embarrassment to his successors.

Back in Spain, Louis tried to get the government to take action against the cruelties and avarice of the Spanish settlers in America, evils which he had witnessed all too often himself but which he had been powerless as a missionary to prevent. He spent the rest of his life training preachers to work on the missions, stressing that the only effective preparation for successful preaching was humble and fervent prayer, "for words without works never have the power to change people's hearts." He died in Valencia after a long illness, on 9 October 1581. He was canonized in 1671 and is the principal patron saint of Colombia. His shrine in Spain was destroyed in the civil war in 1936. There is a striking picture of him by the Spanish painter Zurbarán (1598-1664) in Seville, in which the saint is shown holding a golden bowl out of which a serpent is emerging; this recalls an occasion when an attempt was made to poison him on one of the Caribbean islands.

AA.SS., Oct., 5, pp. 292-488, gives a very early Life by his disciple Fr Antist and a longer one of 1623; *Bibl.SS.*, 8, 342-8; *O.D.S.*, p. 54. On the evangelization of Colombia, see E. Dussel (ed.), *The Church in Latin America: 1492-1992* (1992), pp. 271-6, and bibliog., pp. 478-9.

BB Cyril Bertrand Tejedor and Companions, *Martyrs* (1934)

José Sanz Tejedor was born at Lerma, in the Spanish diocese of Burgos, on 20 March 1888. In 1907 he joined the Brothers of the Christian Schools, taking the name Cyril Bertrand in religion. At the end of his training he was appointed to teach in a difficult school, where he overcame the problems by patience and strength of mind and by following the advice of the founder, St John Baptist de la Salle (7 Apr.), in his book *The Conduct of Schools*. He was appointed to a number of other schools; when these were closed down by the authorities because they were run by religious, he was appointed superior of the community at Santander in 1925. He was so successful in the six years he was there that the reputation of the school grew considerably and pupils left other schools to attend it and, if possible, to be taught by Brother Cyril. In 1933 he was invited to go to Turón, in the Asturias region of northern Spain, to take charge of a school attended largely by the children of local miners; the Brothers ran fourteen schools in the region altogether. While there, in 1934, he made a thirty days' retreat and put himself in the hands of God to follow his will entirely.

There had been political and social unrest in Asturias for some time, following the changes brought about by the proclamation of the Second Republic in 1931; a combination of left-wing parties had introduced anticlerical legislation, especially in connection with the Church's control of education. The general election of 1933 brought a swing to the Right, which led to widespread disturbances and the threat of a national strike. The mining and industrialized areas of Asturias had become very politicized and were the most likely to resist any attempts to change the political complexion of the Republic; when the right-wing government seemed about to do so, the region erupted into armed revolution, on 4 October 1934. The uprising lasted fifteen days and was suppressed only by the use of heavy military force; over a thousand people were killed, and many thousands wounded.

In the early morning of 5 October the rebels arrested Brother Cyril Bertrand and the seven members of his community, along with their chaplain, a Passionist priest named Fr Inocencio. They were imprisoned along with other religious, local priests, and some leading public figures. Four days later, very early in the morning, the eight Brothers, Fr Inocencio, and two officers of the government forces were led out to the cemetery; a large pit had been dug, and the eleven prisoners were lined up on its edge and shot. The rebel leader who had given the order for the executions said later, "The Brothers and the priest quietly listened to the sentence and then walked to the centre of the cemetery at a leisurely yet firm pace. They knew where they were going and went like lambs to the slaughter. It was so impressive that I, hardened as I am, could not help being moved. . . . I think that while walking, and when waiting at the gate, they prayed in a subdued voice." During the short revolution, in addition to the eight Brothers and their chaplain, a total of ten diocesan priests, two Passionists, three Vincentians, two Jesuits, a Carmelite, and six seminarians were executed.

The seven members of the community shot with Brother Cyril Bertrand were all young. Marciano José, born in 1900, had been at Turón only six months; he was a non-teaching Brother because of deafness and other health problems. Vittoriano Pio, born in 1905, and noted for his musical ability, had been a member of the community for only twenty days. Julián Alfredo, born in 1903, had been transferred to Turón in September 1933 because it was thought his quiet strength of character and total commitment would be useful in the difficult situation that was developing. Benjamino Julián, born in 1908 and appointed to Turón in 1933, was noted for his sense of joy and his sound judgment on political matters. Augusto Andrés, born in 1910, had been moved to Turón in 1933 when his previous school had been closed by the government. Benito de Jesús, born in 1910 in Argentina, was a talented writer and very involved in the Eucharistic Crusade. Aniceto Adolfo had been born in 1912 and so was barely twenty-two at the time of his martyrdom. The Passionist priest, Fr Inocencio Arnau, had been born in 1887; he had taught literature, philosophy, and theology and liked to be involved in educational work; he was staying overnight with the community because he had been hearing the confessions of the students in preparation for the First Friday on 5 October.

The eight martyrs were beatified in 1990.

M. Valdizán, F.S.C., *Los Mártires de Turón*, 2 vols. (1985); P. Chico, F.S.C., *Testigos de la Escuela Cristiana* (1989); *Bibl.SS.*, Suppl. 1 (1987), 1231-2.

10

ST FRANCIS BORGIA (1510-72)

Francis Borgia (Francisco de Borja y Aragón) was born at Gandia on the east coast of Spain in 1510, the great-grandson of Pope Alexander VI and King Ferdinand of Aragon, and cousin of the emperor Charles V. He was the eldest son of John, third duke of Gandia, and Joanna of Aragon. He was called to service at the imperial court when he was eighteen, and married Eleanor de Castro in 1529; in the following year he was created marquis of Llombay and began the life of imperial service and honours expected of one so highly born.

In 1539 two events that were to affect him deeply occurred. The death of the Empress Isabella brought home to him the emptiness of earthly honours; in later life he looked on this experience as the start of his conversion to a more spiritual way of life. At the same time he was appointed viceroy of Catalonia and left the imperial court. While still occupied with public affairs he was able to devote more time to prayer and to adopt a more austere way of life. He was influenced by St Peter of Alcántara (19 Oct.) and Bl Peter Favre (11 Aug.), one of the first Jesuits. He proved to be a successful administrator, and was noted for his attempts to rid public life of corruption.

In 1543 he succeeded his father as duke of Gandia and seemed to be well on the way to becoming one of Spain's most powerful and respected nobles. His career suffered a setback, however, when there was opposition to his reforms, and he retired to his private estates, happy to lead a more secluded life and to become involved in a number of good works. These included the foundation of a hospital and of a university for the new Society of Jesus—he had met and been very impressed by the first group of Jesuits to visit his part of Spain. He was a warm-hearted family man, devoted to his wife and children; and he had a large circle of friends, whose wellbeing was his concern throughout his life. In 1546, however, his wife died; he decided to give up public life altogether, renounce all his possessions, and join the new Society, which he did secretly soon afterwards. By 1550 he had settled his affairs and made provision for his eight children, and he set out for Rome to meet St Ignatius Loyola (31 July) and to begin his life as a religious.

Throughout the rest of his life there was a continual tension between his desire to lead a life of seclusion and the demands made on him because of his name and administrative abilities. While in Rome, for example, he became involved in the founding of the Roman College (later the Gregorian University) and in raising finance for its development. A few months later he was back in Spain in a hermitage at Oñate, near Loyola, to prepare for his ordination in 1551. He was able to spend some time in comparative seclusion, writing spiritual treatises, praying, and preaching. He had to be ordered to relax his bodily mortifications, which he later admitted to have been excessive. He could not avoid public duties altogether, however; he was twice required by the emperor to visit Joanna "the Mad", the queen dowager, in her final illness, and the emperor wanted to put him forward for elevation to the cardinalate. To avoid this, he made the simple vows of a professed member of the Society, which entailed the renunciation of all dignities and titles. Charles V abdicated in 1555 and appointed Francis as one of his executors, consulting him on political and spiritual matters. He also became the spiritual adviser to the emperor's daughter, who was viceroy of Spain, and the new king, Philip II, consulted him on important political appointments. This influence in high places made Francis a number of enemies and brought accusations of improper use of his position, which Philip tended to believe. To avoid further trouble, Francis fled to Portugal in 1559, hoping to be able to lead a more secluded life without political involvement. His seclusion was short-lived; in 1561 he was called to Rome by the Society's general, Fr Laínez, to take on the position of vicar general of the Society while Laínez attended the Council of Trent.

His years in Spain had also seen him engaged in establishing the Society there. In 1554 St Ignatius had appointed him commissary for that country, in which he was responsible for founding twelve colleges and a novitiate. During this time he also met St Teresa of Avila (15 Oct.); she described how he gave her "medicine and counsel" for the problems she was having in prayer, an area in which he had, she said, "great experience."

When Laínez died, in 1565, Francis was elected general of the Society. The remainder of his life was dominated by two aims, to strengthen the Society through expansion and careful attention to the spiritual training of its members, and to extend Catholicism through missionary activity abroad and in Europe, especially in the countries that had been affected by Protestantism. He paid particular attention to establishing well-run novitiates in each province of the Society, writing regulations for novice-masters and several letters of spiritual instruction for the novices. Under his direction the *ratio studiorum* was completed and the Constitutions of the Society, first published by his predecessor, revised and completed. He developed the Roman College, began the building of the Gesù church and built the church of San Andrea on the Quirinal next to the Society's Roman novitiate.

He was responsible for establishing a new province in Poland, where the Society was to be all-important in winning that country back to Catholicism, and enlarged and improved the German College in Rome, so that it became a major source of missionaries to work in Germany for the reclamation of large areas to the Church. He overcame some of the opposition that existed in France to the Jesuits and succeeded in opening a number of colleges there. Finally, he was the founder of the Jesuit mission to the Spanish colonies in America, where mission stations were set up in Florida, Mexico, and Peru between 1566 and 1572. Even while he was so heavily involved in this administration he neglected neither his own interior spiritual life nor the more mundane demands of Christian charity. In 1566, for example, when there was a serious outbreak of plague in Rome, he raised large sums of money for relief and sent his priests out to care for the sick in the hospitals and poorest parts of the city.

In 1571 Francis was ordered by the pope, St Pius V (30 Apr.), to travel to Spain and Portugal as part of a papal initiative to build an effective alliance aginst the Turks. Despite increasing ill health, he preached frequently on the journey to large crowds. He died on 30 September 1572, three days after returning to Rome. He was beatified in 1624 and canonized in 1671.

Francis' writings may be divided into three parts, in line with the three periods of his adult life. While he was still duke of Gandia he wrote a number of spiritual works for laypeople, which were published in 1548. These are useful as they show the foundations of Francis' spirituality—a humble knowledge of our nothingness in the face of everything that God has done for us, and a desire to live a life of suffering and to undergo martyrdom in return for God's love. Francis was very fond of using the word "confusion" to describe what must be the state of mind of those Christians who truly realized their lack of a proper response to God's gifts and promptings. His own self-abasement was extreme (he even thought himself more worthy of punishment than Judas) and can be explained only by the comparison he was constantly making between the generosity of God and the selfishness of the sinner.

As a Jesuit he wrote a number of spiritual works of advice for members of his family and the Society, the most important of which was a treatise on prayer, in which he outlined various methods of praying, practical advice on how to avoid distractions and the importance of the sacraments to a life of prayer. He also wrote a treatise on the rosary. Throughout these writings he stressed his favourite themes of self-knowledge and humility, along with the humanity of Jesus, his sufferings, the Eucharist, prayer, and the importance of sanctifying all our daily actions.

When he became general of the Society his spiritual writings were directed toward the sanctification of the members of the Society. Here his series of *Meditations* are noteworthy, especially those based on the liturgical year; others used the feasts of the saints, while another set urged the sanctification of each hour of the day by repeated mental prayer and examination of conscience. His approach to prayer was marked by the use of a clearly defined method, with a stress on Ignatian practices. During these years Francis kept his *Spiritual Diary*, an invaluable document for our understanding of his spiritual life; he prayed continually for the graces he felt he needed and wished to be so totally joined to Christ as to live only for him "as though the world did not exist." He prayed for humiliation and to experience the cross of Christ because he had not given up everything for God: "Christ was crucified and I am without a single wound." The last two lines of the diary, written in 1570, were "I desire to shed my blood for the love of Jesus whenever it may be for his service."

An indication of the opposition to Francis and the suspicion with which some people in Spain continued to regard him is given by his experiences with the Inquisition. In 1559 some of his writings, published in a pirated edition with works of other writers, were placed on the Index of Forbidden Books. The reason appears to have been based on opposition to works of spirituality written in the vernacular, which might have encouraged less-educated laypeople in dubious devotions. Despite the efforts of Francis and his friends to clear his name and remove the slur on the Society, it was not until some years after his death that the inquisitor general withdrew the condemnation.

St Francis is an outstanding example of those people of great wealth and standing in worldly terms who become saints by renouncing everything for Christ's sake. In his case he was not allowed by his superiors to lead the life of seclusion he desired, as they believed that the Church needed his outstanding talents. Involvement in public life, whether political or religious, did not, however, prevent him from developing an interior life of prayer and mortification. It was typical of him that he chose to join the Jesuits, a new and little-known Society subject to misunderstanding and opposition. His efforts on its behalf have led many to regard him as its second founder.

AA.SS., Oct., 5, pp.149-291. The *Opera Omnia* were published in Brussels in 1675; a very large number of letters and other material, including the *Spiritual Diary*, in *Monumenta Historica Societatis Jesu*, 5 vols (1894-1911); modern edition of his *Tratados espirituales* by C. de Dalmases, S.J., (1964). Studies include: P. Suau, *St François Borgia, 1510-1572* (1905); M. Yeo, *The Greatest of the Borgias* (1936); J. Brodrick, S.J., *The Origins of the Jesuits* (1940), and *The Progress of the Jesuits 1556-79* (1946); C. de Delmases, S.J., and J. F. Gilmont, S.J., "Las obras de San Francisco de Borja," *Archivum Historicum Societatis Jesu*, 30 (1961), pp. 125-79; *Dict.Sp.*, 5 (1964), 1019-32.

SS Gereon and Companions, *Martyrs* (date unknown)

It is difficult to distinguish truth from fiction in the case of these martyrs, whom the Roman Martyrology assigned to Cologne during the persecution under Diocletian and Maximian in the early years of the fourth century. Traditionally there were over three hundred of them, and they were said to have been members of a separated detachment of the martyred Theban Legion (22 Sept.). When remains were discovered at Cologne in 1121 they were assumed to be those of the martyrs and were enshrined and venerated, but there is no historical reason to suppose that the relics and the early martyrs were connected.

There is some archaeological evidence for the veneration of a group of martyrs at Cologne before the fifth century, for an inscription says that someone was buried "in the company of the martyrs." St Gregory of Tours (17 Nov.), who lived from *c.* 540 to 594, tells us that at Cologne "there was a basilica built in the place where fifty men of the sacred Theban Legion had been put to death for Christ." He adds that on account of the rich mosaics with which it was adorned, they were called "the golden saints" (*sancti aurei*). It has been suggested that this Latin name may have given rise to the tradition that the soldiers had been from Africa (*Mauri*). Gregory does not mention the name of Gereon. A Cistercian monk, writing in the thirteenth century, invented a detailed *passio* for the martyrs and even had the empress St Helen (18 Aug.) finding their original relics and building a church in their honour at Cologne. That there was a group of soldiers martyred and venerated at Cologne seems certain enough; the rest is conjecture.

AA.SS., Oct., 5, pp. 14-36; *Bibl.SS.*, 6, 216-7. Gereon is mentioned in Bede's martyrology. See also Delehaye, *Origines du culte des martyrs* (1933), pp. 368-81.

St Mihršabor, *Martyr* (*c.* 424)

Mihršabor, or Maharsapor, was born in Persia of noble parents. King Yezdigerd I started to persecute the Christians toward the end of his reign (he died in 420) because of the destruction of a Mazdean temple; the persecution was continued by his successor, Vahram V. Mihršabor was one of the first to be arrested, along with two others named Narses and Sabutaka; after severe tortures these two were executed, but Mihršabor was left in prison for three years in awful conditions and without any light. He was then re-examined by the judge, who found him just as resolute as before in confessing Christ and arguing for the truth of the Christian religion. He was condemned to be thrown into a pit to die of hunger; several days after the sentence had been carried out soldiers opened the pit and found Mihršabor dead, his body reputedly still kneeling as though in prayer and surrounded by a bright light.

The Syriac text of Mihršabor's *passio* was edited critically by P. Bedjan, *Acta martyrum et sanctorum*, 2, pp. 535-9. It is this text that adds the names of the two companions but gives no details about them; the date of 421-2 does not accord with the three years in prison. See also *Bibl.SS.*, 9, 476-7.

St Cerbonius of Piombino, *Bishop* (*c.* 575)

A number of bishops were driven out of north Africa when the Vandals invaded early in the sixth century. Among them were SS Regulus and Cerbonius, who together went to Populonia (present-day Piombino in Tuscany). After a time Cerbonius was made bishop of the place, but when the Lombards invaded he went into exile on the island of Elba, remaining there until his death thirty years later. His body was brought back to Populonia for burial, and he is venerated as the patron of the diocese of Massa Marittima, which includes Piombino.

St Gregory tells a story about Cerbonius in his *Dialogues*: because the bishop gave shelter to some Roman soldiers, he was called before the king of the invading Ostrogoths, who condemned him to be eaten by a bear. The animal, however, refused to harm the holy man, and so Cerbonius was set at liberty. Similar stories are told of some of the early Christian martyrs exposed to wild animals in the Colosseum and elsewhere. A late Life of the saint has him called to Rome to answer the charge of saying Mass at dawn on Sundays to commemorate the resurrection but too early for the people to attend; so many miracles attended his journey to

Rome, however, that he was met by the pope as a saint and sent back with honour. It is not clear what the purpose of such a story was.

The Roman Martyrology used to mention another Cerbonius, bishop of Verona, on this day, but nothing is known of him. The feast of the bishop of Piombino is celebrated by the Canons Regular of the Lateran in Rome because of a tradition that he lived in community with his secular clergy.

AA.SS., Oct., 5, pp. 87–102; *Bibl.SS.*, 3, 1130–1. St Gregory's story is in *Dialogues*, bk. 3, ch. 11; see *P.L.*, 77, 237–40.

St Paulinus of York, *Bishop* (644)

Paulinus was sent to England in 601 by Pope St Gregory (3 Sept.) to support the mission of St Augustine (27 May). In 625 he was consecrated bishop and went as chaplain with Ethelburga, Christian daughter of the king of Kent, to Northumbria, where she was to marry the pagan king, Edwin. Edwin had promised freedom of religious practice to Ethelburga and to think hard about his own conversion, but it proved to be a major task to get him to agree to be baptized. According to Bede's account, Paulinus used every method possible to bring this about, including gifts and letters from the pope, as well as his own apparently considerable powers of persuasion. In the end he was successful (perhaps helped by a more favourable political situation) and in 627 baptized the king, his daughter, and a number of the leading nobles; large-scale conversions followed, and Paulinus once spent thirty-six days at Yeavering in Glendale instructing and baptizing in the local river. He worked also south of the Humber in Lincolnshire and built a stone church in Lincoln, in which he consecrated Honorius archbishop of Canterbury.

Paulinus started the building of a cathedral in York but in 633, after the death of Edwin in battle at the hands of the pagan Penda of Mercia, accompanied Queen Ethelburga when she fled to Kent, where he became bishop of Rochester. The Roman missionaries believed that the support of kings and princes was essential to the success of their work; with Edwin dead, Paulinus presumably thought he could achieve nothing further. Some historians, especially those who favour the Irish missionaries, have argued that a charge of desertion remains unanswered, but Paulinus could have quoted the prudent advice of his mentor in these matters, St Gregory the Great (3 Sept.) in his *Dialogues*: "In this matter we cannot afford to overlook the attitude of the saints. When they find their work producing no results in one place, they move on to another where it can do some good." Gregory had gone on to use the example of St Paul's flight from Damascus and how he had "saved himself for more fruitful labours elsewhere."

Paulinus left the church in Northumbria in the care of a deacon, James, who had accompanied Paulinus on his missionary journeys. Much of the missionary work in the north was undone with the return of a pagan ruler, although James, a very holy person, did what he could to preserve the Faith in the turmoil that followed the invasion, "teaching and baptizing and snatching much prey from the clutches of our old enemy the Devil" (Bede). Christianity was restored under King Oswald (9

Aug.), who called on Irish monks from Iona for a second missionary campaign led by St Aidan (31 Aug.) and based on Lindisfarne. Bede tells us that some of those whom Aidan met were already believers, so Paulinus' work had not been altogether wasted. Paulinus died in Rochester in 644.

St Bede (25 May) is our main source for the life of Paulinus. He tell us that he was "a tall man, stooping a little, with black hair, thin face, and narrow aquiline nose, venerable and awe-inspiring in appearance." His cult was strong in the north of England, where he was venerated as the first apostle of Northumbria, and also in Canterbury and Rochester and a number of monasteries. Five churches were dedicated in his honour. There is some dispute about the dates of his apostolate, which may have started in the north six years or so earlier than Bede said.

AA.SS., Oct., 5, pp. 102-14; Bede, *H.E.*, bk. 2, chs. 9-20, and bk. 3, chs. 1, 14; H. Mayr-Harting, *The Coming of Christianity to Anglo-Saxon England* (1972); B.Colgrave (ed.), *The Whitby Life of Pope Gregory the Great* (1968); *Bibl.SS.*, 10, 163-4; N. K. Chadwick (ed.), *Celt and Saxon* (1963); *O.D.S.*, pp. 384-5.

ST EDWARD THE CONFESSOR (p. 82)
Gold cross and martlets on blue field.

11

St Nectarius of Constantinople, *Bishop* (397)

Nectarius was a native of Tarsus in Cilicia and praetor of Constantinople. When St Gregory Nazianzen (2 Jan.) resigned as bishop in 381, Nectarius was elected in his place. There is a story that the emperor chose him as bishop even though he was not yet baptized and may have been married. The emperor's choice was ratified by the Council of Constantinople, which was sitting at the time, and Nectarius was baptized and ordained. The council also gave Constantinople the right to claim precedence over all other churches except Rome, and Nectarius was often referred to as the first patriarch of Constantinople, though it was some time before the city's pre-eminence and its patriarchal status were acknowledged by the popes.

Nectarius presided over the remainder of the council and was bishop for sixteen years. We know very little of his episcopate except that he constantly opposed the Arian heretics; he was also responsible for doing away with the office of priest-penitentiary and the practice of public penance in the city because of a scandal that had occurred in connection with it. He died on 27 September 397 and was succeeded by St John Chrysostom (13 Sept.). A sermon of his about an unknown St Theodore survives. He features in the Greek Menaion but not in the Roman Martyrology.

AA.SS., Oct., 5, pp. 608-21; *O.D.C.C.*, pp. 958-9. *D.T.C.*, 12, 796-8, deals with the abolition of public penance; the sermon is in *P.G.*, 39, 1821-40. See also *Bibl.SS.*, 9, 831-2.

St Loman of Trim (*c.* 450)

According to Jocelin's Life of St Patrick (17 Mar.), written in the eleventh century, Loman, or Lommàn, was the son of Patrick's sister, Tigris. When Patrick returned to Ireland as a missionary about the year 430, Loman was one of his companions and was left behind to look after the boat and take it up the river Boyne. While his uncle was at Tara converting the high king of Ireland, Loman converted Fortchern, son of the chieftain of Trim, Fedelmid, and later, the chieftain himself and his household. According to Jocelin, Fedelmid gave land at Trim for Patrick to build a church, and Loman later became bishop there.

The so-called Tripartite Life of St Patrick and its sources mention Loman twice, but not as a bishop, while the martyrology of Gorman does list him as a bishop, but without giving any indication of where his see was. There was a later bishop of Trim in the seventh century named Loman, and there may have been confusion between him and the earlier saint. The previous edition of this work gave his feast-day as 17 February, but 11 October is the correct date for it.

Bibl.SS., 8, 86; J. Kearney, *The Problem of St Patrick* (1961), pp. 22, 68; P. Grosjean in *J.E.H.* 1 (1950), pp. 162-9.

St Kenneth, *Abbot (c. 525-600)*

Kenneth, or Canice or Cainnech, was a famous Irish saint, but little is known about him with any certainty. He was born in Glengiven in Derry and as a young man went to Wales to become a monk under St Cadoc (23 Sept.), where he was ordained. Cadoc's excessive praise of the young priest caused jealousies among his brethren, and he was forced to leave. After an alleged visit to Rome he returned to Ireland to study under St Finnian (12 Dec.) at Clonard. He spent some years in Ireland founding monasteries and preaching before going to Scotland, where his presence and cult is evident from a number of place names, including Kilchainnech on Iona and Inchkenneth on Mull. He accompanied St Columba (9 June) on a mission to the pagan king of the Picts and is said to have paralyzed the king's hand to prevent him from murdering them both.

The best known of Kenneth's Irish foundations is at Aghaboe in County Laois; he probably also had a foundation at Kilkenny, where the old cathedral was dedicated to him. He was famous for his zeal as a missionary and his practice of the monastic life; he lived for a time as a hermit and is supposed to have ordered the birds not to sing on Sundays so as not to disturb his prayers. His cult was widespread throughout Ireland, and in Scotland he was honoured particularly in the dioceses of Saint Andrew's and Argyll. His cult also spread to Europe, and he is mentioned in a number of litanies and missals at Reims, Reichenau, Basle, and Frisange (Luxembourg).

AA.SS., Oct., 5, pp. 642-6; a Latin biography was edited by Plummer, *V.S.H.*, 1, pp. 152-69; *The Irish Saints*, pp. 52-6; *D.H.G.E.*, 11, 228-9; A. O. and M. O. Anderson, *Adamnan's Life of Columba* (1961); *Bibl.SS.*, 3, 645-6; *O.D.S.*, pp. 82-3.

St Agilbert, *Bishop (c. 690)*

Agilbert was a Frank by birth who spent several years studying in Ireland, where he was probably consecrated a bishop. When he moved to Wessex he so impressed King Coenwalh, who had recently become a Christian, that the king made him bishop of Dorchester on Thames, a see recently set up by St Birinus (5 Dec.). While in Northumbria he ordained St Wilfrid (12 Oct.) and then attended the Synod of Whitby (663-4), lending his support to the Roman party in the dispute over the date of Easter. Bede tells the story of how Agilbert, when he was ordered by King Oswiu to speak at the synod, asked if Wilfrid could do so in his place, as he would be able to address them in English, whereas he, Agilbert, would have to use an interpreter.

By the time of the synod, Agilbert had already fallen out with his own king and given up his Wessex diocese. Traditionally this has been put down to the king's impatience with Agilbert's inability to speak English and his subsequent decision to introduce an English bishop, Wine, into Agilbert's diocese. The king's decision to divide the diocese was, however, based on political realities: it contained two different tribes, and a second diocese at Winchester made sense. Agilbert took offence at not having been consulted about the division and after attending Whitby returned to Gaul, where he became bishop of Paris in 668. He it was who organized the consecration of St Wilfrid in great splendour at Compiègne. His reputation for learning was considerable: St Theodore, on his way to England to become Archbishop of Canterbury, spent some time with him to learn about the English church. Despite their earlier differences he was still highly regarded by King Coenwalh, and when Wine became bishop of London, Coenwalh invited Agilbert to return to Wessex; Agilbert refused to leave Paris but did send his nephew Eleutherius, who he thought would make a good bishop in his stead.

Agilbert died about the year 690 and was buried at the monastery at Jouarre, where his sister was abbess. His tomb survives. There is no evidence of any early cult of the saint. His relics were examined in the eighteenth century, but no formal recognition of his cult followed. He featured in a calendar of saints drawn up by order of James II in 1686 for the use of English Catholics.

Bede, *H.E.*, bk. 3, chs. 7, 25, 28, and bk.4, ch. 1; *O.D.S.*, p. 7; *Bibl.SS.*, 1, 360. *AA.SS.*, Oct., 5, p. 492, says the editor felt unable to include Agilbert among the saints because there seemed to be no ecclesiastical cult. On the shrine at Jouarre, see *Revue Mabillon* 47 (1957), pp. 258-77.

St Gummarus (775)

Gommaire, or Gommer, was born at Emblehem in modern Belgium and became an important official at the court of Pepin the Short. He accompanied the king on a number of military campaigns and on his return found that his wife had badly mistreated their servants and allowed his affairs to deteriorate into disorder. These domestic troubles provided, for the previous edition of this work, the principal occasion for the exercise of Gummarus' sanctity and were sent by God "to perfect the virtue of his servant and exalt him to the glory of the saints." He restored everything to good order and made restitution to those his wife had cheated. He was unable to reform her, however, and in the end gave up the attempt to cure her wilfulness and retired to live a secluded life. He died as a solitary.

It is not clear how much weight should be attached to these family troubles. He was known for his pious life and generous charity. It is also recorded that at one time he planned to go on pilgrimage to Rome with some friends but was inspired instead to build a chapel near his home, where he often retired for prayer, but without neglecting his wordly affairs. He became a close friend of St Rumold (3 July). He died on 11 October 775, and was buried in his chapel. He became famous as a miracle-worker and his cult spread throughout the Low Countries. By the eleventh century his tomb was looked after by a college of canons who claimed him as their founder. Pilgrim banners in his honour and showing scenes from his life were in widespread use from at least the fifteenth century.

The iconography of Gummarus is interesting for two reasons. First of all, it makes no reference to the domestic troubles which the previous edition of this work makes so central. Secondly, it shows a change in the image of the saint, from earlier depictions of him as a crusading knight to late medieval images of him as a wealthy lord in ermine stole and Merovingian-style hat, holding a pilgrim's staff in his left hand; a healing spring flows from where this staff touches the ground. A seventeenth-century statue in Antwerp cathedral shows him as a Roman centurion, again with an ermine stole.

AA.SS., Oct., 5, pp. 674-97, gives the two versions of his Life, one in prose and the other in verse, written at the end of the eleventh century; a very full discussion is in T. Paaps, *De hl. Gummaire . . . Critische studie* (1944); *Catholicisme*, 5, 93-4; *Bibl.SS.*, 7, 521-4.

St Bruno the Great, *Bishop* (925-65)

Bruno was the youngest son of Henry the Fowler, king of the Germans, and his wife, St Matilda (14 Mar.), and was born in 925. His education began at the cathedral school of Utrecht when he was only four, and he soon acquired a reputation for learning. He was called to the royal court by his brother, who had become King Otto I, also called the Great, and became his confidential secretary at the age of fifteen; soon afterwards he was ordained deacon and given the two abbeys of Lorsch and Corvey to administer. This irregular preferment had good results, as the two abbeys were reformed under Bruno's direction. When he was twenty-five he was ordained priest, but he continued to be heavily involved in politics, accompanying Otto to Italy as his chancellor, an office he had held for some years even though traditionally it had been given only to archbishops.

In 953 Bruno was elected archbishop of Cologne at the instigation of the king and ruled the diocese for twelve years. He was known as a reformer, visiting his diocese regularly, encouraging learning among his clergy, and restoring the monastic spirit in a number of religious houses. He also used his prestige to encourage reform in other German dioceses, and when the duke of Lorraine rebelled against Otto, the king deposed him and put Bruno in his place, thus increasing the archbishop's power and standing and making him, in effect, a powerful prince; the later position of the archbishops of Cologne as prince-bishops was foreshadowed in Bruno's dual position. Bishops at the time in the German lands needed the protection of a central monarch as defence against the interference and depredations of the dukes; for his part the king was happy to use the bishops and build up their power through grants of land and privileges to counterbalance the position of the dukes. The bishops became vassals of the king, doing homage for their lands and becoming key political figures; they and their clergy were used in every sphere of royal government. While this inevitably meant some loss of independence, and royal control of appointments, it enhanced the importance and authority of the Church and gave reforming bishops an opportunity to bring about change.

Bruno set out to restore order in Lorraine after the rebellion and was eventually able to establish peace. He aimed to reform the Church there by appointing bishops of high quality, gaining for himself the nickname "the bishop-maker." His power increased still further in 961 when Otto again went to Italy (where he was crowned Holy Roman Emperor by the pope) and made him co-regent of the empire along with his half-brother William, archbishop of Mainz. On the emperor's return Bruno was once more involved in disputes in Lorraine and was again successful in bringing peace.

Bruno was taken ill unexpectedly in Reims and died on 11 October 965, only forty years old. He had requested that his body be taken back to Cologne to be buried in the abbey church of St Pantaleon, which he had founded. The title "the Great" might seem to belong more fittingly to his more famous namesake, the founder of the Carthusians (6 Oct.), but it was given to Bruno no doubt because of his high standing as the emperor's brother and his position in both Germany and France. He had used his power for the good of the Church as well as the State, and if justification for the existence of prince-bishops were needed, then some might be found in the life of St Bruno of Cologne. His cult was never widespread, however, and was, indeed, limited for a long time to the abbey which claimed his relics; in 1870 it was approved for the rest of the diocese of Cologne.

We have a reliable Life of the saint, written a few years after his death by his disciple Ruotger, in *AA.SS.*, Oct., 5, pp. 698-765; a new edition was edited in 1951 by I. Ott in *M.G.H., Scriptores*, 10; *D.H.G.E.*, 10, 956-7; *Bibl.SS.*, 3, 581-3.

Bd James of Ulm (1407-91)

James Griesinger was born in Ulm in Germany in 1407. When he was twenty-five he went to Italy and became a soldier in the service of the kingdom of Naples. He was shocked by the behaviour of the soldiers and found that they were impervious to all his attempts to improve them, so he left the army and became a legal secretary in Capua. He was so successful in his new career that his master refused to let him go when he wanted to return to Germany. James left secretly, but when he had reached Bologna he was persuaded to become a soldier again. After frequent visits to the shrine of St Dominic (8 Aug.) he became a lay brother in the Dominican house and lived there for fifty years, a model of religious observance and virtue.

James became highly skilled at painting on glass, his main occupation as a lay brother. He was noted for his intense life of prayer and frequently experienced ecstasies. A number of miracles were attributed to his intercession while he was alive and also after his death. He died at the age of eighty-four in 1491 and was beatified in 1825.

There exists a contemporary Life written in Italian by a Fr Ambrosino of Saracino, of which *AA.SS.*, Oct., 5, pp. 793-803, gives a Latin translation. See also J. Procter (ed.), *Short Lives of the Dominican Saints* (1901), pp. 287-91; *Bibl.SS.*, 7, 405-6; H. Wilms, *J. G. aus Ulm* (1922).

St Alexander Sauli, *Bishop* (1534-92)

Alexander Sauli was born of Genoese parents in Milan in 1534. As a boy he showed signs of unusual piety and a special devotion to Our Lady. After receiving a good education, he became for a time a page at the Milanese court of the emperor Charles V but gave up a promising career to join the Clerks Regular of St Paul, or Barnabites, at the age of seventeen. He went to complete his studies at their college in Pavia, where he paid for a new library out of his own money. To test the vocation of this wealthy novice his superiors ordered him to carry a large cross into the marketplace, dressed as a page, and to preach to the people, which he did to great effect. After his ordination in 1556 he was appointed to teach philosophy and theology at the university and became theologian to the bishop, while also making a reputation for himself as a successful preacher. He urged the Forty Hours Devotion and frequent reception of Holy Communion. He was invited by St Charles Borromeo (4 Nov.) to preach in the cathedral at Milan, where he made a great impression on both St Charles and the future Pope Gregory XIV; he became their confessor and counsellor. In 1567 he was elected provost general of his Congregation and was regarded in his lifetime as its father, lawgiver, and living model.

St Charles and Pope St Pius V (30 Apr.) wanted the Barnabites, who had been founded as a reformed Congregation in 1530, to merge with what was left of the wealthy Humiliati friars, who were in need of radical reform. Alexander objected strongly, fearing that the zeal and vigour of his new Congregation might suffer from the laxity of the friars. He was willing to work for the latters' reform but successfully resisted any merger. The friars were soon to be disbanded altogether after one of them tried to assassinate St Charles in 1571.

The pope was impressed by his firmness and reforming zeal, and in 1570 appointed him to be bishop of Aleria in Corsica, a diocese which after years of neglect was in an even worse state than the friars; its clergy were ignorant and its people without the rudiments of religion, while the island itself was split by family vendettas and at the prey of brigands and Barbary pirates. The town of Aleria was in ruins, and Alexander, with three Barnabite companions, had to live in Tallonia.

As bishop he carried through severe reforming measures, visiting his diocese despite the physical dangers, holding synods to enforce the decrees of the Council of Trent, and winning over or dismissing those who opposed him. He worked there for twenty years, and his reforms were so successful that he was known as the apostle of Corsica. He built a seminary and a cathedral, preached to the people, and cared for the sick, especially in the famine and plague which struck Corsica in 1580. He lived in extreme poverty himself without, he said, the means even to build himself as much as a Capuchin's cell. He had visited Rome on a number of occasions and became a friend of St Philip Neri (26 May), who held him up as a model reforming bishop.

Because of his success in Corsica he was offered other sees by the pope, but he refused all preferments until Gregory XIV commanded him to become bishop of Pavia in 1591. He set out to visit his new diocese, but died at Calosso the following year. He was said to have had the gift of prophecy and the ability to quell storms during his life; after his death further miracles were attributed to his intercession. He was beatified in 1742 and canonized in 1904. His body is venerated in the cathedral in Pavia. There is a seventeenth-century statue of him in ecstasy in the basilica in Genoa.

Alexander was a very able canonist and also wrote a large number of pastoral and catechetical works, including the *Doctrine of the Roman Catechism* (1581). He was severe with himself and others and must be counted among the important reforming bishops of the sixteenth century who were in the van of Catholic reform; his life was spent attacking laxity wherever it existed in the Church and in working tirelessly to implement the decrees of the Council of Trent.

AA.SS., Oct., 5, pp. 806-34, gives a contemporary Latin Life; O. Premoli, *Storia dei Barnabiti* (2 vols., 1914, 1922); F. T. Moltedo, *Vita di S. Alessandro Sauli* (1904); on the saint's writings, G. Boffito, *Scrittori Barnabiti* (1933-4); *Bibl.SS.*, 1, 808-12; *N.C.E.*, 12, 1101-2.

St Mary Soledad (1826-87)

The parents of Mary Soledad were Francisco Torres and Antonia Acosta of Madrid. She was the second of their five children, born in 1826 and christened Manuela. She was a quiet child, reputed to have given food to her playmates when they were hungry and to have been more interested in teaching them their prayers than joining in their games. For a time she thought of becoming a Dominican nun, but then a local Servite priest, Miguel Martínez y Sanz, invited a group of local women to form a community in order to help the sick of his parish; Manuela joined this community and so started what was to be her lifelong vocation. She took the religious name Mary Soledad from the Spanish word for "desolate" in honour of Our Lady of Sorrows, to whom she had a special devotion.

Five years later the priest took half the community with him to establish a new foundation in the African colony of Fernando Po, and Mary Soledad was left in charge of the sisters who remained in Madrid. The local bishop was not in favour of their continuing as a religious Congregation, and it looked for a time as though they would have to disband. The Congregation was saved by the support of the queen and the local civil authorities, who valued the work being done for the poor and sick of the capital and whose help had been sought by Mary Soledad. In 1861 the Rule of the Congregation, now named the Handmaids of Mary Serving the Sick, was given diocesan approval, and its work expanded rapidly; an institution for young delinquents was taken over and several new houses set up. The work of the Sisters in the cholera epidemic of 1865 won general praise, but there were internal dissensions, and some of the Sisters left to join another Congregation. The work continued to prosper, however, and in 1875 the first overseas foundation was established in Cuba. Three years later the ancient hospital of St Charles attached to the Royal Monastery of the Escorial was entrusted to the Sisters, and houses and hospitals were opened throughout Spain.

Mary Soledad remained in charge of the Congregation until her death on 11

October 1887. Her last words to her Sisters were, "Children, live together in peace and unity." For thirty-five years she had led the Handmaids of Mary Serving the Sick, not only inspiring them spiritually but also making sure that they were trained and technically equipped for the work they were undertaking. Since her death the Congregation has spread to England, Italy, France, Portugal, and the Americas. She was beatified in 1950 and canonized in 1970 as María Soledad Torres Acosta. In his homily at the canonization Pope Paul VI said hers "was a simple and silent life summed up in two words: humility and charity." Her mission to the sick was not original in the history of the Church, but she approached it so systematically that she was a "lamp of social wisdom," anticipating many of the scientific techniques of modern health care.

A.A.S., 42 (1950), pp. 182-97, for her beatification; 62 (1970), pp. 81-8, for her canonization; *Bibl.SS.*, Suppl. 1, 835-6; E. Federici, *Santa Maria Soledad Torres Acosta ... degli infermi* (1969).

ST WILFRID
Seven voided red lozenges on gold field
(possibly a net for "fisher of men," or
the seven hills of Rome).

12

ST WILFRID, *Bishop* (634-709)

Wilfrid was born in Northumbria in 634. When he was fourteen he went to the monastery at Lindisfarne; the four years he spent there were important, as he seems to have become dissatisfied with the Celtic religious customs followed there. He then decided to go to Rome; on the way he spent about a year in Lyons with the saintly bishop Annemund (28 Sept.; wrongly called Delfinus by Bede). In Rome he was instructed by Boniface, a papal secretary, for some months before returning to Lyons, where he remained with Annemund for three years.

Wilfrid's experiences during these years were even more influential than those at Lindisfarne had been. It was not just that he became versed in the Roman way of doing things. At Lyons he saw and admired a different approach to the bishop's role, one that involved him in politics as a key part of the establishment of authority and order in his region. "If he had regarded men like Aidan [31 Aug.] and Finnan [19 Jan.] as the highest examples of sanctity and episcopal virtue, he would regard them no longer as such once his pilgrimage was over" (Foley). For the rest of his life Wilfrid held an exalted view of the episcopal office, a view which he upheld consistently despite the bitter dissensions and years in exile that were the result. He learned very early on how extreme these results could be: Annemund was murdered on the orders of the queen, and Wilfrid escaped only because he was a foreigner.

On his return to England Wilfrid was appointed abbot of a new monastery at Ripon, which had been founded by King Alcfrith with the help of Celtic monks from Melrose, including St Cuthbert (20 Mar.). These monks had lost the king's favour because they had insisted on following their Irish customs; Wilfrid was appointed to introduce Roman ways. The most obvious difference between the two traditions was in the way of calculating the date of Easter, a difference which meant, for example, that the king and queen might each be keeping the Lenten fast and celebrating Easter at different times as they followed their individual traditions. At the famous Synod of Whitby (663-4), Wilfrid put the Roman case so strongly that he carried the day. Too much has probably been made of this synod: its importance was symbolic rather than essential. It was not the beginning of Roman centralization and the destruction of a native tradition that allowed more room for local initiatives; Roman influences were already strong in England, and the southern Irish themselves had been using the Roman tradition over Easter for some time. But it was important for Wilfrid: soon afterwards he was appointed bishop of Northumbria.

Because he regarded the English bishops as somehow unsound in their beliefs or doubtfully consecrated, he went to Compiègne in France to receive consecration at the hands of the bishop of Paris. The ceremonies were carried out with great splendour, and Wilfrid made sure he had a large retinue to show his wealth and importance. It is said that the twelve bishops who took part in the ceremony carried Wilfrid into the sanctuary on a golden throne. He stayed there for too long, however, and on his return in 666 found that the king had appointed St Chad (2 Mar.) in his place, so Wilfrid retired for a time to his monastery at Ripon. On Chad's resignation he was restored as bishop and settled in York, where he rebuilt the church which had been begun by St Paulinus (10 Oct.). His diocese was very large, stretching from the Humber (indeed, from the Wash at one period) to the Forth, and Wilfrid intended to keep all of it under his own Rule. A large diocese was necessary, he believed, to provide the revenue for the expansion and consolidation of religion through the building of churches and monasteries. It also meant that the bishop would be seen as a man of standing and power. As a recent biographer has said, "There were, therefore, pastoral reasons for not being too humble in public" (Mayr-Harting). He received many favours from the king and queen and was able, for example, to endow a large monastery at Hexham, which was said to have the biggest church north of the Alps.

The archbishop of Canterbury, St Theodore (19 Sept.), had other ideas, however, and he and Wilfrid were soon involved in a dispute that was more important in its implications than the famous Easter controversy. Theodore's ideal of the diocesan bishop was drawn from his experience in Italy and the Mediterranean regions: the bishop was the active pastor of a small area centred on a town, the day-to-day leader of his clergy and chosen for his holiness rather than for the figure he might cut in the corridors of power. Not for him the quasi-prince bishops of Gaul, nor the huge territorial bishoprics of England where what was important was the kingdom or the tribe, not the town or city. While Theodore was wondering what to do with the diocese of Wilfrid, the latter fell out with the king, Egfrith, no doubt because he supported the queen, St Etheldreda (23 June), in her decision not to consummate her marriage but, instead, to become a nun. Wilfrid had other opponents, too, some of whom were jealous of his wealth and position at court; one of his lifelong opponents was the powerful St Hilda of Whitby (17 Nov.), who had been on the losing side at the Synod of Whitby. When the king expelled Wilfrid from Northumbria in 678, Theodore took the opportunity to divide his diocese, first into three and later into five smaller dioceses. Wilfrid took this as tantamount to being deposed and appealed to the pope against Theodore. He set out to Rome to plead his case. His was the first Anglo-Saxon appeal of its kind, though such appeals had been in use in both Gaul and Ireland previously, and too much should not be made of it as an example of Wilfrid's ultra-Roman stance.

The ship in which he sailed from England was blown off course and Wilfrid landed in Friesland. There he stayed for the winter and following spring, preaching to the people, converting many, and thus starting the English mission to that part of

Europe, which was carried on so fruitfully by St Willibrord (7 Nov.). Here we see a different side of Wilfrid—the pastoral missionary, using his considerable eloquence to persuade and convince rather than to confront. He had also a very practical grasp of the skills of fishermen and helped the Frisians to develop their abilities; as Bede says, the people "began to hope more readily for heavenly things from the ministry of him whose ministry had yielded temporal benefits."

In Rome, Wilfrid persuaded the pope that he should be restored to his see, but the pope also upheld the division of his former diocese, allowing Wilfrid, however, to choose his own suffragan bishops. On his return to Northumbria he still met with hostility from the king, who accused him of getting the pope's support by bribery and put him in prison for nine months before expelling him again. This time Wilfrid went to work as a missionary among the people of Sussex and Wessex; he met with the same success as he had in Friesland, and he was able to found a monastery at Selsey. This became the base for a diocese, which was later transferred to Chichester. He worked in those parts for about five years, until Theodore persuaded the new king of Northumbria, Aldfrith, to restore him. Yet again Wilfrid quarrelled with the king—the cause is not clear—and was in exile again from 692 to 703, having been deprived of his bishopric and of the abbeys of Hexham and Ripon. He appealed again to Rome, and was eventually restored to his two abbeys, ending his life as bishop of Hexham, not without further skirmishes with the king. Wilfrid died in 709 at the monastery of Oundle in Mercia (present-day Northamptonshire), one of the several monasteries he had founded outside his own diocese. He divided his considerable wealth among the poor, his former companions in exile, his churches, and the abbots of his monasteries "so that they might purchase the goodwill of kings and bishops"—he had an eye to the main chance to the end.

There is no doubt that Wilfrid was triumphalist in his approach to being a bishop. He enjoyed wealth and power and seemed to revel in the ins and outs of politics. He stood on his rights too often, perhaps, for our modern liking, but everything he did was directed toward the advancement of the Christian faith in a country still half-pagan and still ruled by all-powerful and often arbitrary kings and princes. His latest biographer calls him a man of the world with outstanding gifts and able to present Christianity in an attractive way to all levels of society. He was interested in learning, in the liturgy, in well-ordered monasticism, in founding churches, and in the unremitting labour of the missionary (Mayr-Harting). Whenever possible he led by example; he suffered exile and prison for his belief in the **need for strong episcopal independence if the Faith were to survive the vicissitudes of politics and the arbitrariness of kings. He is one of the great figures of the Anglo-**Saxon church, different in his sanctity from the ascetic and retiring Irish monks and bishops but witnessing all the same to a life devoted to God and spent in the service of the Church.

He was venerated at Ripon and Hexham; later, as his relics were transferred to Canterbury and Worcester, his cult spread throughout the country. Forty-eight churches were dedicated to him; the crypts of his churches at Ripon and Hexham survive. He was usually depicted as a bishop in all his attire or as a missionary to the pagan peoples.

We have an early Life written by his disciple Eddius Stephanus and edited by B. Colgrave, *The Life of Bishop Wilfrid by Eddius Stephanus* (1927; 1985); Bede *H. E.,* esp. bks. 4, chs. 13, 14; 5, ch. 19; *Bibl.SS.*, 12, 1092-4; *O.D.S.*, pp. 492-4; H. Mayr-Harting, *The Coming of Christianity to Anglo-Saxon England* (1972) and *Saint Wilfrid* (1986); D. P. Kirby (ed.), *St Wilfrid at Hexham* (1974); W. T. Foley, *Images of Sanctity in Eddius Stephanus' Life of Bishop Wilfrid* (1992).

St Maximilian of Lorch, *Bishop and Martyr* (? 281)

According to a late Life of this saint, written about the year 1300, Maximilian was born at Celeia (Cilje, in former Yugoslavia) sometime in the third century. He visited Rome on pilgrimage, and Pope Sixtus II (257-8) gave him the task of evangelizing the Roman province of Pannonia, where he worked for over twenty years. He became bishop of Lorch, south-east of the Austrian town of Linz, and was martyred back in Cilje in 281. He is considered to be the apostle of Noricum (the east-central area of the Alps) and is patron of the diocese of Passau.

All we know for certain is that at the beginning of the eighth century a bishop of Salzburg built a chapel over the tomb of a certain Maximilian at Bischofshofen, to the south-east of Salzburg. Presumably there was already a cult of the saint, perhaps as a missionary bishop, in the area. Tenth-century documents refer to him variously as a confessor, a martyr, and a bishop. Relics of a Maximilian and a Roman martyr Felicity were translated in 976 by the bishop of Passau, who was keen to add importance to his see and so made out that he was the successor of the archbishops of Lorch, the first of whom had been Maximilian. Whether these two Maximilians were the same person or not is not clear.

He is probably the same saint as is venerated as bishop of Capodistria. The Roman Martyrology mentions him under both 12 and 29 October.

AA.SS., Oct., 6, pp. 23-58, gives the Life of 1300; see also I. Zibermayr, *Noricum, Bayern und Osterreich* (1956); *Anal.Boll.* 77 (1959), p.385; *Bibl.SS.*, 9, 23-5.

SS Felix and Cyprian, *Bishops*, and Many Others, *Martyrs* (*c.* 484)

The Roman Martyrology for today commemorates those who died in North Africa during the persecutions under Huneric, the Arian king of the Vandals. He intensified the efforts of his predecessor to destroy Catholic Christianity in his kingdom, burning churches and forbidding meetings for prayer. All the ancient historians of the period mention the ferocity of the persecution, which we can date from 482. It appears that very large numbers (accounts say 4,966) of Catholic Christians, bishops, priests, and laypeople, young and old, healthy and infirm, were gathered together and marched in groups to different centres; there attempts were made to get them to adopt Arianism, but these failed. Some of them were then forced into the desert, where they died either from the harsh conditions or from the cruelty of the tribes who attacked them; some were sold as slaves, while others were sent into exile. A contemporary eyewitness, Victor, bishop of Vita, described their sufferings and how some of them went to their deaths singing psalms after they had been kept locked up in prison in terrible conditions; he adds that some Christians joined the prisoners voluntarily in order to achieve martyrdom.

Amongst those martyred was Felix, bishop of Abbir, whom Huneric refused to spare even though he was very old and half-paralyzed; he had to be carried into the desert. Cyprian also was a bishop; he and Victor spent their time and money caring for those who were suffering until he was arrested himself and sent into the desert, where he died from the hardships he had to endure.

Victor of Vita is our only source of detailed information about these martyrs; his *History of the Persecutions in the Province of Africa* is printed and discussed in *AA.SS.*, Oct., 6. pp. 83–96; see also *Bibl.SS.*, 5, 559–60. The previous edition of this work noted that it was curious that no identifiable mention of the group occurs in the ancient calendar of Carthage or in St Jerome's martyrology.

St Edwin, *Martyr* (584–633)

The ancient kingdom of Northumbria was made up of two principal areas, Bernicia and Deira (roughly speaking, present-day Northumberland and Yorkshire). Edwin was a prince of Deira who spent many years in exile because Northumbria was ruled by King Ethelfrith of Bernicia. When Ethelfrith was killed in battle in 616, Edwin became king in his place and soon became *bretwalda*, or over-king, with authority over the other Anglo-Saxon rulers. He was not a Christian at this time, and so when he sought to marry Ethelburga, daughter of the Christian king of Kent, doubts were raised in case he interfered with her practice of her religion. He gave assurances that this would not happen, and so Ethelburga travelled north, with St Paulinus (10 Oct.) as her chaplain and missionary bishop.

According to Bede, Edwin was a cautious person who hesitated for a long time over whether to become a Christian or not. Three things seem to have persuaded him to change: an escape from assassination, the memory of a vision and a promise he had made while in exile, and a warm letter of encouragement from Pope St Gregory the Great (3 Sept.). The king called his council together and took their advice; one of the nobles described human life as a "sparrow flying quickly through your hall as you sit at supper on a winter's day. . . . The fire burns in the middle, and the hall where you sup is warm . . . and the bird enters by one door and flies straight out at the other. While it is inside, the winter storms do not touch it, but when it has passed through this short moment of comfort it passes from winter to winter and disappears. . . . Even so short is the life of man, and of what follows it, and what preceded it, we know nothing at all." If the new religion helped them to understand these things better, then they should accept it. Edwin's pagan high priest denounced the ancient religion as being of no value; the nobles called on Paulinus to teach them more about God and finally accepted Christianity. Edwin and his chief followers were baptized at York in the year 627.

Edwin then made Paulinus bishop of York and started the building of a stone church there, on the site of the present minster. For the next five years he worked to spread Christianity throughout his kingdom, which he extended and pacified to such an extent that Bede tells us that "there was such perfect peace in Britain, wherever the rule of King Edwin extended, that, as people still say, a woman and her new-born baby could walk throughout the island from sea to sea unharmed." In 633, however, he was defeated and killed in the battle of Hatfield Chase by a combined force of the Welsh king Cadwallon and the pagan king Penda of Mercia.

Whether Edwin should be regarded as a martyr or not is open to question. He was certainly venerated as such in England; it is likely that there was a cult at Whitby and York, but the loss of the liturgical books of the abbey of Whitby (where his body was venerated) leaves a major gap in the sources. The fact of the translation of his body, however, may be taken as the equivalent of canonization in those days. Pope Gregory XIII allowed him to be featured among the martyrs in the chapel of the English College in Rome. One or two ancient churches were dedicated to him.

The previous edition of this work concluded that his claims to sanctity were less doubtful than those of some other royal saints, English and other. This appears to be barely fair: Bede is a reliable source in these matters, and he tells us that Edwin was a just and successful ruler who adopted Christianity only after considerable thought and then did all he could to convert his peoples without resorting to force.

Bede, *H.E.*, bks. 2, chs. 5, 9-18, 20; 3, ch. 1; B. Colgrave (ed.), *The Earliest Life of Gregory the Great* (1968); D. P. Kirby, "Bede and Northumbrian Chronology," in *E.H.R.* 78 (1963), pp. 514-27; N. K. Chadwick, *Celt and Saxon* (1963); H. Mayr-Harting, *The Coming of Christianity to Anglo-Saxon England* (1972); *Bibl.SS.*, 4, 935.

St Ethelburga of Barking, *Abbess (c. 670)*

Ethelburga may have been born in Lincolnshire; she came from a wealthy, perhaps even a royal, family and was the sister of St Erkenwald (13 May), who later became bishop of London. He had founded a monastery for monks and nuns at Barking in Essex, and he appointed Ethelburga to be its abbess. There is a story that Erkenwald invited a French nun to be prioress at Barking under his sister, to teach her the true monastic traditions. Bede says of her that she lived according to the Rule, "devoutly and in an orderly manner, providing for those she ruled, as was also manifested by heavenly miracles." Among the examples he gives of these miracles, one concerns a vision one of the nuns had that foretold Ethelburga's death; he adds, "And no one who knew her holy life can doubt that when she departed this life the gates of our heavenly home opened at her coming." She died between 664 and 678. When the same nun was herself dying, Ethelburga appeared to her and comforted her, telling her exactly when she would die.

Traces of a liturgical cult can be found in some medieval calendars and antiphons.

Little can be added to Bede's account in *H.E.*, bk. 4, chs. 6-10, but see also *AA.SS.*, Oct., 5, pp. 648-52, for a short Life; for the Life written by Goscelin of Canterbury, see *Anal.Boll.* 58 (1940), p. 101. See also *Bibl.SS.*, 5, 118.

13

ST EDWARD THE CONFESSOR (1005-66)

Edward was the son of Ethelred II, the Unready, and his Norman wife, Emma. He was born in 1005 (possibly 1004) and because of the troubled state of the country was sent abroad to Normandy when he was about ten years old. He remained there until 1041, when he was recalled to England, where he became king in 1042. His most recent biographer suggests that it was in Normandy that Edward learned certain qualities that were to be to his advantage as king: "opportunism and flexibility, patience, caution, a grasp of the oblique approach . . . wordly wisdom . . . prepared to accept whatever fate had in store" (Barlow). He survived for a relatively long reign and kept his enemies, internal and external, at bay; the country his successor, Harold, took over in 1066 was more peaceful, united, and stable than had been the case in 1042 when Edward had become king.

It is his record as king that must be established if we are to assess his saintliness and not any claimed incidental holy actions. It is, however, difficult to be certain about many aspects of his reign and his own character and motivations. As his cult developed, the reputation of his reign became more and more enhanced as a supposed golden age; he was very popular and for a long time was one of the leading patron saints of England. Later Lives stressed his holiness, the miracles worked through his intercession, his lifelong chastity, his kindness to the poor, and his generosity to the Church, especially to monks. Some writers have even dismissed him as a holy simpleton, making out that he had none of the qualities of the strong ruler demanded by the troubled times and that he was in reality a monk *manqué*. It was clearly to the benefit of the monks of Westminster Abbey to encourage any account that added to his saintliness and to his renown as a miracle-worker, for they had his shrine, which they wanted to become a leading attraction for pilgrims. It was Osbert of Clare, prior of Westminster in the 1130s, who produced the first saintly Life of Edward and did so much to promote the royal cult. It was also useful to later kings to be able to claim a royal saint among their predecessors, especially one who linked them to the Anglo-Saxon past and legitimated their rule.

Some elements in the traditional accounts of the reign can almost certainly be dismissed: his life of chastity and the non-consumation of his marriage, for example; there is neither trustworthy evidence to support it nor any obvious reason why Edward and his wife, Edith, should have chosen such a way of life. Again, most of the miracle stories are late and somewhat dubious, though the earliest Life, written within a year or two of the king's death, mentions four or five cures brought about by the use of water in which Edward had washed his hands. Later, his aid was to be invoked especially against skin disorders and epilepsy; it is claimed that he was the first of the kings of England to have touched for the king's evil (scrofula), but the evidence is at best uncertain. There is, finally, a story that he did away with the unpopular heregeld tax, which had gone toward the upkeep of the army, and gave what had been collected to the poor; it is unlikely, however, that the suspension of the tax was more than temporary.

We are on surer ground with his abilities as king. He defended the country from external enemies and protected his royal authority from over-ambitious subjects. He seems to have wanted to avoid war if at all possible but was resolute in gathering an army and navy and deploying them against the threat of invasion. He also made a number of foreign alliances to strengthen his position. The greatest threat to his authority at home came from Earl Godwin and his family. He tried to tie the earl into an alliance by marrying his daughter, Edith, but when Godwin threatened rebellion in 1051, Edward did not hesitate to exile him and his family and to send Edith into seclusion in a convent. He soon had to give way and allow Godwin to return and re-establish his position. This, and his general flexiblity and caution, can be taken as weakness and a failure to stand up to consistent opposition; on the other hand, there is a virtue in not driving one's enemies to extremes and in preserving the country from civil war. The return of Godwin did not weaken Edward during the rest of his reign, and the eventual settlement had been reached without any fighting. The peace was genuine and a welcome contrast with preceding reigns.

Despite his later reputation he does not seem to have been a particularly generous benefactor of the Church, except in the case of Westminster. A sensible use of ecclesiastical appointments was an essential part of establishing royal authority and good government, and his judgment in these matters was sound, although in the case of Stigand, later archbishop of Canterbury, administrative ability was given too much weight over religious considerations. If he appointed foreigners to English sees, it was because of the quality of the men concerned and not part of a desire to destroy the Englishness of the Church. His reign saw some important local reforms; certainly there were no scandals, and links with Rome were strengthened.

His decision to refound the abbey at Westminster was the result of a vow which he is said to have made while in Normandy: he would go to Rome as a pilgrim if God restored the fortunes of his family. When he became king he was unable to leave the country to fulfill his vow and so asked the pope to be released from it. This was granted on condition that he should endow a monastery dedicated to St Peter. Edward chose an existing house at Thorney to the west of London, gave it rich grants of land and money, and started the building of a magnificent Romanesque church, the forerunner of the existing Westminster Abbey. He was too ill to attend the opening of the choir of the new church and died on 5 January 1066 (a Westminster tradition says 4 January); he was buried in the abbey. In 1102 the tomb was opened and the body was found to be intact and was translated to a new site. Attempts were made to have the king canonized, but the upheavals of Stephen's reign seem to have prevented it. Finally, in 1161, Henry II persuaded Pope Alexander III, whom he was supporting against rival claimants, that the canonization should go ahead. A second translation of the body, still incorrupt, took place two years later in the presence of St Thomas Becket (29 Dec.), when the sermon was preached by St Aelred of Rievaulx (12 Jan.); a final translation took place in 1269. The relics survived the Reformation and are still in Westminster Abbey. In 1689 the feast was extended to the whole of the Western Church and the date of the first translation, 13 October, was fixed as the feast-day.

It is important to see Edward's reign in its own right and not as a prologue to the Norman invasion. There was much more success than failure in it, and the king was neither piously inept nor a mere puppet of others. Beneath the layers of holy legend it is possible to see a ruler of both caution and vigour, determined to keep his country intact, yet flexible enough not to cause extreme reaction. His reputation for holiness probably started during his life, and there is no reason to doubt his generosity to the poor. The contemporary Anglo-Saxon Chronicle expressed sadness at the loss of "so dear a lord, a noble king."

In art the saint is most commonly shown holding the ring which he is supposed to have given as alms to a poor man who was St John the Evangelist in disguise, or else doing charitable works. The best-known English picture of him is in the Wilton diptych (*c.*1390) in the National Gallery in London, in which he features with St Edmund and St John the Baptist presenting Richard II to Our Lady. He also features in the Bayeux Tapestry.

Contemporary accounts of the king's reign are in *A.S.C.* for the years 1042-66; a collection of early lives in H. R. Luard (ed.), *Lives of Edward the Confessor* (1858); for the earliest known Life, F. Barlow (ed.), *The Life of King Edward Who Rests at Westminster* (1962); Aelred of Rievaulx's totally hagiographical but influential *Life of St Edward*, trans. and ed. by Jerome Bertram (1990). See also M. Bloch, "La vie d'Edouard le Confesseur par Osbert de Clare," *Anal.Boll.* 41 (1923), pp. 5-132; Bloch's dating is questioned by R. W. Southern, "The First Life of Edward the Confessor," *E.H.R.* 58 (1943), pp. 385-400. The best modern account, critical of most of the saintly elements, is F. Barlow, *Edward the Confessor* (2d ed., 1979); see also his *The English Church 1000-1066* (1963); *Bibl.SS.*, 4, 921-6; *O.D.S.*, pp. 149-51; B. W. Scholz, "The Canonization of Edward the Confessor," *Speculum* 36 (1961), pp. 38-60; L. E. Tanner, "Some Representations of St Edward the Confessor," in *Journal of the Brit. Archaeological Association* 15 (1952), pp. 1-12. On the creation and role of royal saints, see S. Ridyard, *The Royal Saints of Anglo-Saxon England* (1988).

SS Faustus, Januarius, and Martial, *Martyrs* (*c.* 304)

The Roman Martyrology mentions these three martyrs, and the poet Aurelius Prudentius, writing in the fourth century, refers to them as the "Three Crowns of Córdoba," which the city would be happy to take before Christ as its offering on judgment day. According to their *passio*, which unfortunately is of no historical value, they were cruelly tortured in turn to get them to sacrifice to the gods. Faustus proclaimed, "There is only one God, who created us all," while Martial cried out, "Jesus Christ is my comfort. There is only one God, Father, Son and

Holy Ghost, to whom homage and praise are due." In the end the three were condemned to be burned alive, and the sentence was carried out at Córdoba in Spain, probably during the persecution under the emperor Diocletian (284-305).

The fact of their martyrdom and the place where it occurred are not open to doubt; the cult is an ancient one and the three names are given in inscriptions of the fifth or sixth century, and there is an entry for today in the *Hieronymianum*: see *C.M.H.*, pp. 530, 554. *AA.SS.*, Oct., 6, pp. 187-95, gives the *passio*. See also *Bibl.SS.*, 5, 500.

St Comgan, *Abbot* (Eighth Century)

Comgan is said to have been the son of an Irish prince named Kelly, the ruler of the province of Leinster. Comgan succeeded his father and ruled until he was attacked by a group of neighbouring princes. Defeated and wounded in battle, he fled to Scotland, taking with him into exile his sister and her children, one of whom became the abbot St Fillan (19 Jan.). Comgan settled at Lochalsh, opposite the island of Skye, and built a monastic settlement there; seven men who had fled with him became its first monks. Comgan ruled the monastery as abbot for many years, living a life noted for its austerity and penance.

When he died, his nephew Fillan took his body to Iona for burial and built a church there in his honour. This was the first of several churches dedicated to Comgan throughout Scotland, some of which used other forms of the name such as Cowan, Coan, and Congan; the place names Kilchoan and Kilcongen may also reflect his cult.

AA.SS., Oct., 6, pp. 223-6, gives the lessons from the Aberdeen Breviary, as no early Life exists. *K.S.S.*, pp. 310-11, gives a list of church dedications. See also *Bibl.SS.*, 4, 132; *O.D.S.*, pp. 109-10.

St Gerald of Aurillac (*c.* 855-909)

Gerald was born into a noble family in south-central France about the year 855. Chronic ill-health prevented him from taking up the usual military career, and so he received the normal education of a cleric as well as that of a young nobleman. When he became count of Aurillac he continued to be more interested in study and religious matters than in military affairs and gave away much of his wealth to the poor; he dressed and ate modestly and frugally, rising early every morning to recite Matins and attend Mass. In a violent age he strove to rule his lands justly and to safeguard his people from bloodshed and the attacks of marauding bands.

After a pilgrimage to Rome he built a new church at Aurillac, dedicated to St Peter, and also founded a monastery there. He thought of becoming a monk and received the monastic tonsure but was persuaded by the saintly Gausbert, bishop of Cahors, to remain in the world, where he could do more to help other people. He was blind for the last seven years of his life and died in 909 at Cézénac in Quercy; he was buried in the monastery that he had founded at Aurillac. So many pilgrims visited his shrine that the church was rebuilt in 962.

Apart from two official documents, all our knowledge of Gerald comes from a Life written about the year 940 by St Odo of Cluny (18 Nov.). This is largely reliable and gives an attractive picture of the saint; indeed, the previous edition of this work called it "one of the freshest and most attractive character-sketches which have survived" from the period. It describes many of the miracles for which Gerald was famous. Odo obviously felt some need to justify this aspect of his work, for he prefaced the Life with the words: "Many doubt whether the things that are said about the blessed Gerald are true, and some think that they are certainly not true but fantastic." He goes on to explain why God used Gerald to work miracles: "It seems that the divine dispensation performs these things in our age and through a man of our time, because everything which the saints did or said in the past has been forgotten," and the purpose of the miracles was to "revive enthusiasm for downtrodden religion." But the Life is not all miracles, and Odo gives us a picture of a ruler who must have been a civilizing influence in a rough world: "The poor and the wronged always had free access to him, nor did they need to bring the slightest gift to recommend their cause." As the modern translator of the Life tells us, the picture of Gerald, when his cavalcade had camped for the night on one of his journeys to Rome, standing outside his tent after his prayers were over so that he would be accessible to anyone who wanted to talk to him, "is one that is pleasant to contemplate."

St Odo's Life has been translated into English in G. Sitwell, O.S.B., *Lives of Odo of Cluny and Gerald of Aurillac* (1958); see also *Vies des Saints*, 10 (1952), pp. 413-26; *Bibl.SS.*, 6, 170-1.

St Coloman (1012)

Coloman, or Colman, was a Scottish or Irish pilgrim on his way to Jerusalem. He reached the Danube at Stockerau, a town about six miles up-river from Vienna. It was a time of civil war in the region, with sporadic fighting between the peoples of Austria, Moravia, and Bohemia. When Coloman arrived in the area he was taken as a spy, and, as he was unable to explain his true mission because he did not know the local language, he was hanged, on 13 July 1012. The fact that he suffered this unjust sentence patiently was taken to be a sign of sanctity, and this seemed to be confirmed when his body was found to be incorrupt three years later, when it was removed to the nearby monastery of Melk. A large number of miracles were attributed to his intercession.

Coloman has traditionally been regarded as a martyr, and the Roman Martyrology gives him that title. There is no evidence, however, that would support the claim that his death was in defence of the Church or its teachings. He was never formally canonized, but his local cult was strong and he came to be venerated as a minor patron of Austria. A large number of churches in Austria, Hungary, Bavaria, and the Palatinate in Germany were dedicated to him, especially in mountainous regions. On his feast-day a special blessing of horses and cattle is held in a number of places, because his intercession is regarded as especially effective in protecting and healing those animals. He is also prayed to by young women who are hoping to find a suitable husband. In order to add to his importance, a totally imaginary royal ancestry was invented for him. His cult has interesting folkloric aspects, but it is not clear how it started or why it became so strong.

AA.SS., Oct., 6, pp. 357-62, prints a Life by an abbot of Melk. See also J. F. Kenney, *Sources for the Early History of Ireland* (1929), 1, pp. 613-4; *Bibl.SS.*, 4, 96-7.

St Maurice of Carnoët, *Abbot* (1115-91)

Maurice was born in 1115 at Croixanvec in Brittany. His parents were peasants, who eventually settled in the district of Loudéac, where Maurice spent his early years. He had a good education and seemed destined to follow a successful career; he was ordained priest and appointed master of studies. He wanted a life of solitude, however, and so decided to become a monk, joining the Cistercian monastery at Langonnet, near Quimper. His zeal for the strict observance of the Rule was so great that he was elected abbot only three years after his profession.

He became well known for his prudence and wisdom, and was widely consulted. He remained as abbot for several years and then retired to find greater solitude. In 1170, however, he was persuaded to become abbot of a new foundation which had been set up by Duke Conan IV of Brittany, probably on Maurice's advice. The new monastery was on a wild site at Carnoët, which called for heavy physical labour to bring it under cultivation. Maurice governed it for fifteen years with conspicuous success, and his own reputation for holiness became so great that a number of miracles were attributed to him, including changing water into wine and ridding the monastery of a plague of mice and the local countryside of dangerous packs of wolves. He died in 1191, and his tomb became a place of pilgrimage; the monastery changed its name in 1200 to Saint Maurice de Carnoët. He has been venerated by the Cistercians since then as well as by a number of dioceses in Brittany. Pope Clement XI (1700-21) allowed a full liturgical celebration of his feast-day where his cult was established, but he was never canonized.

A Latin Life exists in two forms: see *AA.SS.*, Oct., 6, pp. 378-83. A popular account was published by L. Le Cam, *St Maurice, abbé de Langonnet* (1924), and another with the same title by A. David in 1936. See also *Bibl.SS.*, 9, 205-6, and *Vies des Saints*, 10, p. 124.

St Daniel and Companions, *Martyrs* (1227)

In 1227 six Franciscan missionaries left Tuscany for Morocco to work among the Muslim population; their names were Samuel, Angelo, Leo, Domnus, Nicholas, and Hugolino. They were fired by the great missionary enthusiasm that was so evident among the members of the young Franciscan Order, even though it was obvious that their mission was a dangerous one—especially as only seven years earlier five other Franciscan missionaries had been martyred in Morocco (16 Jan.), and the civil authorities there had forbidden all Christian proselytizing. As they travelled through Spain they were joined by Brother Daniel, minister provincial of Calabria, who became their superior. They reached Morocco on 20 September, and after spending ten days with some European merchants preparing for their mission, they went out to preach in the streets of Ceuta in Latin and Italian, as they did not know the local language.

Their appearance caused an uproar, and they were badly treated by the crowds before being taken before the kadi for interrogation. At first he took them to be mad, with their rough clothes and shaven heads, and put them in prison. From there Daniel wrote to the Europeans among whom they had stayed, describing what had happened and adding, "Blessed be God, the Father of mercies, who comforts us in all our tribulations!" When the authorities found out they were Christian missionaries, the Franciscans were led out and invited to give up their religion. They continued to affirm their belief in Christ and to attack Islam, and so were ordered to be put to death. Each of the missionaries went to Brother Daniel and asked for his blessing and his permission to die for Christ; they were beheaded in turn outside the walls of Ceuta. Their bodies were mangled by the local people, but some of the Christian merchants rescued the remains and buried them. Later the relics were taken back to Spain, and in 1516 the Friars Minor were allowed to celebrate their feast-day liturgically. A number of churches claim the relics, but nothing certain is known about their whereabouts. The Roman Martyrology commemorated them on 10 October, but the *Acta Sanctorum* gives their details under 13 October, which seems to have been the day of their death.

AA.SS., Oct., 6, pp. 384-92; *Anal.Franc.*, 3 (1897), pp. 32-3, 613-6; A. Lopez, *La Provincia de España OM* (1915), pp. 61-5, 329-30; D. Zangari, *I sette SS. Fratri Franc. martirizzati a Ceuta* (1926); *Bibl.SS.*, 4, 469-70.

Bd Magdalen Panattieri (*c.* 1444-1503)

Maddalena Panattieri was born and lived all her life in the small town of Trino-Vercellese on the borders of Lombardy and Piedmont in northern Italy. She became a member of the Third Order of St Dominic, taking a vow of celibacy and joining a group of women tertiaries who devoted their lives to good works and devotion. She soon made a name for herself in the town, caring for the poor and children and involving herself in prayer and penance for the conversion of sinners. She was particularly concerned about usurers, exhorting and reprimanding them openly. At the same time her own spiritual life was developing to the point where she reached the heights of contemplative prayer and frequently experienced ecstatic visions. Because of her reputation she was appointed to give conferences to women and children in a chapel adjoining the Dominican church and was so successful that priests and religious began to attend as well, and Domincan novices were sent to listen to her. By her efforts the Domincan friars in the town were persuaded to adopt a stricter observance of their Rule, and she invited the reformer, Bd Sebastian Maggi (16 Dec.), to visit the town to inaugurate this reform.

The townspeople attributed to Magdalen the fact that their town was spared from attack and destruction during the French invasions in the Italian Wars; she is said to have foreseen some of the calamitous results of these wars. She died on 13

October 1503, already venerated in the town as a saint and with miraculous powers attributed to her. Her tomb very quickly became a shrine, attracting large numbers of pilgrims. This popular cult was confirmed by Pope Leo XII in 1827. Her relics were destroyed, perhaps in a bombardment in 1639. In 1964 a skeleton was discovered which some people claimed to be that of the saint, but no conclusive proof of the connection exists, and the ecclesiastical authorities have made no pronouncement on the matter.

The previous edition of this work claimed that her life was "notably lacking in eventfulness, and she seems to have been spared all external contradiction and persecution." One should add to this that she was an excellent example of the Christian requirement to carry out the ordinary duties of one's chosen way of life as wholeheartedly as possible. She is also witness to the reforming spirt that was influencing the Church in the late fifteenth century, a spirit sometimes more evident among laypeople than among the clergy.

AA.SS., Oct., *Auctarium*, gives a full account, including the Life by Marchese. See also M. C. de Ganay, *Les Bienheureuses Dominicaines* (1924), pp. 358-68; J. Procter (ed.), *Short Lives of the Dominican Saints* (1901), pp. 291-4; *Bibl.SS.*, 10, 77-8.

Bd Honoratus of Biala Podlaska (1829-1916)

Florence Wenceslaus John Kozminski was born on 16 October 1829 at Biala Podlaska, in Poland. His parents were comfortably-off, devout Catholics who had a considerable influence on his early upbringing and education. In 1844 he attended the School of Fine Arts in Warsaw to study architecture as his father had done. But after the sudden death of his father in the following year, Wenceslaus was affected by anti-religious teachings and gave up all religious practice; for a time he became an ardent campaigner against the Church, trying to convert his companions to his new outlook.

In 1846 he was falsely accused of having taken part in a conspiracy against the Russians, who ruled Poland at this time, and was imprisoned under terrible conditions; for a time he feared he would be condemned to death for treason. While in prison he contracted a serious illness, probably a form of typhus; he also experienced severe internal trials and was tempted to give up his religious faith altogether. Finally, however, on the feast of the Assumption in 1846 he recovered his religious faith, and when he was released from prison the following year publicly confessed his former apostasy, attributing his conversion to the grace obtained for him by Our Lady and the prayers of his mother. In December 1848 he joined the Capuchin Friars Minor and took the name Honoratus in religion. Four years later he was ordained priest and began his pastoral work in and around Warsaw as a confessor, preacher, and prison chaplain. He also taught religion in the local schools and colleges and, along with Maria Angela Truszkowska, helped to found the Congregation of the Sisters of St Felix. In an attempt to increase the piety of the people he founded a number of "Circles of the Living Rosary."

After the unsuccessful Polish uprising of 1863, the Capuchin house in Warsaw was suppressed, and Honoratus and the other members had to move to Zakroczym. They remained there until 1892, living in difficult conditions, constantly watched by the secret police, and forbidden by the Russians to leave the monastery or move elsewhere. Honoratus spent many hours each week hearing confessions and giving spiritual direction to the crowds from Warsaw and other parts of the country who visited him. He developed a special apostolate of the confessional and was tireless in his efforts to win over those who had strayed from their faith or religious practice, as he himself had done in his youth. He was also impressed by those who wanted to devote themselves to some form of the religious life but found it impossible to do so because of the attitude of the government. Many of these thought of emigrating, but Honoratus decided that what was needed was a new form of religious society which would enable them to stay and devote themselves to God's service where they were needed most, in Poland. He thought that the Third Order of St Francis provided the model for what was required, as its members could take simple vows and live in community without any of the outward signs of being members of a religious Order. They continued their everyday occupations and performed a secret apostolate among their fellow-workers. Between 1874 and 1895 twenty-six of these Congregations were set up; they had specific roles as well as a general apostolate— some purely religious, such as preaching, some social, such as involvement in working for higher wages for rural workers. They were an early form of the modern secular religious institute. Honoratus wanted to put them under episcopal control, but the Polish bishops were frightened of being involved; when a degree of tolera- tion was granted in 1905, however, they sought to take them over and change their nature. In this they were supported by Rome, and Honoratus, although deeply disappointed by the action of the bishops, submitted to their wishes and gave up all involvement in the groups.

The house in Zacroczym had been closed by the Russians in 1892, and Honoratus had moved to Nowe Miasto, where he lived under the same restrictions as before and continued his pastoral work, especially in the confessional. In 1895 he was appointed commissary general of the Capuchins in Poland. He wrote a number of spiritual books and Lives of saints. He died after a painful illness on 16 December 1916 and was beatified on 16 October 1988.

Notitiae, 24 (1988), pp. 939-41; *A.A.S.*, 80 (1988), pp. 1814-6, gives the authentication of a miracle attributed to Bd Honoratus. See also C. and C. Billot, *Honorat Kozminski* (1982); *Bibl.SS.*, Suppl. 1, 721-3, with photograph.

14

ST CALLISTUS I, *Pope and Martyr* (222)

What we know about the early life and career of Callistus, or Calixtus, is told by St Hippolytus (13 Aug.), an unfriendly source, as he quarrelled with him about the doctrine of the Trinity, and also about penance, and led a group in opposition to him. Hippolytus' story is that Callistus was a slave who was put in charge of a bank by his master, a Christian. He lost the money of some Christian depositors and fled from Rome but was recaptured and sentenced to work on the treadmill. Those who had lost their money had him released so that he could try to recover it, but he was arrested again, this time for brawling in a synagogue, perhaps while trying to recover money from the Jews, and was sentenced to work in the mines on Sardinia. He was among the Christians released at the request of the emperor's mistress, Marcia. He was later freed from slavery.

When Zephyrinus became pope in 199 he put Callistus in charge of the Christian burial-ground on the Via Appia, a task which he carried out very well. It is still known as the cemetery of St Callistus. The pope made him a deacon, and he seems to have become a papal counsellor and to have been an able administrator. He was later elected pope himself, about the year 217, but not without the opposition of St Hippolytus, who later denounced him for laxity with regard to the readmission to Communion of public sinners and the ordination of divorced men as priests. His non-rigorist approach to church discipline in general was condemned by Tertullian. His Trinitarian beliefs also came under suspicion, and he faced accusations of being unorthodox, but these were unfounded. On the whole, Callistus appears to have been a firm upholder of Catholic doctrine and good discipline, but we know too little about him from trustworthy sources to be sure of the detail.

He died in 222. There are grounds for believing that he was martyred, perhaps during a popular disturbance, but his *acta* are of no historical value. He was buried on the Via Aurelia. His tomb was discovered in 1960; it contains sixth-century frescoes of his martyrdom. The Roman church of St Callistus in Trastevere may be on the site of an earlier church built by Callistus himself, on land granted by the emperor to the Christians rather than to some inn-keepers. The emperor, Alexander Severus, is supposed to have declared that it would be preferable to have the rites of any religion on the site rather than a tavern.

Very little can be learned about the life of Callistus from either the *Liber Pontificalis* or the worthless *passio* (*AA.SS.*, Oct., 6, pp. 401-48); for the acts of his pontificate attacked by Hippolytus, see L. Duchesne, *History of the Early Church*, 1 (1912); B. Altaner and C. B. Daly, "The Edict of Callistus," in *Studia Patristica* 3 (1961), pp. 176-82; *D.A.C.L.*, 2, 1657-1754; *Jedin-Dolan*, 1 (1980), pp. 244-5, 258ff.

St Justus of Lyons, *Bishop (c. 390)*

Justus was born in the Vivarais region of Gaul and served as a deacon in the church at Vienne. He became bishop of Lyons and gained a reputation for the severity of his attitude toward those who needed correction and for his attachment to discipline and good order. He attended the Synod of Valence in 374, and was one of three bishops from Gaul to attend the Council of Aquileia in 381. The main business of the council was to deal with the Arians, and Justus gained the respect of St Ambrose (7 Dec.), who wrote to him later on at least two occasions on biblical questions.

It appears that Justus wanted to give up his active pastoral life as bishop and become a solitary; instead of returning from Aquileia to Lyons, he went off to Egypt and joined a monastery. He had tried to do this once before, but the opposition of his flock had prevented it despite Justus' claim to have sound canonical reasons for abdicating. He had, he said, been responsible for a man's death and so was debarred from carrying out his priestly duties. This had come about when a murderer had sought sanctuary in his church; Justus had handed him over to the magistrate on condition that his life would be saved, but he had been killed by the people.

There are two different accounts of what happened when the church of Lyons discovered what Justus had done. According to one tradition, they sent a priest named Antiochus (in some accounts Martin) to persuade Justus to return. When Antiochus found that his arguments were in vain, he stayed with Justus till the latter's death in 390; on his return to Lyons he was elected bishop in succession to Justus. The latter's body was taken back to Lyons and buried in the church of the Machabees, which was later renamed after him. According to the other tradition, Justus did return to Lyons with the messenger, taking with him information about the veneration of the Machabees; he died and was buried there. This second tradition is more likely to be true, since the translation of the body from Egypt would be unlikely at that time, and some early martyrologies give a date for his return.

AA.SS., Sept., 1, pp. 365-7, gives an early Latin Life which is mainly reliable. Justus is mentioned on five different days in the *Hieronymianum* (see *C.M.H.*, pp. 566-7), evidencing a well-established cult; Sidonius Apollinaris described in a letter the enthusiasm of the crowds who flocked to his shrine on his feast-day—*M.G.H., Auctores Antiquissimi*, 8, pp. 89-90. See also *D.A.C.L.*, 10, 191-3; *Bibl.SS.*, 7, 31-2.

St Angadrisma (*c. 695*)

Angadrisma, or Angadrême, lived in the diocese of Therouanne, in northern France. Her upbringing was strongly influenced by St Omer (9 Sept.), the bishop of the diocese, and her cousin, St Lambert of Lyons (14 Apr.), who was a monk at Fontenelle at the time. It was presumably their influence that persuaded her to become a nun, against the wishes of her father, who had promised her in marriage to a young local lord, St Ansbert (9 Feb). In order to avoid the marriage, Angadrisma prayed that she might become physically repulsive and was as a result struck down with leprosy. Ansbert married someone else (and later became bishop of Rouen), and Angadrisma was free to receive the religious habit from the hands of St Ouen (24 Aug.), at which time her leprosy disappeared. She lived an exemplary life as a nun and later became abbess of a convent near Beauvais. A number of miracles were attributed to her, including stopping a fire that threatened to destroy the convent by holding up the relics of its founder, St Ebrulfus (29 Dec.). She was over eighty years old when she died. She is one of the patrons of Beauvais, and her help is invoked against fires and public calamities.

When the convent was destroyed by the Normans in 851, her relics were transferred to the church of St Michael in the town; during the French Revolution they were moved again, to the cathedral.

AA.SS., Oct., 6, pp. 538-44; *M.G.H., Scriptores rerum Merov.*, 5, for a Life of St Ansbert written in the eighth century; *Bibl.SS.*, 1, 1184-5.

ST TERESA OF AVILA
Gold heart with red IHS and silver rays on black field.

15

ST TERESA OF AVILA, *Doctor and Foundress* (1515-82)

Teresa de Ahumada y Cepeda was born in Avila in 1515. Her father, Don Alonso Sánchez de Cepeda, had married again after the death of his first wife, and Teresa was the third of the nine children of his second wife, Doña Beatriz de Ahumada. The family was wealthy, and Don Alonso was highly respected in Avila, although his father had been a Jewish *converso* in Toledo and so lacked the racial purity that was so essential for full social acceptance in sixteenth-century Spain—and for escaping the suspicions of the Inquisition, which never believed that *conversos* made genuine Christians. They were, indeed, excluded from many offices of State and from most of the principal religious Orders in Spain. Teresa, so open about so much of her life, kept quiet about her ancestry; but it may, perhaps, have influenced her later views on the unimportance of family titles and the need to treat everyone as equal.

Her childhood was happy, ordinary, and pious. Too much should not be made of her early liking for the Lives of the martyrs, which she read avidly, for they were the adventure stories of the day. She and her older brother Rodrigo were struck by the idea of heaven lasting "for ever, for ever, for ever," as they were fond of repeating, and decided that death at the hands of the Moors would be an easy way of gaining it. They ran away from home but were soon brought back by an uncle. Foiled in their attempt to become martyrs they decided that the next rank of sanctity, that of the hermits, was more within their grasp, and so they built cells for themselves in the garden. These childish pieties were not important in themselves but may have been early signs of Teresa's lifelong ability to act on her convictions and to inspire others to follow her: she was only seven at the time, while Rodrigo was eleven.

Teresa grew into an attractive and charming girl, with the grace, as she called it, of always being able to please people. She became very fond of reading romances, a habit she was careful to hide from her father, and mixed with rather worldly friends, including some cousins. She liked dressing up and enjoyed wearing jewellery and using perfume. When she was writing her autobiography much later in life she was very harsh on herself when dealing with these years, but there seems to have been nothing but teenage trivia and frivolity and perhaps an unwise romantic attachment. Don Alonso, left to look after his large family after the early death of Doña Beatriz (when Teresa was thirteen), decided that his daughter would be better off away from home and so sent her to a local Augustinian convent, which served as a finishing school for well-to-do young women. Society allowed them a choice between only two careers, marriage or the religious life. Teresa was attracted to the latter but also dreaded it; she does not seem to have considered marriage in any positive way. It is interesting that she later told her nuns how fortunate they were to have avoided its drawbacks—which she gave as having to submit totally to a man and running the risk of an early death through too much childbearing.

Eventually, after a serious illness and a long mental battle, she decided to join the local Carmelite Convent of The Incarnation. Her father refused his permission, but she went ahead and left home secretly in November 1536 to begin her religious life. Don Alonso withdrew his opposition, and Teresa felt that she had taken a step which would at least enable her to save her soul; she did not claim to have any particular vocation to the Carmelite way of life—her choice of convent was dictated as much by the presence of a close friend there as anything else. Nor was there anything in that particular convent to distinguish it from the many she might have chosen. The nuns had a fairly relaxed lifestyle; visitors of every kind were admitted freely, and the nuns could spend time away from the convent when they wished. It was not well endowed, and genteel poverty characterized it rather than luxury, but one's previous social status in the world was not lost on entering, and the over-large community of about 180 nuns was split into cliques and factions. Those who were able to could have their own servants living in the convent with them. At the same time, the nuns attended chapel several times a day for the divine office, went to confession at least fortnightly, took the discipline, and fasted regularly; if there was little to remind a visitor of the original ideal of a life devoted to contemplation, there were no scandals either. Teresa lived in comparative comfort with her own oratory, kitchen, and guest room (in which her younger sister Juana was able to stay for a time).

A year or so after her solemn profession she fell ill, and her father took her away from the convent to be cured. A pious uncle gave her a book on prayer by Francisco de Osuna called *The Third Spiritual Alphabet*. Osuna, a Franciscan, had been influenced by the *devotio moderna*, part of a northern European movement for reform, which inspired many of those in Spain who were seeking to reform the religious Orders and help laypeople to develop a more personal spirituality. The book was a beginner's guide to mental and contemplative prayer, and Teresa learned from it the importance of recollection and the possibility of opening her soul to a passive reception of God in the prayer of quiet. She wrote later that she had been delighted with the book and had "determined to follow that way of prayer with all my might." Her copy, much used and heavily scored, still exists.

Her illness, however, got very much worse; she suffered almost complete paralysis, was declared to be consumptive, and after a fit thought to be dead. It took about three years for her to return to good health. Unfortunately, this also meant a return to the rather worldly life of The Incarnation, and she was caught up again in its distractions. Despite what she had learned and begun to practise from Osuna, Teresa gave up mental prayer, justifying this to herself on the grounds that she was not worthy to talk to God so intimately and that her health did not allow her to practise it. The result was that the external practices of religion and her penances were not balanced by interior prayer, and this added to the sense of frustration she was beginning to feel. Her confessor told her to return to simple meditation as a form of mental prayer and to receive Communion every fortnight. She still found it very difficult to pray: "Over a period of several years I was more occupied in wishing my hour of prayer over and in listening whenever the clock struck, than in thinking of things that were good. . . . I would rather have done any severe penance . . . than practise recollection as a preliminary to prayer. . . . I used to feel so depressed that I had to summon up all my courage to make myself pray at all."

While these years between her recovery in 1543 and her "second conversion" in 1555 seemed barren, they were very important both for her personal spiritual development and her ideas on what a convent should be. She persevered in her attempts to pray despite an apparent lack of success; she learned from one of her confessors (most of whom did not understand her) how to examine her conscience not according to sins committed or not committed but according to the good which she had impeded by opposing the graces given her by God. It was a slow conversion during which, as she said, "On the one hand God was calling me, on the other I was following the world." Her sense of her own sinfulness and worthlessness, which she expressed in language which strikes us today as highly exaggerated, increased as she became more aware of the presence of God. She began to experience interior visions and voices, and occasionally enjoyed the higher reaches of contemplative prayer. She was encouraged by both St Francis Borgia (10 Oct.) and St Peter of Alcántara (19 Oct.) to accept that these experiences came from God, and she was helped by reading the *Confessions* of St Augustine. Another penitent she drew strength from was St Mary Magdalen (22 July), who came to her assistance as she was meditating on Christ's sufferings. Teresa wrote later: "From that day I have gone on improving much ever since in my spiritual life." She knew she had become too dependent on human relationships, and part of her conversion lay in breaking with these so that she relied on God alone.

Her ideas about convent life also developed during these years. This was partly a reaction against the way of life practised in The Incarnation; the community was far too large to be a genuine community with a common purpose; it was too open to worldly distractions, and its nuns were too fond of their social standing and creature comforts. What Teresa wanted was a poor, small community (limited to about a dozen nuns) subject to the rules of strict enclosure. But she was also influenced by the general desire for reform that had been active in Spain for several decades: people like Osuna, Peter of Alcántara, Ignatius of Loyola, Francis Borgia, John of Avila, and John of the Cross all witness to a reforming force that was affecting the Spanish church, and the religious Orders in particular, and which was to influence the Council of Trent in its reforming agenda and decisions. Teresa also knew what was happening in Europe as a result of the Protestant Reformation; her knowledge was sketchy and her understanding imperfect, but she had heard of the attacks on the Church in France by the Calvinists, and she was determined that her community would pray, suffer deprivation, and do penance to remedy the situation. Another reforming founder would hardly be noticed, one would have thought, yet when Teresa proposed to found a house that would follow the strict Carmelite Rule, there was an uproar of opposition.

Some of this opposition came from her Sisters at The Incarnation, who felt their way of life threatened; no doubt some of them also wondered how genuine Teresa was, with her raptures and other spiritual experiences—Spain had had a large number of pious visionaries, especially women, some of whom had been found to be frauds. The Inquisition was especially vigilant about this, searching out anything that smacked of private inspiration or illuminism: choral prayer was the correct thing for religious, it claimed, not mental prayer. Osuna's work was put on the Index of Forbidden Books, along with a book by St Francis Borgia, and Teresa's works were to come under suspicion later.

But the most serious opposition was aroused because of her determination to found her new house in poverty and to seek neither endowments for it nor dowries from its Sisters. It needed all her stubbornness and the insistence of her interior voices to keep her to this key element in her reform. The arguments of theologians, the local bishop, the cathedral chapter, her provincial, and the municipal authorities almost wore her down, but, as she wrote: "When I fell to prayer again and looked at Christ hanging poor and naked upon the Cross, I felt I could not bear to be rich. So I besought him with tears to bring it to pass that I might be as poor as he." The opposition was not all unreasonable: there were so many religious in Spain, and most towns already had so many houses to support that a new convent that was to be totally reliant on alms could hardly be expected to survive. Teresa was to meet this point of view very often in the future: in Seville, for example, where she made a foundation some years later, there were already twenty-four convents and eighteen monasteries; local people might well have thought that enough was enough!

Eventually the new Carmelite convent of St Joseph's opened in Avila in 1562. Teresa had four companions to begin with, and they set about living what they believed was the original Carmelite Rule. They did not wear shoes, hence their name Discalced Carmelites, and their life was one of prayer and penance, although Teresa warned against excessive bodily mortifications. She had an intense dislike of "long-faced saints that make both virtue and themselves abhorrent"; she believed that the holier her nuns became "the more sociable they should be with their sisters." They relied entirely on voluntary alms and did not beg; the extent of their poverty may be gained from a statement in the early Constitutions: "When there is anything to eat, dinner shall be taken at half-past eleven." The number of nuns reached its full complement of thirteen, and the first five years or so of her time at St Joseph's were the happiest of her religious life.

In 1567 St Joseph's was visited by the father general of the Carmelite Order, who was keen to reform his subjects according to the decrees of the Council of Trent. Teresa seemed to be the perfect instrument for this, and he gave her permission to found other convents and two reformed houses for friars—an extraordinary vote of confidence. In the next nine years she founded twelve houses, travelling about Spain in appalling conditions, facing opposition most of the time, and suffering from increasing ill health. We have hundreds of her letters from this period, which give a vivid picture of a very human person with a shrewd business sense. She was very demanding of her friends—she could be querulous if she thought they were neglecting her, and she chided, encouraged, and teased as occasion demanded. Her travels made her well known, and, as Allison Peers put it, if princes and prelates respected her, muleteers and peasants adored her.

At the same time her own spiritual life was developing and her sense of God became so intense that she experienced a mystical union or spiritual marriage with God; in trying to explain this she used a number of similes: "It is as if a tiny streamlet enters the sea, from which it will find no way of separating itself, or as if in a room there were two large windows through which the light streamed in: it enters in different places but it all becomes one." In this state all that the soul desires is for God's will to be done, and there is a constant awareness of God's presence. Her life in these years showed that it was possible to combine a life of the deepest contemplation with great activity and attention to secular business. But there could be problems, as she wrote to her brother in 1577: "For over a week I have been in such a condition that, if it were to go on, I should hardly be able to attend to all my business. . . . I have had raptures again, and they have been most distressing. Several times, I have had them in public—during Matins, for example. It is useless to resist them and they are impossible to conceal. I get so dreadfully ashamed that I feel I want to hide away somewhere. I pray God earnestly not to let them happen to me in public. . . . Latterly I have been going about as if I were drunk."

External trials increased. Her reform programme was almost ended altogether after 1576 when there was a serious attempt made by the "Calced" or unreformed friars to stop it. Teresa's friend and ally, St John of the Cross (14 Dec.), was kidnapped and imprisoned; the superior of the Discalced and her closest friend, Fr Gracián, was put under house arrest, while the papal nuncio to Spain described Teresa herself as a "restless, disobedient and contumacious gad-about woman, who under the cloak of piety has invented false doctrines, left the enclosure . . . against the orders of the Council of Trent and her own superiors, and has gone about teaching . . . contrary to the injunctions of St Paul who said that women were not to teach." Nuns at The Incarnation who voted for her to be their prioress were excommunicated, and the new convents were forbidden to accept any more novices. Teresa wrote to the king, Philip II, who had always supported the reform, and she even went to see him to enlist his help. As a result partly of royal intervention, partly of the gradual winning over of the nuncio, peace was made in 1580 when the Discalced Carmelites were given the status of being a separate province from the Calced—the first step toward complete independence as a distinct Order in 1594.

Teresa made four more foundations between 1580 and 1582 and arranged for a fifth to be made by St John of the Cross. Despite her growing reputation as a saint she still faced strong opposition; and with her health rapidly getting worse, so that travelling became even more hazardous for her, these last foundations were no easier than the earlier ones. There were troubles, too, with some of her prioresses. Early in 1582 she felt she was dying and wanted to be taken back to Avila; she could get no further than her convent at Alba de Tormes, where she died on 4 October, constantly repeating the words, "A broken and contrite heart, Lord, thou wilt not despise. . . . Cast me not away from thy face." After all, as she told her Sisters, she had always been a faithful daughter of the Church, and she trusted that would be counted to her credit.

Her cult spread rapidly throughout Spain, and there was an unseemly rush to get her body or whatever parts of it could be removed as major relics. She had lived in an age of refomers and founders, yet to her contemporaries she had stood out from the rest; some even wanted her to be declared patron of Spain alongside the great St James (25 July). She had not been known as a miracle-worker during her life, but very soon miracles were associated with her relics. The first edition of her works was published in 1588 and two Lives by 1600; a popular "golden legend" made up of stories and myths illustrating both her human qualities and her mysticism was soon in circulation. The official process of inquiry into her sanctity began in 1591; in 1614 she was beatified and a Mass and Office allowed in her honour; and in 1622 she was canonized, on the same day as Ignatius Loyola, Francis Xavier, and Philip Neri—a stunning foursome! In 1688 her feast-day was extended to the Universal Church, an honour previously only allowed to women saints who had been virgin martyrs. In 1970 she was given the title Doctor of the Church.

Much of what we know about Teresa comes from her own writings. In addition to her letters she wrote *The Book of the Foundations, The Way of Perfection, The Interior Castle,* her autobiography (*The Life of the Holy Mother Teresa of Jesus*), *Thoughts on the Love of God* (a commentary on part of the Canticle of Canticles), the *Constitutions,* and a number of minor works such as the *Spiritual Relations.* It was a prodigious output for someone so active—and one so lacking in formal education. Her main source was her own lived experience, but her thought was also rooted in the scriptures and particularly the Gospels. Most of what she wrote she did under obedience to her superiors or confessors, as she had little belief in her ability. When asked to write something on prayer, for example, she replied, "For the love of God let me work at my spinning wheel and go to choir and perform the duties of the religious life, like the other sisters. I am not meant to write. I have neither the health nor the intelligence for it." But she did write something, and the result was one of the greatest spiritual classics, *The Interior Castle.*

In 1970 Pope Paul VI declared her to be a Doctor of the Church in recognition of her outstanding contribution to mystical theology and Christian spirituality. She had found new ways of describing a Christian's progress in the spiritual life, making use of lively similies and homely language. Central to her spirituality is the imitation of Christ; she prayed, "Where you are I wish to be, where you will travel I wish to travel." She urged her Sisters, "Look at the crucified one"—his poverty, his total renunciation and humility, his silence under injuries, and his relationship with his Father. Unlike previous writers, the humanity of Christ was important for

Teresa even at the highest level of prayer, no matter how detached from bodily things the contemplative might become. Indeed, Jesus and his humanity were for her the essential means of entering the higher levels of the spiritual life; other divine mysteries may be the object of the contemplative's concentration, but for Teresa such experiences were always "in the company of Christ our Lord, at once human and divine."

She was the first woman in the history of the Church to write systematically and at length about the spiritual life. The lasting value of her writings is shown by the fact that in the twentieth century there have been over six hundred complete or partial editions of her works, and they have been translated into every major language. They provide food for spiritual writers, theologians, and everyday Christians. As Paul VI said, Teresa had lived what she wrote about; her writings are noteworthy for their wisdom and show her to have been "a mother of wonderful simplicity and yet a teacher of remarkable depth." So, for example, while she describes the highest planes of contemplative prayer with remarkable skill and clarity, she can also talk of prayer as being simply a friendly conversation with someone we know loves us.

Her legacy is consequently rich and many-sided. There is her stress on prayer, which must include private meditation and contemplation as well as the office and Mass; the danger of activity without prayer; the possibility of mixing activity and contemplation in a balanced and productive way. There is an equal insistence on self-knowledge: "Self-knowledge is so important that, even if you were raised right up to the heavens, I should like you never to relax your cultivation of it. . . . However sublime your contemplation may be, take care both to begin and to end every period of prayer with self-examination." Once, when she was thinking how it distressed her to eat meat and to do no penance, she heard her voices say, "Sometimes there is more self-love in such a thought than a desire for penance." She was always questioning her own actions and motives under a "microscope of meticulous honesty" (du Boulay). But while self-knowledge is important, one must not become self-centred: one focus, of course, must be God and the discerning of his will; the other must be the Church. To ignore the "ecclesial dimension" in Teresa's thought would be to miss an essential element: we are praying with and for the Church at all times. The more aware we become of Christ the more aware we become of the duty to work with him in achieving his plan of salvation through the Church.

Her convents are her most obvious legacy. Modelled on Carmelite spirituality and on her own experience of forty-seven years of convent life, they are also witness to her borrowings from the best in other traditions, be it the newly-formed Jesuits, the Dominicans, or the Franciscans, especially St Clare (11 Aug.). Here again we meet the ecclesial dimension: her Carmels are powerhouses of prayer for the Church and, especially, its clergy. While she anticipated the decrees of the Council of Trent in many areas of her reform, toward the end of her life she was very much aware of its ideals for the religious life and incorporated them into her thinking.

For modern Christians her letters have a particular appeal: she could be completely detached from the world at one moment, and the next show how hurt she was by being let down by her friends. That tension between the demands of the Christian life and the demands of everyday living is faced by every Christian; the tension is not resolved by isolating the two into separate compartments but by striving to seek God's will in the mundane as well as the mystical. Part of Teresa's lasting appeal as a saint and mystic is that she became holy without ceasing to be human. There are, of course, things in her life that are daunting and seemingly impossible to imitate, but there is also encouragement for beginners and those who fall, and one is always aware that she had lived what she was writing about.

She has been portrayed in art very often. Probably the best-known image is in the church of Santa Maria della Vittoria in Rome—Bernini's great baroque statue of the saint at the moment of the piercing of her heart by the divine love (the so-called transverberation), expressing both suffering and ecstasy. It has been condemned as ambiguous in its sensuality, and it is not to modern taste; it is, however, remarkably faithful to Teresa's own account of her experience. A more lifelike image is that in the painting done in Seville in 1575 by Brother Juan de la Miseria; Teresa said on seeing it, "God forgive you, Brother Juan! How ugly and bleary-eyed you have made me!" Most of her contemporaries thought it a reasonably good likeness; its artist did not have the skill of a great portrait painter, but it shows a peaceful, rather round face of someone with assurance and common-sense rather than one caught up in heavenly things. After her canonization in 1622, baroque artists revelled in her mysticism. There is a painting of her by Rubens in the Metropolitan Museum, New York.

Three early Lives exist: by Fr Francis de Ribera, first published in 1590; Diego de Yepes (1599), and Julian of Avila (1881)—these exist in various editions; *AA.SS.*, Oct., 7, pp. 109-790 gives the *acta*; see *A.A.S.*, 62, pt. 2 (1970), pp. 590-6, and 63 (1971), pp. 185-92, for the declaration of her as Doctor. The basic scholarly edition of her works is that in Spanish by Father Silverio, 9 vols. (1915-24); this text was used by E. Allison Peers (trans. and ed.), *The Complete Works of St Teresa of Jesus*, 3 vols. (1946), and *The Letters of St Teresa of Jesus*, 2 vols. (1951). For a new French edition, see Mère Marie du Saint-Sacrement, *Oeuvres Complètes de Thérèse d'Avila* (1995). The most complete modern bibliography is in *Teresianum* 34 (1983), pp. 355-451. From the huge number of studies and biographies see *Bibl.SS.*, 12, 395-419; *Dict.Sp.*, 15 (1991), 611-58, has an up-to-date bibliography and an excellent discussion of Teresa's writings; E. Allison Peers, *Mother of Carmel* (1945), and *St Theresa of Jesus and Other Essays and Addresses* (1953); Elizabeth Hamilton, *The Great Teresa* (1960); Fr Thomas and Fr Gabriel, *Saint Teresa of Avila: Studies in Her Life, Doctrine and Times* (1963); Stephen Clissold, *St Teresa of Avila* (1979); J. Blinkoff, *The Avila of St Teresa* (1989); S. du Boulay, *Teresa of Avila* (1991); A. Sicari, *Nuovi ritratti di santi*, 3 (1992), pp. 43-61. The letter to her brother is quoted from J. Cumming (ed.), *Letters from Saints to Sinners* (1996), pp. 50-3.

St Thecla of Kitzingen, *Abbess (c. 790)*

Thecla was one of the nuns sent in 748 or 749 by Tetta, abbess of Wimborne in Wessex, to help St Boniface (5 June) in his missionary work in Germany. She probably went about the same time as her kinswoman, St Lioba (28 Sept.), under whom she was a nun for a time in the abbey of Bischofheim. Boniface then made her abbess of Ochsenfurt, and after a time she became abbess of Kitzingen on the river Main as well. Her name does not appear in Kitzingen's list of its abbesses, perhaps because it seems she continued to live at Ochsenfurt; she may be the person referred to in the Kitzingen list under the name Heilga, "the saint." She was noted for her humility, gentleness, and charity not only among her Sisters but also among the local people. We have the text of a short letter written by St Boniface to her, St Lioba, and the community; in it he appeals to their Christian charity and asks their prayers for the success of his mission. After Thecla's death about the year 790 the house at Ochsenfurt declined fairly quickly, being overshadowed by its close neighbour at Kitzingen. There is some late evidence of a cult in the area around the abbey, and in the fifteenth century there was a ruined chapel named after her on an island in the river Severn in Wales. Her shrine was destroyed during the sixteenth-century Peasants' Revolt.

She is shown in art with a dark veil over her head and upper body, stroking a lioness; this is no doubt due to a confusion with the martyr of the same name, thrown to the beasts in 304 and commemorated with St Timothy of Gaza (19 Aug.).

Although we know so little about Thecla, there is no doubt of her existence. She shares in the collective importance of the Anglo-Saxon mission to Germany led by Boniface, which was a key factor in the evangelization of that country in the eighth century. The nuns who joined the mission tended to do so about fifteen or twenty years after its start, but their work as rulers of large abbeys was crucial in the consolidation of Christianity and the encouragement of learning.

AA.SS., Oct., 7:1, pp. 59-64, gathers together the scattered references to Thecla. See also *Bibl.SS.*, 12, 181-2; *Vies des Saints*, 10, pp. 462-4.

St Euthymius the Younger, *Abbot (c. 820-98)*

This Euthymius was called the "Younger," or the "New," to distinguish him from St Euthymius the Great (20 Jan.), who had lived about four hundred years earlier. His baptismal name was Nicetas, and he was born at Opso, near Ancyra in modern Turkey. He married while still quite young and had a daughter named Anastasia. In 842, however, at the age of eighteen, he left his wife and child and went off to join a laura (a community of anchorites living separately but with a common master or abbot) on Mount Olympus in Bithynia; the former edition of this work added that the circumstances of his leaving his family "look curiously like desertion." There is about his life an air of restlessness and agitation. For a time he put himself under the direction of St Joannicius (4 Nov.) and then under a monk named John, who gave him the name Euthymius and later sent him off to the monastery of Pissidion.

The abbot of the monastery was deposed in 858 for his part in the ecclesiastical intrigues of Constantinople, and Euthymius took the opportunity to leave for the famous Mount Athos, where he hoped to be able to live a more solitary life. Before he left he was given the Great Habit, the outward sign of the highest degree to which the Eastern monk can aspire. On Mount Athos he joined up with a hermit named Joseph, and tradition has it that the two were soon competing with each other in rather bizarre ascetic trials—fasting for forty days on vegetables to begin with, and then seeing which of them could stay in his cell for three years. This proved too much for Joseph, but Euthymius persevered and was warmly congratulated by his brethren when he eventually emerged from his seclusion. Such stories of ascetical prowess are common in the accounts of Eastern monks and hermits and were no doubt meant to indicate the spiritual standing of the saints concerned rather than real events.

Euthymius spent some time at Salonika (hence he is sometimes referred to as "Euthymius the Thessalonian") and seems to have lived for a time in a tower as a stylite. He preached to the crowds who went to see him and used his power of exorcism to heal those who were possessed. Before returning to Mount Athos he was ordained deacon and, in 867, priest. But he could not escape the crowds who visited him even there and so fled to an island with two other monks; driven from there by pirates, he joined up again with his former fellow-hermit Joseph. After Joseph had died, Euthymius had a vision which directed him to return to the monastic life as he had been long enough in solitude. He was to restore a ruined monastery dedicated to St Andrew the Apostle. He did this, and when disciples joined him he was able to set up a monastic community which he ruled as abbot for fourteen years. He then visited his native town of Ospo and gathered a number of recruits, including some members of his own family. These included some women, and so he built a separate monastery for them. When he felt that both houses were well established he handed them over to the local bishop and retired again to the solitude of Mount Athos. He died on 15 October 898. His life seems to have lain somewhat uneasily between his search for solitude and his energy as a monastic founder. His relics are venerated in Thessalonika.

Euthymius features in the Greek lists of saints as Euthymius the New; he was unknown in the West until the text of a Greek Life was published at the beginning of the present century; the Life was written originally by his disciple Basil, who later became metropolitan of Salonika, as his master had foretold. See *B.T.A.*, 4, pp. 122-3; *Catholicisme*, 4 (1954), 729-30; *Dict.Sp.*, 4, 1723-4.

St Richard Gwyn, *Martyr (c. 1537-84)*

Richard Gwyn was born at Llanidloes, Powys, in Wales, about the year 1537. He was educated at St John's College, Cambridge, but had to leave after two years because of a lack of funds. He returned to Wales and became a schoolmaster at Overton in Clywd, where he married; he and his wife had six children, of whom three survived. Under threat of being fined for not attending the local parish church, for a time he conformed to the new religion which had been established by the Act of Conformity of 1559. He later repented of this and moved to Overstock to open a new school. He was arrested as a recusant in Wrexham in 1579 but managed to escape. In 1580 the Privy Council ordered the bishops to become more active in arresting recusants, especially those who were schoolmasters, as these were thought to be particularly dangerous because of their influence over the young. Richard was arrested and imprisoned in Ruthin Castle but refused to conform; when he was taken in chains to the local church he made so much noise that the preacher could not be heard. As a punishment he was put in the stocks and fined. He was released for a time but was unable to pay the fines imposed for non-attendance at church and so was re-arrested. He was taken before the Council of the Marches along with other recusants and tortured to get him to reveal the names of local Catholics. While he was in prison he wrote a number of poems in Welsh, polemical and rather bitter in tone, in which he urged his compatriots to adhere to the old "Mother Church" and attacked the new religion and its ministers. One of the poems is a song of praise for the assassination of the Protestant William of Orange.

Eventually he was brought to trial at Wrexham, the eighth time he had appeared before the assizes there, and was accused of reconciling a person to the Catholic religion (a capital offence according to the law of 1581) and of upholding the supremacy of the pope. The evidence against him was false and had been obtained by bribery, but he was condemned to death for refusing to recognize the royal supremacy. His wife and one of their children were brought into the courtroom to be warned not to follow his example, but she replied by offering to die alongside her husband; she was sure, she said, that the judges could find evidence against her if they spent a little more money. On the scaffold Richard announced that he recognized Elizabeth as his lawful queen but could not accept her as head of the church in England; he was hanged, drawn, and quartered on 15 October 1584 in Wrexham. He was beatified in 1929 and canonized in 1970 as one of the Forty Martyrs of England and Wales; he is honoured as the proto-martyr of Welsh recusants because he was the first to suffer death in Wales itself. The editor of his poems said of him, "Though he had his moments of weakness, he was a very amiable character, a devoted husband and father, a teacher of youth who won and kept the strong affection of his scholars."

A.A.S., 62 (1970), pp. 558-60, 745-53; *M.M.P.*, pp. 102-5, where Challoner uses the English name White instead of the Welsh Gwyn; *D.N.B.*, 61, p. 70, also writes of him under the name White, which it says Gwyn adopted at Cambridge; *O.D.S.*, p. 222; T. P. Ellis, *Catholic Martyrs of Wales* (1933), pp. 18-33; *Blessed Richard Gwyn* (1960); *B.T.A.*, 4, pp. 202-4. *C.R.S.*, 5 (1908), pp. 90-9, prints the Welsh poems with an English translation.

16

ST HEDWIG (*c.* 1174-1243)

Hedwig (or Jadwiga) was born in Bavaria about the year 1174, the daughter of Berthold, count of Andechs. When she was only twelve she was married to Henry, duke of Silesia. Together they founded a large number of religious houses, the best known of which was a convent for Cistercian nuns at Trebnitz, near Breslau in modern Poland, the first convent for women in Silesia. These foundations helped both to develop the religious life of the people and to spread a common German culture throughout their lands. They also established hospitals and a house for lepers. Their seventh and last child was born in 1209, and Hedwig persuaded her husband to take a mutual vow of chastity. They lived largely apart, with Hedwig taking up residence close to the nunnery at Trebnitz and often sharing the austere life of the nuns. She recommended fasting to those who wanted to live holier lives, saying that it could "master concupiscence, lift up the soul, confirm it in the paths of virtue, and prepare a fine reward for the Christian."

Much of the rest of Hedwig's life was spent in trying to keep the peace between her warring sons Henry and Conrad and in attempts to make peace between her husband and his enemies. When Henry died in 1238, she comforted those who mourned him with the words, "Would you oppose the will of God? Our lives are his; our will is whatever he is pleased to ordain, whether our own death or that of our friends." She took the habit at Trebnitz but did not take any religious vows, remaining free to administer her property for the good of the poor. We are told that she took great care to instruct the uneducated in their religion, on one occasion having an old woman share her room so that they could go through the Our Father together whenever there was a free moment. After ten weeks of patient teaching, the old woman could repeat and understand the prayer.

When her son Henry II was killed in 1240 fighting the Tartar invaders, Hedwig knew of his death three days before a messenger arrived from the battlefield. Other miracles were attributed to her; she cured a blind nun, for example, and had the gift of prophecy, foretelling her own death in October 1243. She was canonized in 1267, and her feast was extended to the Western Church in 1706.

AA.SS., Oct., 8, pp. 198-270, for a thirteenth-century Life; a manuscript copy of this from 1323 is illustrated with scenes from the life of the saint, reproduced in H. Riesch, *Die heilige Hedwig* (1926); E. Markowa, *The Glowing Lily* (1946); *Bibl.SS.*, 4, 933-4; E. Walter, *Studien zum Leben der hl. Hedwig* (1972).

ST MARGARET MARY ALACOQUE (1647-90)

Margaret Alacoque was born in 1647 in Janots in Burgundy. She was the fifth of seven children, and her father was a notary of some distinction in the town. He died when Margaret was eight years old, and she was sent away to school with the Poor Clares. She impressed the nuns with her piety and was allowed to make her First Holy Communion earlier than was usual at the time. For her part, she was attracted to the life of the convent. When she was nine, however, she was afflicted with a painful rheumatic illness, which kept her bed-ridden until she was fifteen. She returned home to find that the house was controlled by relatives of her father, who treated her and her mother badly. When she recovered, it was suggested that she should marry, and she seems to have considered this as a serious possibility. By the time she was twenty, however, she had made up her mind to become a nun, a decision she later claimed had been helped by a vision of Our Lord. She was confirmed and took the name of Mary, which she added to her baptismal name of Margaret. Finally, in 1671, she entered the Visitation convent at Paray-le-Monial.

Margaret Mary was already well advanced in prayer and the spiritual life. She found it impossible to follow the methods of meditation which the novices were expected to use, as she had progressed to what mystical writers describe as the prayer of simplicity; she was aware of Our Lord as some sort of sensible presence, often as crowned with thorns, and she seemed to be directed by his voice. This urged her to ask for "humiliations and mortifications," and these she found in the work she was assigned to do in the convent. She was slow and clumsy, and perhaps rather absent-minded; she annoyed the infirmarian when working as her assistant and was treated with scorn and ridicule as a result. In due course she was professed, and, as she wrote, "Our Lord was pleased to accept her as his bride, but in a way that she felt herself incapable of describing."

It was shortly after this that Margaret Mary received the first of the revelations that were to make her famous. As she knelt before the Blessed Sacrament she heard our Lord speaking to her "in so plain and effective a manner as to leave no room for doubt, such were the results this grace produced in me, who am always afraid of deceiving myself about what I assert to take place interiorly." She was to be the instrument, she was told, for spreading the love of Jesus' Sacred Heart and making it known throughout the world. Then it was as though he took her heart and put it within his own before returning it "burning with divine love." Over the next eighteen months she received further revelations amplifying this basic message. The Sacred Heart was to be depicted as a heart of flesh; she and others should make reparation for the coldness and insults Our Lord received in return for his love; a special feast should be established on the Friday after the Octave of Corpus Christi; faithful Catholics should receive Communion on the first Friday of each month and should spend an hour in prayer every Thursday evening in remembrance of his sufferings in Gethsemane.

When Margaret Mary tried to carry out these instructions she met with strong opposition and even hostility from her superior and some of the other nuns. Theologians who were invited to pass judgment on her revelations condemned them as delusions and suggested that she needed to eat more. She was supported by Bd Claude de la Colombière (15 Feb.) when he became confessor to the nuns, and he became one of her first disciples in spreading the devotion. But her trials were not at an end. She was asked in a vision to become the sacrificial victim for the short-comings of the nuns in the community and for the ingratitude of some of them toward the Sacred Heart. Not surprisingly, some of the community took exception to Margaret Mary's portrayal of herself in this way, and their resentment lasted for the rest of her life. In addition to these external trials she suffered from strong temptations to despair, vanity and self-indulgence; she was also troubled with ill health.

A later superior appointed Margaret Mary as her assistant, and she also became novice-mistress; in this latter role she was highly successful, and it also provided her with opportunities to spread devotion to the Sacred Heart. The new feast was kept in the convent in 1686, and two years later a special chapel was built in honour of the Sacred Heart, and the devotion began to be accepted in other Visitation houses and to spread throughout France. The writings of Claude de la Colombière were important in helping to bring about this expansion, as was the work of St John Eudes (19 Aug.).

While serving a second term as assistant superior Margaret Mary was taken ill in October 1690. Just before her death she said, "I need nothing but God, and to lose myself in the heart of Jesus." She died while being anointed. She was canonized in 1920.

Devotion to the Sacred Heart did not begin with St Margaret Mary. Its origins appear to go back to the thirteenth century and St Gertrude (16 Nov.). There is no doubt, however, that the devotion in its modern form started in France in the seventeenth century and was given a tremendous impetus by the story of the revelations made to her and the subsequent writings of Bd Claude. France at the time was, perhaps, ready for a message that stressed the love of God as expressed most obviously in the suffering human heart of Jesus; this was an antidote to the rigorism and coldness of the Jansenist tendencies that were becoming so prevalent. As Margaret Mary wrote, "This divine heart is an ocean full of all good things, wherein poor souls can cast all their needs; it is an ocean full of joy to drown all our sadness, an ocean of humility to drown our folly, an ocean of mercy for those in distress, an ocean of love in which to submerge our poverty." The number of religious Orders, Confraternities, church dedications, popular hymns, statues and pictures relating to the Sacred Heart; the popularity, at least before the Second Vatican Council, of the practice of the Nine First Fridays; the consecration of the world to the Sacred Heart by Leo XIII and the annual renewal of this dedication on the feast of Christ the King ordered by Pius XI; the gradual enhancement to the highest rank of the liturgical standing of the feast of the Sacred Heart—Margaret Mary's revelations and almost entirely hidden life have borne remarkably rich fruit.

The most important sources for the Life of St Margaret Mary are the autobiographical sketch made under obedience about five years before she died, 133 of her letters, and a number of spiritual notes and memoranda in her own handwriting; these were definitively ed. by L. Gauthey, 3 vols. (3d ed., 1915); an Eng. trans. of the autobiography was published in 1961 by V. Kerns. See also *M-M. Alacoque, Oeuvres choisies* (1962). For general accounts, see *Bibl.SS.*, 8, 804-9; *O.D.S.*, p. 10. Many popular Lives exist in almost every European language. On the devotions and theology, see *D.T.C.*, 3, 320-51; *Dict.Sp.*, 2, 1023-51; J. B. O'Connell, *The Nine First Fridays* (1934); *N.C.E.*,12, pp. 818-22; *O.D.C.C.*, pp. 514, 872, 1220-1; M. Walsh, *A Dictionary of Devotions* (1993), pp. 226-8; B. Häring, *The Sacred Heart of Jesus and the Redemption of the World* (1983); A. Callahan, *Karl Rahner's Spirituality of the Pierced Heart: A Reinterpretation of Devotion to the Sacred Heart* (1985).

St Gall (*c*. 550-640)

Gall, or Gallech or Gilianus, was born in Ireland, probably in Leinster, and became a monk at the great monastery at Bangor under the direction of St Comgall (11 May) and St Columban (23 Nov.). The house was noted for its learning, and Gall is said to have been well versed in the scriptures, poetry, and grammar; some accounts say he was ordained priest there. When Columban left Ireland about 590 on his missionary journey to Gaul, Gall was one of the twelve monks who accompanied him and was to become the most famous of Columban's disciples. They first founded the monastery at Annegray, and then, two years later, that at Luxeuil, in the Vosges mountains; both houses followed a very strict rule and introduced several usages of the Celtic church.

Columban and his monks were expelled from the area in 610, apparently for rebuking the royal court, and settled for a short time at Bregenz on Lake Constance. They were in trouble again in 612, and Columban left for Bobbio in Italy. Gall did not accompany him, perhaps because of illness—one account says that Columban thought Gall was malingering and so ordered him not to say Mass again during Columban's lifetime as a punishment; Gall obeyed this unjust order because of his vow of obedience. He remained in the part of Swabia that is now Switzerland and established himself as a hermit on the river Steinach. At various times he was offered a bishopric and elected abbot of a monastery, but he refused both offices, preferring a life of solitude with occasional preaching expeditions. He gathered a group of disciples around him who lived according to the Rule of St Columban, and his reputation for holiness grew steadily. He died at Arbon, where he had gone to preach, about the year 640.

Walafrid Strabo wrote a Life of St Gall in the ninth century in two books, the second of which is devoted to the miracles that took place in connection with his tomb and relics. He also says that the saint had "plenty of practical sense." St Gall was one of the principal missionaries in what is now Switzerland (his feast is kept there as well as in Alsace, parts of Germany, and Ireland), and his cult is ancient. His shrine in the abbey survived until the Reformation; when it was opened his bones were found to be very large. His personal fame was exceeded by that of the Benedictine abbey which grew up on the site of one of his hermitages by the

Steinach about a hundred years after his death. This bore his name, as did the town that grew up around it, and became one of the most important monasteries in Europe, with an outstanding, very ancient library and scriptorium. It was closed in 1805, but its library remained more or less intact and is still housed beside the church, which is now a cathedral.

Gall was often represented with a bear, illustrating a legend that he removed a thorn from a wild bear's paw and the animal, in gratitude, helped him in his building work by carrying logs for him. He was usually shown wearing the Benedictine habit, as supposed founder of the great abbey.

We have three main Lives of St Gall: the first was written about a century after his death, the second by Abbot Wetting dates from the early part of the ninth century, and Strabo's from about twenty years later; all three have been edited by B. Krusch in *M.G.H., Scriptores rerum Merov.*, 6, pp. 251-337. Strabo's Life was trans. by M. Joynt, *The Life of St Gall* (1927). See also *AA.SS.*, Oct.,7, pp. 856-909; B. and H. Helbling in *Schweiz. Zeitshrift für Geschichte* 12 (1962), pp. 1-62; *O.D.C.C.*, pp. 317, 546; *O.D.S.*, p. 194; J. M. Clark, *The Abbey of St Gall as a Centre of Literature and Art* (1926).

St Mommolinus of Noyon, *Bishop* (*c.* 686)

Mommolinus, or Mommélin in French, was a native of the Coutances region in Normandy. He became a monk at Luxeuil and was sent with two companions, SS Bertram and Bertinus (5 Sept.), to St Omer in Artois, to work as a missionary among the Morini people. They established a monastery at what is now Saint-Mommélin, and Mommolinus became its superior. After several years of missionary work they moved to a new monastery, St Peter's, at Sithiu. When St Eligius (1 Dec.), bishop of Noyon, died in 660, Mommolinus was chosen as his successor; it was said that he was chosen by the king, Clotaire III, because of his knowledge of German. Among his first acts was to establish a monastery in the town of Saint-Quentin and to make Bertram its superior. He governed his extensive see for twenty-six years, dying about the year 686. His name occurs as witness on a number of charters. A basilica was built over the place where he had been buried.

There are two short Latin Lives of the saint, the more important of which is in *AA.SS.*, Oct., 7, pt. 2, pp. 980-4. See also *Vies des Saints*, 10, pp. 510-2.

St Lull, *Bishop* (*c.* 710-86)

Lull was born in Wessex and became a monk at Malmesbury before joining his cousin St Boniface (5 June) as a missionary in Germany. Boniface ordained him priest before sending him to Rome to consult Pope St Zachary (15 Mar.). On his return in 752 he was consecrated bishop and succeeded to the see of Mainz in 754 when Boniface left for Frisia. When the latter was martyred in 755, Lull arranged for the body to be taken back to Fulda and buried in the abbey Boniface had founded. Most of Lull's episcopate was taken up by quarrels with St Sturmi (17 Dec.), abbot of Fulda and himself a former disciple of Boniface. The main cause of the dispute was the exemption the abbey claimed from the bishop's jurisdiction, a privilege Lull himself may have been instrumental in obtaining when in Rome. At one stage Lull deposed the abbot in favour of his own nominee, but the intervention of King Pepin led to the restoration of Sturmi.

Lull was an energetic pastor, governing the diocese of Mainz with zeal, founding monasteries at Hersfeld and Bleidenstadt, and attending a number of councils in France and Germany. He was keen to spread learning and to have an educated clergy, and his letters show him sending to England and other countries for books. On one occasion he wrote to his former master, Dealwine, to ask for some writings of St Aldhelm (23 May) to comfort him in his exile; he also asked for prayers, using the affected style of his day: "I beseech your Grace's clemency with my deepest entreaties that you may deign to support the ship of my insignificance with your kind prayers, so that, protected with a shield by your intercessions and prayers, I may deserve to reach the harbour of salvation and to obtain pardon for my sins in this earthly prison-house." Another letter, to the archbishop of York, touches on some of the troubles of the missionary: "Truly, for the sake of Christ's name it behoves us to glory in insults and tribulations and in the exaltation of his Church, which is daily afflicted, burdened and harassed. . . . I importune your Excellency with humble prayer to be a continual intercessor for the safety of my soul. For I am driven by incessant sickness of body and anxiety of mind to leave this wretched and most perilous life, to render account to the faithful and stern Judge."

In general the letters give a picture of a careful and committed bishop, keen to enforce canon law, and ordering prayers and Masses to be said and fasts held to save the harvest and, on another occasion, for the repose of a deceased pope. He seems to have received letters from people in various countries, including the abbot of Wearmouth, in Northumberland, who ordered Masses to be said for the deceased in Germany whose names Lull had sent him; the practice of exchanging the names of the deceased seems to have flourished between bishops and abbots in different parts of Europe. In 781 he received the *pallium* as Mainz was restored to the metropolitan status it had had under St Boniface. The profession of faith to the pope that he made on this occasion survives—the only one of the kind that we have for the eighth century.

Toward the end of his life Lull retired to the monastery at Hersfeld, where he died in 786. He is regarded by some as the greatest of Boniface's disciples and succeeded him as the leader of the English mission to Germany; he kept up Boniface's custom of keeping in touch with England by means of regular correspondence and followed his master's policies faithfully. His cult was popular in Germany but not in England.

Nine letters of St Lull are extant and were published in *M.G.H., Scriptores*, 1, pp. 352ff. The letters quoted above are in *E.H.D.* (2d ed.), 1, pp. 815 and 834–5, along with a selection of letters to Lull. A Life written at Hersfeld two centuries after his death is not very reliable but is printed in *AA.SS.*, Oct., 7, pt. 2, pp. 1050–91; see also W. Levison, *England and the Continent in the Eighth Century* (1945), which prints Lull's profession of faith, pp. 238–40.

St Anastasius of Cluny (*c.* 1085)

Anastasius was a native of Venice and a man of considerable learning. By about 1050 he was a monk at Mont-Saint-Michel, where the abbot turned out to be far from satisfactory, being accused of simony. As a result, Anastasius left the monastery in order to live as a hermit on an island off the coast of Normandy. A few years later St Hugh of Cluny (29 Apr.) persuaded him to join the monastery there. After seven years there he was on his travels again, this time sent to Spain by the pope, St Gregory VII (25 May). We do not know the precise reason for his mission, but it may have been to persuade the Spaniards to change over from their Mozarabic liturgy to the Roman one. Whatever the reason, Anastasius was soon back, first as a hermit in the Pyrenees and then in Cluny, where he stayed for another seven years before leaving to become a hermit once again, this time near the city of Toulouse. He preached to the local people and is said to have shared his solitude with the former Cardinal Hugh of Remiremont, who had at one time been papal legate to France and Spain but who had been deposed and even excommunicated for repeated acts of simony. Anastasius was recalled to Cluny in 1085 for some unknown reason but died on the way and was buried at Doydes. He may have been the author of an "Epistle to Geraldus," a treatise on the Real Presence. The Huguenots destroyed his shrine during the religious wars in France in the sixteenth century, but his cult continued.

A Life, written by a certain Galterius, is printed in *AA.SS.*, Oct., 7, pt. 2, pp. 1125-40. See also *Bibl.SS.*, 1, 1057.

St Bertrand of Comminges, *Bishop* (1123)

Bertrand was born about the middle of the eleventh century at L'Isle-Jourdain (Gers, France) and was related on his mother's side to the counts of Toulouse. He had the usual upbringing of those destined for a military career, but instead of following in his father's footsteps as the local lord, he decided to become a priest. He was made a canon at Toulouse and then archdeacon; it was noted that he obtained both these promotions on merit and without asking for them, still less using bribes to obtain them. About the year 1075 he became bishop of Comminges. (The diocese was abolished in 1801 and its territory was incorporated into Toulouse and Tarbes.) His first task was to rebuild the city, which had been destroyed several centuries earlier; he also built a cathedral there dedicated to Our Lady. From 1222 the town was renamed Saint-Bertrand-de-Comminges.

He set about the spiritual reformation of his diocese with such zeal that he met with considerable opposition, not all of it peaceful. He carried out a number of visitations and showed that he was a reforming bishop, keen to implement the Gregorian reforms; he went on a number of preaching expeditions to the more remote and mountainous parts of his diocese, where travel was difficult and sometimes dangerous. He himself lived in community with his canons, under the rule of St Augustine, as an example to the clergy of the diocese. He attended the Synod of

Poitiers in 1100, during which King Philip I was excommunicated and the assembled bishops were stoned by the people. Another time, he was involved in an incident at Auch when some local monks tried to set fire to the church because they felt aggrieved over their rights.

A number of miracles were attributed to him while he was alive and after his death, and one of these gave rise to the so-called pardon of Comminges, or the Great Pardon. When the diocese was overrun by enemy soldiers who stole all the local cattle, Bertrand interceded with their leader to return the animals to avoid the ruin of his people. The leader insisted on payment, which Bertarnd promised but had not made by the time he died. The enemy leader was himself captured and imprisoned by the Moors, and Bertrand appeared to him and led him to safety in payment of his debt. This event is commemorated locally every year on 2 May, and Pope Clement V (1305-14), who had himself been bishop of Comminges and whose baptismal name was Bertrand, granted a plenary indulgence to be gained at the cathedral there whenever the feast of the Finding of the Cross (3 May) fell on a Friday. This grant was approved by later popes down to the eighteenth century.

Bertrand died on 16 October 1123; he was canonized some time before 1309, probably by Honorius III (1216-27), who had ordered an inquiry into the circumstances of how Bertrand had come to be listed locally as a saint. He features in the thirteenth-century tympanum depicting the Adoration of the Magi, which can be seen in the cathedral at Saint-Bertrand-de-Comminges.

AA.SS., Oct., 7, pt. 2, pp. 1140-84, prints a Life said to be by a contemporary notary of Auch; see also P. Bedin, *St Bertrand de Comminges* (1912); *Bibl.SS.*, 3, 129-32, and *Catholicisme*, 1, 1505-6.

St Gerard Majella (1726-55)

Gerard Majella was born in 1726 at Muro Lucano, fifty miles south of Naples. He showed signs of great piety as a child, and after making his First Communion at the age of ten he was allowed to receive every other day, a very unusual practice for the time. When his father died, Gerard was apprenticed to a tailor (his father's trade); he was ill-treated by other workers both while he was learning his trade and afterwards when he became a servant in the household of the bishop of Lacedogna. The bishop himself, a man of ungovernable temper, also mistreated him. Before this he had tried to join the Capuchins, but they rejected him because of his youth and delicate health. After the bishop's death in 1745 Gerard returned home to live with his mother and sisters and set up as a tailor in the town. He gave away about two-thirds of the money he earned, either to the poor or for Masses for the souls in purgatory; at the same time he led an increasingly austere life and spent some hours each night in prayer.

When he was twenty-three he attended a mission given by priests from the newly-founded Redemptorist Congregation. He asked if he could join them as a lay brother and, after an initial refusal again because of his health, was accepted. The founder of the Redemptorists, St Alphonsus de'Liguori (1 Aug.), was impressed by his hard work and humility and intervened on his behalf to have the period of the novitiate shortened. Gerard was professed as a lay brother in 1752, adding to the usual vows one always to do whatever seemed more pleasing to God. A contemporary biographer tells the story of Gerard as a novice praying before the Blessed Sacrament and suddenly crying out, "Lord, let me go, I pray thee! I have work that I *must* do."

Gerard spent the three years of his religious life working as a tailor and infirmarian and in accompanying the priests on missions and retreats where his ability to read the secrets of people's souls was highly valued; more than twenty cases of his being able to bring sinners to repentance in this way are recorded. He was subject to ecstasies and levitation (it was said that on one occasion he was carried through the air for half a mile) and had the gifts of prophecy and infused knowledge. Above all, he was famous for the phenomenon of bilocation—attending a sick man in a cottage while talking to a friend in the monastery at the same time, for example. (The previous edition of this work carried a note to say that examples of bilocation, when proved, are usually explained either by the imagination of the beholder being impressed by the image of a person not physically present, or by the production by God of a real external image of an absent person, or by the person being seen through all the intervening space as though he were present.)

Gerard's reputation for holiness was so great that he was appointed as spiritual director of a number of communities of nuns, something most unusual for a non-ordained person. He wrote letters of advice to religious superiors and priests; they contain plain, straightforward statements of the ordinary Christian duties as applied to a particular way of life: he stressed gentleness to a prioress, vigilance to a novice, tranquillity to a parish priest, and conformity to God's will to everyone. He became known as a miracle-worker, and the number of people wanting to see him and ask for his help became so great at one stage that he had to be moved to another house. There he worked as the porter and managed to feed and clothe large numbers of beggars every day without anyone being certain where his supplies came from.

He was suffering from consumption, and in October 1755 he foretold the day and the time at which he would die; his forecast was correct, and he died on the night of 15-16 October. Pope Pius IX described him as "a perfect model for those of his own condition, the lay brothers," while Leo XIII referred to him at the time of his beatification in 1893 as "one of those angelic youths whom God has given to the world as models." He was canonized in 1904. He has been called the "most famous wonder-worker of the eighteenth century," and although some doubt has been thrown on the authenticity of some the accounts of his miracles (see below), he is still an outstanding figure.

Not long after his death he was being invoked as the patron of women in childbirth, though no particular event in his life justified such a devotion; by the end of the nineteenth century it had spread very widely throughout the Catholic world. In 1955, the second centenary of his death, there were worldwide petitions to have him declared the special patron of mothers. According to Walsh, the latter seems to be a popular modern devotion, again with no obvious foundation in the saint's life, although the way he supported his widowed mother might be cited in partial support. Another possibility is that his fame as a miracle-worker gave rise to the dissemination of a great many images of him, in some of which he is shown carrying a cross and a skull. In Central America, this led to him being identified with a Voodoo underworld figure who protected women in childbirth.

There is a contemporary Life by Fr Tannoia, trans. into English in *Lives of the Companions of St Alphonsus* (1849), pp. 243-453; see also *Propylaeum*, pp. 458-9. For his writings, see *Lettere e Scritti di S. Gerardo Maiella* (1949). See also J. Carr, *To Heaven Through a Window* (1946). A critical note is struck by N. Ferrante, C.SS.R., in *Bibl.SS.*, 6, 192-6, and in his *Storia meravigliosa di S. Gerardo* (3d ed., 1965), particularly with regard to Tannoia's Life and the more popular accounts; too much credence should not be given to the wonders related in some of the earlier depositions. M. Walsh (ed.), *Butler's Lives of Patron Saints* (1987), pp. 196-9, reprints most of the earlier account in *B.T.A.*

ST IGNATIUS OF ANTIOCH
Gold heart with red inscription on red field.

17

ST IGNATIUS OF ANTIOCH, *Bishop and Martyr*, (*c.* 37 - *c.* 107)

Ignatius was a Syrian, born about the year 37, who became bishop of Antioch about the year 69. He is said by some to have been a disciple of St John the Evangelist. He gave himself the nickname *Theophorus*, "God-bearer," because he was so certain of the presence of Christ within him. He was put to death as a Christian in Rome (he was, perhaps, a Roman citizen) during the reign of Trajan about the year 107 (some writers date his death later, between 110 and 117).

On his way to Rome he met St Polycarp (23 Feb.) and was warmly received by the various churches he visited. He wrote seven letters to churches in Asia Minor and to the Christians in Rome; these are important for the picture they give of Christianity in the first century and are our main source of information about Ignatius himself. They reveal him to have been a deeply spiritual and learned person, with a strong desire for martyrdom. He was concerned to heal dissensions in the churches and stressed the role of the local bishop as the authority to be followed and of the Eucharist as a source of unity, "the medicine of immortality, the antidote against death which gives eternal life in Jesus Christ . . . the bread that is the flesh of Jesus Christ, this flesh which has suffered for our sins." He also stressed the true humanity and divinity of Jesus and his bodily death and resurrection, the source of the Christian's new life. He wrote to the Christians at Ephesus, "You are all bearers of God, bearers of his temple, bearers of Christ, and so you are adorned with no other ornament than the counsels of Jesus Christ."

According to legend, as Ignatius approached Rome the Christians went out to meet him, rejoicing that he was with them but sad that they might soon lose him. It seems that they still hoped somehow to gain his release, but he repeated what he had urged in his letter to them, not to stand in the way of his going to the Lord: "I am afraid that your affection for me may do me harm; for it is easy for you to do what you will, but hard for me to attain to God, unless you are kind to me." He then prayed for the Church, for an end to persecution, and for love and unity among Christians. He was hurried off to the Colosseum, thrown to the lions, and died almost immediately. In his letter he had described himself as the "wheat of God (to) be ground by the teeth of wild beasts to become pure bread." He had continued, "Then shall I be truly a disciple of Jesus Christ, when the world shall not even see my body. . . . But, even if I do suffer, I shall do so as a freedman of Christ. In Christ I shall rise again, a free man. Now, in my bondage, I must learn to forget all my desires."

As has been said already, Ignatius had a strong desire for martyrdom, and his writings give us for the first time a Christian theology of martyrdom. According to this, the Christian must imitate Christ in all things, including his passion. For himself, Ignatius believed he was only truly a disciple when he imitated the Lord's sufferings, and death suffered in the name of Jesus would be the climax of his achievement as a Christian. This is not to be understood in the sense of the Christian's having to parallel in physical detail the sufferings of the passion, as some later writers were to assert, but in the sense that suffering and death allow the Christian to find God through being one with Jesus, who opened up life to us through his death. For Ignatius, moreover, this sharing in the passion of Christ must be part of the whole life of the Christian through the practice of holiness and an active apostolate, through self-denial and being open to the Spirit. There is a link here, of course, with what has been said about Ignatius' stress on the importance of the Eucharist, for in the Eucharist the Christian is associated with the passion and is united with Jesus in a unique way.

Ignatius' feast used to be kept on 1 February in the Western Church but after 1969 this was changed to 17 October, in line with the custom of the church at Antioch. Other Eastern churches celebrate his feast on 20 December, the supposed date of his arrival in Rome.

Ignatius has been frequently portrayed in Christian art, usually depicted in full episcopal vestments, as in the sixth-century mosaics in Santa Sophia, the Chartres statues, and the baptistery in Florence. Another image is of the removal of the saint's heart bearing the name "Jesus"; Botticelli's painting of this is in the Uffizi in Florence and Fra Angelico's *Adoration of the Saints and Angels,* in the National Gallery in London, shows the mitred saint holding a heart in his left hand.

AA.SS. Feb., 1, pp. 13–37; J. B. Lightfoot, *The Apostolic Fathers* pt.2 (1885); C. C. Richardson, *The Christianity of St Ignatius of Antioch* (1935); V. Corwin, *St Ignatius and Christianity in Antioch* (1960); *Bibl.SS.,* 7, 653–65. See *Dict. Sp.,* 7, pt. 2 (1971), 1250–66, on his theology and views on martyrdom as outlined above. Controversy about the authenticity of his letters continues; for an up-to-date account see C. Trevett, *A Study of Ignatius of Antioch in Syria and Asia* (1992); also, J. Rius-Camps, *The Four Authentic Letters of Ignatius* (1980). There is a complete translation in W. R. Schoedel, *Commentary on the Letters of Ignatius of Antioch* (1985). See also S. Tugwell, O.P., *Apostolic Fathers* (1989).

St John Kolobos (*c.* 409)

John was nicknamed Kolobos, a Greek word meaning "small"; he is generally known in English as "John the Dwarf." As a young man he retired into the Egyptian desert of Skete to live a life of solitude. His master was Ammoes, and among the tasks he set John to test his obedience was that of planting a walking stick and watering it until it blossomed. John did so for three years and eventually was rewarded when the stick took root and produced some fruit. Ammoes carried the fruit into the church and distributed it with the words, "Take and eat the fruit of obedience." It should be added that the story is also told of another John, of Lycopolis, and may more properly belong to him. John Kolobos cared for Ammoes for the last twelve years of his life without a word of thanks or appreciation until the master lay dying, when he described John as "an angel and not a man."

John's ideal of the perfect monk was someone who kept to his cell, tried to have God ever before his mind, and watched over his natural inclinations. He himself had a naturally quick temper and a rather high opinion of his own abilities; he curbed these characteristics so successfully that he developed a reputation for humility and thoughtful speech. He tried not to take part in discussions about what was happening in the world lest he be distracted from the things of God and lose that interior peace which he regarded as essential for holiness. He was extremely forgetful, but whether this was caused by his absorption in spiritual matters or by nature is not clear; it led to many stories being told about his absent-mindedness and inability to concentrate on the work in hand, and it was clearly a source of annoyance to his brethren, not least to St Arsenius (19 July).

In the tradition of the Desert Fathers, John built a monastery near Wadi al-Natrun for the disciples who had gathered round him. He is said to have lived in "a pit," which almost certainly means a narrow ravine or cave of which the area around the monastery is full. When some Berbers raided Skete about the year 400, John crossed the Nile toward the Red Sea and settled at Clysma, near Suez, close to where St Antony (17 Jan.), one of the founders of Western monasticism, is said to have lived. In the sayings attributed to him John praises humility and endurance and sees spiritual combat as a necessity. He could be severe and sometimes put his disciples through humiliating tests. Before he died, in his seventies, his brethren asked him for a final message; he did not want to be remembered as an important teacher, so he simply said, "I never followed my own will, nor did I ever teach another what I had not first practised myself." He died early in the fifth century, possibly in 409, with the reputation of being one of the most eminent of the Egyptian Desert Fathers, and his cult spread rapidly. His relics were translated from Clysma to his own monastery in 805. The ruins of the monastery have been discovered and accurately identified as that of St John.

John's life is known from two main sources, a Life by Bishop Zacharias written in the late seventh century and the *Apophthegmata Patrum*, or Sayings of the Fathers; both need to be used with caution, as there were many monks named John and it is not always possible to distinguish between them. See *AA.SS.*, Oct., 8, pp. 39-59; *Bibl.SS.*, 6, 666-9; *The Coptic Encyclopedia* 5 (1991), pp. 1359-62, which also gives a full modern bibliography.

St Nothelm of Canterbury, *Bishop* (*c.* 740)

Nothelm, whom Bede describes as "a devout priest of the church of London," became archbishop of Canterbury in 734 or 735. Two years later he received the *pallium* from Pope St Gregory III (10 Dec.). He is remembered principally for the help he gave to Bede in the writing of the latter's famous *Ecclesiastical History*. Nothelm was the mouthpiece of Albinus of Canterbury, on whom Bede relied for his knowledge of Christianity in Kent and southern England and of the work of the first missionaries sent by St Gregory. Nothelm also worked in Rome and found in the archives there documents relevant to the establishment of the English mission. In particular, he brought back a copy of St Gregory's *Replies* to St Augustine (27 May), which dealt with queries about how the English converts should be treated, and which Bede used in his work. While some doubts have been expressed about both the authenticity of the *Replies* and Nothelm's searches in Rome, there is not enough evidence to undermine Bede's account and his favourable picture of Nothelm.

We know very little about Nothelm as archbishop of Canterbury. He consecrated at least three bishops and held a synod, which agreed to the division of the Mercian diocese. He was consulted by St Boniface (5 June), to whom he sent a copy of St Gregory's *Replies*. He was interested in the interpretation of the scriptures, sending a list of thirty questions on the Books of Kings to Bede; Bede wrote a treatise on the Books in reply.

Nothelm died in 739 or 740 and was buried in the church of St Augustine in Canterbury. His cult was a local one. In 1091 his remains were moved to the new apse and reburied with those of the other archbishops around the body of St Augustine.

Bede, *H.E.*, preface; *AA.SS.*, Oct., 8, pp. 117-24; on the question of authenticity, see M. Deanesly and P. Grosjean, *J.E.H.* 10 (1959), pp. 1-49, and P. Meyvaert, *R.H.E.* 54 (1959), pp. 879-94. See also *Bibl.SS.*, 9, 1075; *O.D.S.*, p. 362.

St Seraphino (1540-1604)

Felice da Rapagnano was born at Montegranaro near Ascoli Piceno in Marche in 1540. His parents were very poor, and he spent his early years as a shepherd. His parents died when he was still young, so he was looked after by an elder brother, who turned out to be a severe taskmaster and rather cruel in his treatment of Felice. While he was working as a servant in a nearby house he heard the daughter of the family reading aloud from the Lives of the Saints and other spiritual books, and this gave him the idea that he might have a religious vocation. He was encouraged by the daughter, who directed him to try the Capuchins, and eventually he was allowed to enter as a lay brother at the age of eighteen; he took the name Seraphino in religion.

He met with many difficulties and had to move around the Marche region from monastery to monastery. No matter how diligently he fulfilled the duties given him, he seemed to be unable to please his superiors and the other friars and so was spared neither reproofs nor punishments; they tried to get rid of him at the first opportunity. For his part he accepted what was happening with humility and added additional mortifications to these external trials. His spiritual life developed to a high degree. He spent three hours every night before the Blessed Sacrament and did not return to bed after attending Matins as the other friars did. Eventually he settled in Ascoli Piceno, where he became doorkeeper. His duties brought him into contact with the poor, and he developed his own mission to them, feeding them with vegetables from the friary's garden, giving them spiritual advice, and curing the sick by making the sign of the cross on them. His approach was a mixture of great simplicity and mature judgment that was extremely effective in leading people to God. He had the gift of discerning spirits, was able to settle disputes, and could foretell the future and so was sometimes consulted by both civic and ecclesiastical authorities on important matters. When it was rumoured that he was on the move again, the local authorities wrote to his superiors to prevent his departure.

At one time he had wanted to go and work among the infidels as a missionary, as St Francis had done, but his superiors refused him permission and he lived his religious life almost entirely in the obscurity of a lay brother's vocation, and yet he managed to be a messenger of peace and good will. He was reputed to have worked many miracles, such as passing through a swollen river dry-foot and unharmed, having the vegetables which he had cut for the poor grow again overnight, and curing the sick. He died on 12 October 1604 at Ascoli Piceno and was canonized in 1767. His relics are in the Capuchin church of Santa Maria in Solestà, which was restored on a number of occasions in his honour.

AA.SS., Oct., 6, pp. 128-60; G. da Fermo, *Gli Scrittori Cappuccini delle Marche* (1928); *Bibl.SS.*, 11, 850-2.

BB Ursuline Nuns of Valenciennes, *Martyrs* (1794)

The Ursuline convent at Valenciennes in the north-east of France had been established in 1654; its nuns had run schools and looked after the poor of the neighbourhood. After the French Revolution had broken out in 1789 a large number of religious houses were forcibly closed, including that at Valenciennes, and so the nuns took refuge in another house of their Order at Mons, across the frontier in the Austrian Netherlands (modern Belgium). The Austrians invaded France and took Valenciennes, and so the nuns returned to their convent and reopened their schools. The town was recaptured by the French Revolutionary armies, but the nuns decided to stay. Shortly afterwards, in September 1794, they were arrested on the grounds that they were emigrées who had returned to France without permission and were running religious schools. They were imprisoned, and five of them were brought to trial on 17 October; they stated quite openly that they had returned to the town to teach the Catholic religion and were sentenced to death. As they were being led out to the guillotine in the marketplace one of them, Marie Augustine Dejardin, spoke to the mother superior: "Mother, you taught us to be valiant, and now that we are going to be crowned, you weep!" Five days later the superior, Marie Clotilde Paillot, and the remaining five nuns were also executed, with the superior declaring publicly, "We die for the faith of the Catholic, Apostolic and Roman Church!" A lay sister, Cordule Barré, was overlooked by the commissioners but climbed into the tumbril of her own accord and was executed along with the rest; they went to their deaths singing the Litany of Our Lady. They were among the last to be executed under the Revolution.

Eleven of the Ursuline nuns were beatified as martyrs in 1920. Among them were two, Lilvina Lacroix and Anne Marie Erraux, who had been Bridgettines, and

Anne Josephine Leroux, who had been a Poor Clare; all three had joined the Ursulines when their own Orders had been suppressed. The names of the other nuns were Marie Vanot, Laurentine Prin, Ursula Bourla, Louise Ducrez, and Scholastique Leroux (sister of Anne Josephine).

J. Loridan, *Les Bienheureuses Ursulines de Valenciennes* (2d ed., 1920); *N.C.E.*, 14, p. 516. For a general account of the Martyrs of the French Revolution, see 2 Jan.

St John Baptist Turpin du Cormier and Companions,

Martyrs (1794)

At the beginning of 1794 there was a fresh outbreak of religious persecution in the town of Laval in the region of Mayenne in France. Since the start of the Revolution in 1789 there had been a number of oppressive laws and decrees against priests, religious, and laypeople; what happened in January 1794 marked a change to active and, indeed, fierce repression. A revolutionary commission began to indict and try people on religious charges, and within a month had sentenced 359 men and 102 women to death. Among these were twenty-two priests, three religious, and a seminarian. The trials took place amid great confusion and without proper procedures; the accused were not allowed to defend themselves and were frequently ordered to answer a simple yes or no to the questions. The judges seemed to be intent on making as many as possible of the priests and religious apostasize. When none of the accused agreed to renounce their religion they were condemned to death; as the sentences were announced the accused replied, "*Deo gratias.*" Fourteen priests were executed on one day; the last of them to die was John Baptist Turpin du Cormier, who recited the *Te Deum* as he mounted the scaffold and kissed the spot where the blood of the others had fallen. The date was 21 January.

On 17 October of the same year, another priest, Jacques Burin, was killed by soldiers because he had been carrying on a secret apostolate among the people. A pious woman, Françoise Mézière, who taught in a parish school, was executed in February, and two nuns of the Congregation of Charity of Chapelle-au-Riboul (now known as the Sisters of Notre Dame d'Evron) were executed in March, while another, an Augustinian who had been working in a hospital, was executed in June.

A cult of the martyrs started straightaway, and the mass grave at Croix-Bataille became a place of pilgrimage, at first privately and then, after the Revolution, in public. The remains were moved to a more suitable tomb, and a canonical process, the first step toward canonization, was begun in 1839. It was felt, however, that such a process would only cause further trouble by re-awakening old enmities and hatreds, and it was not continued. It was restarted in 1917 and introduced formally in Rome in 1944, leading to the beatification of nineteen martyrs in 1955. These were chosen, from the hundreds who died in the persecution around Laval, after rigorous investigation of the circumstances of their deaths to ensure that no possible political motive could be attributed to the executions.

The names and dates of the martyrs are: priests: Jean-Baptiste Turpin du Cormier

(1732-94), parish priest and rural dean of Laval; Jean Marie Gallot (1747-94), assistant parish priest and chaplain to the Benedictines; Joseph Pellé (1720-94), chaplain to the Clarisses; René Ambroise (1720-94), assistant priest; François Duchesne (1736-94), collegiate priest; Julien Morvin de la Gérardière (1733-94), assistant priest at a local parish; Jean-Baptiste Triquerie (1737-94), a Conventual Franciscan; Jacques André (1743-94), curate; André Duliou (1727-94), parish priest; Louis Gastineau (1727-94), chaplain; François Migoret-Lamberdière (1728-94), parish priest; Julien Moulé (1716-94), parish priest; Augustin Philippot (1716-94), parish priest; Pierre Thomas (1729-94), hospital chaplain; Jacques Burin (1756-94), curate. The nuns were Françoise Trahet and Jeanne Véron (Notre Dame d'Evron), and Marie Lhuillier (Augustinian).

A. Batard, *Les Martyrs de Laval pendant la Terreur* (1925); G. Cesbron, *Les Martyrs de Laval* (1955); *Vies des Saints*, 13, pp. 105-14; *Bibl.SS.*, 7, 1130-3. For a general account of the Martyrs of the French Revolution, see 2 Jan.

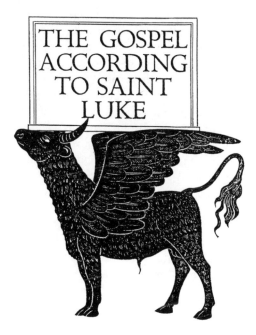

ST LUKE
The Bull Calf of St Luke, by Eric Gill.
Wood engraving and type from The Four Gospels *(1931).*

18

ST LUKE, *Evangelist* (First Century)

We do not know enough about Luke, the writer of the third Gospel and the Acts of the Apostles, to provide even a basic biography. His name was probably derived from the Latin Lucius or Lucanus. According to a fairly early and widespread tradition he was unmarried, wrote his Gospel in Greece, and died at the age of eighty-four in Boetia. According to Eusebius, the ecclesiastical historian, Luke's home was in Antioch. St Gregory Nazianzen (2 Jan.), who died in 390, tells us that Luke's missionary work was undertaken in Greece and that he was martyred; this seems to be very doubtful. Later traditions say he was one of the seventy disciples sent out by Jesus (see Luke 10:1), and one of the two disciples who met Jesus on the way to Emmaus (Luke 24:13-35).

There is a Luke mentioned by St Paul in his Epistles, and there is some debate about whether this is the evangelist or another person of the same name. When writing to the Colossians (4:14), Paul talks of "my dear friend Luke, the doctor"; in his second letter to Timothy (4:10) he says, "only Luke is with me"; and in his letter to Philemon (24) he calls Luke one of his "colleagues." It has usually been assumed that the Luke referred to in these passages is the same Luke who wrote the Gospel and the Acts of the Apostles. This, however, may not be so—the name was a common one, and it is interesting that Paul nowhere refers to his Luke as a writer. On the other hand, if we take the obvious meaning of "we" in Acts 16:10, for example, to mean Luke and Paul together, then Luke accompanied Paul on some of his journeys and shared in the troubles and persecution he suffered, and so could be the Luke mentioned by Paul. All that we have for certain are the Gospel and the Acts, and from these we can draw out some of the qualities and theological ideas of their author. The two books were written as two volumes of a single work, and it is important to see them together to understand their author more fully.

Luke opens his Gospel with a Prologue to tell us why he wrote it. Many other people, he says, have drawn up accounts of what had happened "among us," according to what they had heard from eyewitnesses and "ministers of the word," and so he had decided to write an "ordered account" himself, after carefully going over the whole story from the beginning. This would help Theophilus, the important person for whom he was writing, to see how authentic the teaching he had received was. With this Prologue we seem to be straightaway in the presence of a writer who was concerned about his sources and about producing a carefully planned account. Presumably he was not himself an eyewitness of everything "from the outset." The Prologue, and that to Acts, indicate Luke's cultural background and read like contemporary Greek prefaces written in a classical Greek style. He changes this style when he goes on to write about the birth of John the Baptist and uses the popular form of spoken Greek that was in use by educated people of the time. In other places he uses the Greek of the Old Testament Septuagint, the version of the Old Testament current among Jews who lived in the Diaspora outside Palestine, and he had a detailed knowledge of synagogue life. But he was writing for a non-Jewish readership, translating all Hebrew and Aramaic terms, and insisting that the salvation brought by Christ's life, teaching, and death was for everybody and not just the Jews (see, for example, 3:6 and 24:47, and Acts).

Luke tells us of events and sayings not found elsewhere in the Gospels. He is an accomplished storyteller, knowing how much detail to include and able to give us revealing character-sketches, as with the prodigal son (15:11-32) and the crafty steward (16:1-8). He gives us the fullest account of Jesus' birth, including the Annunciation and Visitation and the detail of the Nativity itself. For this reason, and the fact that Luke gives her a more central role in his writings than the other evangelists, older commentators argued that Luke must have obtained this information from Mary herself, but this was just a pious supposition. It is much more likely that he was relying on earlier oral traditions, such as he was referring to in his Prologue, though it is possible that one of these sources was the group of women disciples who accompanied Jesus and to whom Luke gives some prominence in his account (see 8:1-3). As with everything he wrote, however, Luke was concerned to present not just a historical account of what had happened but a carefully worked-out theological treatise that would help to convey his message to the reader.

Other parts of his Gospel are also peculiar to him: he relates six miracles and eighteen parables not mentioned by the other evangelists, and he has a long section (9:51-18:14) which is built around the theme of Jesus' journey to Jerusalem. This last is important and illustrates one of Luke's key theological ideas: the Holy City is central in the plan of salvation, and it is from there that the evangelization of the world must start. His gospel account starts and ends in Jerusalem, and it is in the Holy City that the apostles receive the Spirit and go out to preach to the world at the beginning of Acts.

All the time Luke presents events and teaching in a way that is his own. He is concerned, for example, to remove any blame for the crucifixion from the Roman authorities, perhaps because one of his aims in writing was to persuade them to recognize Christianity as a lawful religion throughout the empire. In other passages he brings out the kindness and sensitivity of Our Lord—the parable of the prodigal son (15:11-32), for example, and Christ's words to the women of Jerusalem (23:27-31). He underlines Christ's mercy to sinners and his concern for the outcasts of society—the parable of Dives and Lazarus (16:19-31); the stories of the woman who was a sinner (7:36-50) and of Zacchaeus (19:1-10); the promise to the repentant thief (23:39-43). Luke himself appears to share this sensitivity: he treats the apostles more kindly than does Mark, for example, omitting some of their misunderstanding of Christ's words and excusing their conduct on other occasions (see 9:45, for example).

Another marked feature of Luke's writings is the role he gives the Holy Spirit. The Spirit is instrumental in the Incarnation (1:35, and see also 2:25-7), guides the life of Jesus (4:1, 14, 18; 10:21), and will guide the disciple in the Christian life (11:13, 12:12). And it is in Acts that Luke gives us the full account of the coming of the Spirit at Pentecost and of the remarkable effect this had on the apostles (Acts 2). There is an important continuity here: the Spirit will guide the Church as it guided Jesus, and so the Church will be the continuation of Jesus' earthly life and ministry.

As well as stressing the role of the Spirit, Luke places considerable importance on prayer, again both in the life of Jesus (see 3:21, 5:16, 6:12, 9:18, 22:39-46) and for the Christian (11:1-9, 18:1-8). Finally, among the features unique to Luke or stressed more by him than by the other evangelists is the number of times he remarks on the role or presence of women in the events he is describing: the Visitation and Elizabeth (1:5-66); the widow of Nain (7:11-17); the woman who was a sinner (7:37-50); Mary Magdalen and several others (8:1-3); the woman in the crowd who blessed his mother (11:27); the women of Jerusalem (23:27-31); and of course the prominence given to Mary in the whole nativity account. In Acts, too, Luke notes the presence of Mary and other women with the apostles (1:14).

At the end of his Gospel Luke tells us how Jesus, immediately before his Ascension, explained to the apostles how his message of repentance would be preached to all nations (24:47). This theme is taken up in Acts, where Luke stresses again and again that salvation could be gained only through Jesus, "for of all the names in the world given to human beings, this is the only one by which we can be saved" (4:12). This fundamental fact demands a response from those who hear it: once Jesus has been preached as the crucified, risen, and glorified Lord, the would-be disciple must respond by faith, repentance and conversion, and baptism. Moreover, the disciple's response must continue and be evident in a Christ-like life. This means the following of Jesus as the Way, bearing witness to him in everything that is done, and prayer. It also involves a detached attitude to material possessions, an attitude that is much more evident in Luke's writings than elsewhere in the New Testament and that covers detachment from family ties as well. The community of goods and living described by him in Acts (4:32-35) is the perfect response of the early disciples in this regard. The fact that Luke himself seems to have been at ease in an affluent society gives these points additional weight.

In Acts Luke also sets out to show the divine origin of Christianity by stressing the miracles worked as the result of the Spirit's outpouring at Pentecost (2:1-12, 43); the way the first Christians lived in harmony (2:44-47); the way the gospel spread so quickly, and the special divine help given to both St Peter and St Paul (12 and 16). As in his first work, Luke is at pains to show throughout Acts that the gospel is for all people: he gives the details of the conflict between the apostles and the Jewish converts on this point (see, for example, 11:1-18, and again note the role of the Holy Spirit).

Part of Acts reads like a diary kept by Luke of his journeys with St Paul (see the start of the "we" passages in 16:10). In these chapters Luke shows himself to have been a keen observer and recorder of places and events. His account ends rather abruptly, however, with Paul under house arrest in Rome for two years; we can only surmise why Luke did not complete his story with the obvious ending, the death of Paul. Was this because he wrote his pro-Roman books at this exact time, to explain the new religion for which Paul had been imprisoned and to defend him when he came to trial? If this is true, then Luke was writing in the sixties of the first century; most modern scholars, however, favour a somewhat later date, between the years 70 and 85, leaving the "unfinished" nature of Acts an unanswered question.

Luke is the patron saint of the medical profession. He is also the patron saint of painters, especially of portrait painters, because of an ancient tradition, which dates from the sixth century, that he painted a portrait or icon of Our Lady. Later on other pictures were attributed to him as well. An extension of this patronage has led him to be regarded as the protector of craft workers in general, and of lace-makers in particular. Because his writings contain so much accurate detail he became the patron saint of notaries. Finally, since his symbol as an evangelist is an ox (perhaps because of the Temple sacrifice mentioned in the nativity narrative), he is also the patron saint of butchers.

Luke was usually depicted in art writing his sacred books, accompanied by his symbol of an ox. A later Flemish custom was to show him painting Our Lady, and there is a well-known painting attributed to Raphael on the same theme. His feast-day was celebrated throughout the Church from early times, and in England twenty-eight ancient churches were dedicated to him. What were claimed to be his relics were venerated in Constantinople, where the emperor Constantius II, who died in 361, had had them transferred from Thebes in Boetia.

AA.SS., Oct., 8, pp. 282-313; C. K. Barrett, *Luke the Historian in Recent Study* (1961); G. B. Caird, *Saint Luke* (1963); *Bibl.SS.*, 8, 188-222, with an interesting range of illustrations; P. Esler, *Community and Gospel in Luke-Acts* (1987); *O.D.C.C.*, pp. 12-3, 844-5. For a thorough critical study and commentary, see J. Fitzmyer, S.J., *The Gospel According to Luke*, 2 vols. (1981), in the Anchor Bible series, esp. 1, pp. 1-258; see also, in the same series, J. Munck, *The Acts of the Apostles* (1967). On the role of women in Luke's writings see Carla Ricci, *Mary Magdalene and Many Others: Women Who Followed Jesus* (1991; Eng. trans. 1994).

St Justus of Beauvais (date unknown)

The 1954 Roman Maryrology said that Justus was a young boy who was beheaded for being a Christian in the region of Beauvais during the persecution under Diocletian; this would place the date of his martyrdom some time between 303 and 313. His cult was very popular throughout north-western Europe; in Belgium it was centred on the abbey of Malmédy, where the monks were said to have obtained the martyr's body "for a good price" in the tenth century. In England King Athelstan gave Winchester the martyr's head in 924, but the monks at Auxerre claimed he had only a part of it. The diocese of Coira in Switzerland claimed to have received some relics in the eleventh century. At Beauvais his name was included in the Canon of the Mass and his feast-day had its own proper preface, while his name was given to nearby Saint-Just-en-Chaussée, at the crossroads where he was said to have been killed.

There was considerable confusion, however, between this Justus and other saints of the same name, and it is not possible to discover any trustworthy details of his life or execution. The oldest version of his *passio* dates from the eighth century. There is a detailed but obviously fabulous legend about him, including the story that when the soldier struck off his head the boy continued to live and even directed his relatives where he should be buried. A similar story is told of the St Justin who is venerated in Paris, whose supporters seem to have borrowed it from today's saint.

AA.SS., Oct., 8, pp. 323-42; *Bibl.SS.*, 7, 24-5; *Anal.Boll.* 52 (1954), p. 269.

19

SS JOHN DE BREBEUF AND COMPANIONS, *Martyrs* (1642-9)

Between September 1642 and December 1649 eight Jesuit missionaries were murdered in North America, mainly by members of the Iroquois and Mohawk peoples. They were canonized as a group in 1930, and in 1969 their feast-day was extended to the Universal Church as the proto-martyrs of North America and fixed as 19 October. The best known of the group are Joan de Brébeuf (1593–1649) and Isaac Jogues (1607–46); the others are Antoine Daniel (1601–48), Gabriel Lalemant (1610–49), Charles Garnier (*c.* 1605-49), Noël Chabanel (1613-49), René Goupil (1608-42), and Jean de la Lande (? -1646); the last two were not priests but missionary helpers. There are shrines to their memory at Auriesville, New York, and Midland, Ontario, which are popular places of pilgrimage.

It was in 1615 that three Jesuit priests landed in Quebec to help the Franciscan missionaries working in the area. Two of these were John de Brébeuf and Charles Lalemant; the third was Ennemond Masse, who had been part of an earlier group that had gone out in 1608 but had been driven away by English pirates. Brébeuf was an unlikely choice, as when he had entered the Jesuit house of studies in Rouen he had not been strong enough to follow the usual courses of study or to teach for any length of time—he seems to have suffered from tuberculosis.

Brébeuf spent the first winter with the Algonquins, living in appalling discomfort but learning their language and customs. In a letter of 1636 he described some of the hardships: the "minor martyrdom" of being kept awake almost all night by fleas, the log cabin where the smoke was "so heavy, stifling and continuous, that unless you are quite used to it, for five or six days at a time you can hardly read a couple of lines of your breviary." He complained of never being left alone, and hints at other problems when he writes, "One difficulty I cannot go into in detail, the risk of following their impurity if God is not so firmly with you that you can resist that poison."

The following year he went into the country of the Hurons, who had settled along the eastern shore of what is now Lake Huron. He was accompanied by another Jesuit and a Franciscan; they travelled about six hundred miles by canoe and on foot and finally set up a base at Tod's Point. His companions were soon recalled and Brébeuf was left alone among the Hurons; he hoped that the more settled way of life of the latter would lead to greater success in evangelizing them than had been the case with the more nomadic peoples. But they blamed him, and especially the cross on the top of his cabin, for all their ills, and he failed to make a single convert before he and the other French settlers were forced out by the English and returned to France.

In 1632 they were able to go back to Canada. Antoine Daniel arrived in 1632, and Brébeuf and Masse joined him in the following year. The head of the mission, Fr Le Jeune, started to send back to France a series of reports on their work designed to get the support of Catholics at home; these became known as the "Jesuit Relations," and they often contained letters of the missionaries, especially of Brébeuf. They were successful in arousing interest in the missionary work and in persuading others to join them.

John de Brébeuf, Antoine Daniel, and another Jesuit, Darost, went off to the Huron lands to try a second campaign of evangelization. Travelling was extremely hazardous, especially by canoe, and they had to motivate themselves to keep going. As Brébeuf wrote, "Anyone who thinks of his loving Saviour taunted by cruel enemies and ascending Calvary under the weight of the cross will find it sheer joy to shoot these rapids. . . . The discomfort of a canoe is no problem for anyone who remembers our Lord crucified." Their knowledge of the language enabled them to get to know the Hurons' approach to religion, which seemed to them to be based almost entirely on fear. Brébeuf wrote, "We began our catechizing with the memorable truth that their souls, which are immortal, all go after death either to paradise or to hell. It is thus we approach them in public or in private. I explained that it rested with them during life to decide what their future lot was to be." The Hurons were more impressed when prayers to the Christian God seemed to end a drought and averted famine, but they were still slow to become converts. Unlike some other missionaries of the time, the Jesuits did not baptize any adults, except the seriously ill, unless they had been properly prepared over a long period and gave some sign of likely perseverance. The Jesuits decided that little progress would be made until some of the younger Hurons could be properly trained to work as missionaries among their own people, and so Antoine Daniel left for Quebec with a few children to set up a seminary.

In 1636 five more Jesuits joined the mission, two of whom were to become martyrs—Isaac Jogues and Charles Garnier. Jogues had been born in Orleans, while Garnier was from Paris; both had joined the Jesuits at a young age and after their ordination had been sent to Canada. Isaac Jogues was twenty-nine years old, Charles Garnier thirty. By May of the following year Brébeuf was able to write, "We are listened to gladly, we have baptized more than 200 this year, and there is hardly a village that has not invited us . . . at last it is understood that we have come . . . solely to teach them, and to procure for them their souls' health and happiness that will last for ever." But there were still many obstacles to be overcome. At one point the missionaries were condemned to death because of continuing suspicion that they brought evil, and they were saved only by Brébeuf's eloquence.

A second mission station was established at Teanaustaye, with Gabriel Lalemant in charge of both; John de Brébeuf left to look after Sainte-Marie, a settlement some way from the Huron villages which became an administrative centre for the missionaries and French settlers. A hospital, fort, and cemetery were set up there, and missions went out to other peoples in the area but with little success. Gabriel

Lalemant wrote, "We have sometimes wondered whether we could hope for the conversion of this country without the shedding of blood," and John de Brébeuf and Isaac Jogues were praying that they might be allowed to share in suffering and martyrdom. Brébeuf, for example, wrote, "For two days without break I have felt a great desire for martyrdom. . . . My God and my Saviour Jesus, what return can I make to you for all the benefits which you have conferred upon me? . . . I make a vow . . . to you never to fail, on my side, in the grace of martyrdom, if by your infinite mercy you offer it to me some day."

It was Isaac Jogues and his assistant, René Goupil, who were to face suffering and death first. In 1642 they were ambushed by a group of Iroquois, the bitter enemies of the Hurons, and severely tortured and mutilated, losing their nails and then their fingers; at night they were laid out naked on the ground in chains and had hot coals and ashes thrown on them. Eventually René Goupil was tomahawked to death when he was seen to make the sign of the cross over some children. He had originally been a Jesuit novice but had to leave because of his health; he had then become a surgeon and gone to Canada, where he had offered his medical services to the missionaries and become one of their helpers. He died on 29 September 1642.

Isaac Jogues remained a slave for a time and was then rescued through the good offices of Dutch settlers. He returned to France, where he received permission to continue to say Mass despite his mutilated hands. By 1644 he was back in Canada and was chosen to be part of a deputation to the Iroquois, who had asked for peace. This was successful, but the Mohawks (part of the Iroquois) suspected that some of the religious objects left behind by Isaac Jogues were the cause of a serious epidemic, and when he and an assistant, Jean de la Lande, later visited some of their villages, they were attcked by the Mohawks after they had been invited to a meal; both were tomahawked and beheaded, on 18 and 19 October 1646.

By this time the mission to the Hurons was showing signs of success and there were hopes that a period of peace would see large numbers converted. The Iroquois, however, began a new campaign against them and in 1648 attacked Teanaustaye, where Antoine Daniel was in charge. He refused to leave, making what arrangements he could for the safety of the Christian converts and caring for the wounded. He went to plead with the attackers but was shot by arrows and his body thrown into the chapel, which was then burned. He died on 4 July 1648.

Within a year, on 16 March 1649, the Iroquois attacked the village where John de Brébeuf and Gabriel Lalemant were stationed. Gabriel Lalemant had been the last of the martyrs to arrive in New France; two of his uncles had already served as misionaries there, and after his ordination he had taken a vow to offer his life as a sacrifice on the missions. The two priests were captured and subjected to atrocious tortures; John de Brébeuf was killed on 16 March, Gabriel Lalemant the day after. Later in the same year the Iroquois attacked the Tobacco nation, among whom Charles Garnier had established a mission station in 1641, and set about slaughtering the people. Charles Garnier was the only priest present at the time, and he did what he could to give absolution to the dying and baptize those who had been catechumens. He was shot by one of the Iroquois but continued trying to reach a dying person whom he thought he could help, until he was tomahawked and killed. The date was 7 December 1649.

The next day Noël Chabanel, who had been Charles Garnier's missionary companion, was shot and killed, this time by a Huron Christian who had apostasized and who later admitted his crime had been motivated by revenge for the evils he believed the missionaries had brought upon his family. Noël Chabanel had been a reluctant missionary, unable to adapt to the harshness of the life or learn the Huron language and accept their customs. Despite his natural feelings of revulsion, however, he had taken a vow to remain working on the mission in North America until he died.

John de Brébeuf had written in his spiritual diary: "How I grieve, my God, that you are not known, that this savage country is not yet wholly converted to faith in you, that sin is not yet blotted out!" This was the motive that encouraged him and his fellow-martyrs to persevere in what were terrible conditions, facing the likelihood of torture and death as a way of giving something back to Jesus, who had, in Brébeuf's words, "been so gracious as to die for me."

The primary sources of information about the martyrs are their own letters and the official reports, or "Relations," sent back to France; for these see R. G. Thwaites, *Jesuit Relations and Allied Documents, Travels and Explorations of the Jesuit Missionaries in New France*, 73 vols. (1897-1901; new ed., 1959). Recent study of these has examined how far the missionaries tried to understand the cultures and religions of the peoples they were trying to convert. There is some evidence of a slowly developing awareness of some of the complexities involved, but the missionaries were men of their time and shared the contemporary European insensitivity toward other peoples and assumptions of their own cultural superiority. Their overall aim of conversion and their need to relate their experiences to a European frame of reference prevented any genuine appreciation of others' beliefs and practices. See M. Pomedli, "Beyond Unbelief: Early Jesuit Interpretations of Native Religions," in *Studies in Religion* 16 (1987), pp. 275-87. The extracts from Brébeuf used above are taken from the *Office of Readings*, 3, p. 349, and from J. Cumming (ed.), *Letters from Saints to Sinners* (1996), pp. 177-8; a detailed description of Isaac Jogues' tortures can be found on pp. 236-9. See also R. Latourelle, *Etude sur les Ecrits de S. Jean de Brébeuf* (1953); W. and E. M. Jury, *Sainte-Maries Among the Hurons* (1953); M. Twomey, *A Parade of Saints* (1983), pp. 93-6. The previous edition of this work gives the feast under the date of 26 Sept.; it also gives some details of the tortures inflicted on the martyrs.

ST PAUL OF THE CROSS, *Founder* (1694-1775)

Paolo Francesco Danei was the eldest son of an impoverished noble businessman and was born at Ovada, near Genoa in northern Italy. He tried the life of a soldier against the Turks in 1714 but gave it up after a year and led a life of seclusion and prayer until 1720. In that year he was moved by a vision to found a Congregation especially devoted to the passion of Christ; he wrote its Constitution while on retreat and was allowed to accept novices from 1725. He and his brother were ordained priests by Pope Benedict XIII in 1727, and in the same year they established a house on Monte Argentaro.

Paul's aim was to combine an austere monastic life, based on devotion to the passion, with preaching to the poor; the principal theme of the preaching was to be the passion. The life was extremely rigorous, and many novices gave up and left; but the work of preaching, combined with a ministry to the sick, was successful and gained Paul and those who stayed with him considerable recognition. Papal approval of the new Congregation was given in 1741 and 1746, on condition that the Rule became somewhat less severe. Three houses (known as "Retreats") existed by 1747, and final approval was given in 1769, when the Congregation was granted the privileges of the older religious Orders. Its members were known as the Discalced Clerks of the Most Holy Cross and Passion of Our Lord Jesus Christ, or Passionists; they took a fourth vow to spread the memory of Christ's passion to the faithful. Their habit was black, with a large badge consisting of a white heart surmounted with a cross and bearing the words, "Jesu XPI Passio."

Paul was elected superior general in 1747. He was a very effective preacher, and he and his priests were in demand throughout Italy for retreats, parochial missions, and spiritual direction. Most of Paul's correspondence deals with ascetical theology and prayer. In one letter, for example, he wrote, "This fire [*i.e.* love] which penetrates the inner core of one's being, changes the lover into his beloved. And on a higher level where love is merged with sorrow and sorrow mingled with love, there results a certain blend of love and sorrow that is so complete that the love can no longer be distinguished from the sorrow nor the sorrow from the love." He urged his followers to behave in such a way that it would be clear to everybody that they bore the image of Christ crucified, "who is the pattern of all that is gentle and attractive. . . . Bury yourselves, therefore, in the heart of Jesus crucified, desiring nothing else but to lead all men to follow his will in all things."

He spent long periods in adoration before the Blessed Sacrament and continued to practise extreme austerities and bodily mortifications. He recommended three things to his priests: "The spirit of prayer, the spirit of solitude and the spirit of poverty. With these the Congregation will shine before God and before the world." It was poverty that he was most insistent about, writing on another occasion: "It is certain that the spirit of religious perfection will flourish in the Congregation so long as the love and practice of voluntary poverty remain in their vigour and intensity." He also stressed the importance of obedience: "Let obedience be blind: let all think in a lowly manner about themselves, let them study and love to be despised, that they may the more easily attain to religious perfection." His priests were to "count that day lost on which [the] will has not been exercised by submission."

From one point of view Paul was a contemplative at heart, most content when living a life of solitude and prayer. Yet he showed how it was possible to combine this with a very active and practical missionary life; nor was this an optional extra. Paul's intense devotion to the passion, and his understanding of how great God's love was, as proved by the sufferings of his Son, made it essential to try to spread that knowledge and love to others, by both preaching and example.

After 1769, when final papal approval was granted to the Congregation, Paul lived mostly in Rome near the basilica of SS John and Paul, which the pope had given them after the death of Paul's brother, John, in 1765. A few years before he died he founded a Congregation of enclosed, contemplative nuns, who also took an additional vow to practise devotion to the passion. By the time of his death in October 1775 Paul had a reputation as a miracle-worker, with the gifts of healing and prophesying and the ability to read people's spiritual condition. He was canonized in 1867.

Paul left a small number of important spiritual writings. He wrote a Diary during a long retreat in 1720, which gives the principles underpinning his spirituality and preaching: the norm for the Christian must be participation in the life of Jesus; suffering is a gift from God which allows the Christian to partake more fully in Christ's suffering on the cross and in his glory; the way to enter into communion with the Trinity is through the humanity of Christ. This key document was neglected for a long time after Paul's death and given a critical edition only in 1964. Paul was also a regular letter writer; over two thousand of his letters have been published in five volumes. He had an easy, simple style even when writing in a hurry, and his letters are full of enthusiasm and humour. His short work, *Morte Mystica* (Mystical Death), gave suggestions on how to live the religious vows as a sharing in Jesus' death on the cross in order to be reborn to a new life. The book disappeared from circulation after Paul's death, apparently because of some hesitation over its intense mysticism; it was discovered and published in 1976. Finally, there was a work intended to help uneducated laypeople, *The Passion of Jesus Christ in Forty Short Meditations*—whether this was written by Paul himself is in some doubt, but it is certainly based on his preaching and letters.

The Congregation did not spread beyond central Italy until 1840. In that year a house was opened in Belgium, and then in 1841 the first group of Passionists began working in England, a country Paul had always been interested in. They developed a very fruitful mission in the new industrial areas where the majority of Catholics lived, making a name for themselves by insisting on wearing their distinctive habit in public and by their often emotional preaching. One of them, Bd Dominic Barberi (27 Aug.), received the future Cardinal Newman into the Church. The Congregation spread to the United States in 1852, to Spain in 1878, and then slowly to South America, Australia, and France. It was not until 1924 that houses were opened in Germany and Poland.

Paul's letters were edited by A. Casetti and C. Chiari, *Lettere*, 5 vols. (1924 and 1977); these also contain the Diary and *La morte mistica*. For the Diary see also E. Zoffoli (ed.), *S. Paolo della Croce. Diario spirituale* (1964). The extracts above are from the *Office of Readings*, 3, p. 351, and from T. S. Gregory, "St Paul of the Cross 1775-1995," *The Tablet*, 18 Oct. 1975. The first Life was written in 1786 by Bd. B. M. Strambi, C.P; trans. as *Saints and Servants of God*, 2 vols. (1853). There are many modern Lives; see P. Edmund, *Hunter of Souls. A Study of the Life and Spirit of St Paul* (1946); C. Alméras, *S. Paul, le fondateur des Passionistes* (1957; Eng. trans., 1960); E. Zoffoli, *S. Paolo della Croce, storia critica*, 3 vols. (1963-8)—the starting point for further study. See also *Bibl.SS.*, 10, 231-57; *O.D.S.*, pp. 382-3; *O.D.C.C.*, pp. 1039-40, 1052;

Dict.Sp., 12:1 (1984), 540-60, with a very good bibliography; the paragraph above on Paul's writings is dependent on this. On the Congregation, see E. Zoffoli, *I Passionisti* (1955), and *Le monache passioniste. Storia e spiritualità* (1970); F. Giorgini, *La communità passionista* (1980); *N.C.E.*, 10, pp. 1066-8.

St Ethbin (Sixth Century)

Ethbin, or Egbin, was born in Britain of noble parents. When his father died, Ethbin, who was fifteen at the time, was entrusted to St Samson (28 July), one of the most important missionary bishops of the day. Later, Ethbin moved to Brittany and became a monk under St Winwaloe (3 Mar.). The monastery was destroyed by the Franks, and Ethbin seems to have moved to Ireland, where he died about twenty years later after living as a hermit; the place cannot be identified with any certainty, and no cult developed in Ireland—indeed, he is not mentioned in any of the Irish calendars. It has been suggested that the place where he lived as a hermit was near Senlis, in northern France, and not in Ireland at all. His relics are claimed by two French churches, at Montreuil and Pont-Mart. His name is certainly Anglo-Saxon and not Celtic.

The previous edition of this work printed one of the several miraculous stories which are told in his Life. One day he was out walking with St Winwaloe when they saw a leper lying helpless by the road. Winwaloe asked Ethbin what they should do, and Ethbin suggested they follow the apostles' example and bid him get up and walk. Winwaloe was moved by Ethbin's faith, followed the advice, and the leper was healed.

AA.SS., Oct., 8, pp. 474-88, gives an untrustworthy Life. See also Baring-Gould and Fisher, 2, pp. 466-7; R. Largillière, *Mélanges d'hagiographie bretonne* (1925); *Bibl.SS.*, 5, 113-4; *O.D.S.*, p. 162.

St Aquilinus of Evreux, *Bishop* (*c.* 620-95)

Aquilinus, or Aquilin, was born in Bayeux about the year 620 and spent several years as a soldier and a courtier under Clovis II. While he was away on a military campaign against the Visigoths, his wife took a vow to observe chastity for a year in return for his safety. They eventually met at Chartres; together they decided to devote their lives to God and the service of the poor and made the vow perpetual. Aquilinus was about forty years old at this time. They settled in Evreux and worked there for about ten years until, on the death of the bishop, St Aeternus, Aquilinus was chosen as his successor. He was one of the bishops who attended the Council of Rouen in 688-9. He was not happy at the thought of all the distractions the life of a bishop would entail, so he built himself a cell by the cathedral and lived as much like a hermit as possible, praying and doing penance on behalf of his flock. During his last years the bishop lost his sight, but he retained his reputation as a zealous pastor and was said to have worked a number of miracles. He died about the year 695, and the oratory where he was buried was named after him and became the chapel of the local seminary; it was destroyed in the bombardment of 1940.

At various times his feast-day has been celebrated in October, February, and July; the Evreux Breviary mentions two saints of the same name. A large number of churches were dedicated to him.

AA.SS., Oct., 8, pp. 489-510, prints a twelfth-century Life, which seems to be an expanded version of an earlier one. See also J-B. Mesnel, *St Aquilin* (1909); *Bibl.SS.*, 2, 330-1; *Catholicisme*, 1, 751-2.

St Frideswide (*c.* 680-727)

It seems likely that an area of what is now west Oxfordshire was ruled in the late seventh century by Dida of Eynsham. He built a number of minsters, including one at Oxford; and his daughter, Frideswide, was abbess of a double monastery in the same place, on the site of what is now Christ Church; the town of Oxford grew up around these buildings. Legend has it that she had been the object of unwanted advances from a neighbouring ruler and had fled, first to Binsey and then to Oxford. Her monastery became important both religiously and as a landowner, but its records were destroyed in an attempted massacre of some Scandinavians who had taken refuge in the church.

There is eleventh-century evidence for the existence of her shrine, and her relics were translated in 1180, after the monastery had been refounded about 1120 as a house for Augustinian canons. They were moved again in 1289. In the fifteenth century she was officially adopted as patron of the university, and her shrine was visited ceremonially twice a year by the chancellor and other members of the university. In 1525 Cardinal Wolsey dissolved the priory, with permission from the pope, in order to build Cardinal College. The priory church became the college chapel, but Frideswide's shrine was left intact until it was despoiled by the dissolution commissioners in 1538. The chapel became the cathedral church of the new diocese of Oxford in 1546, and the college was refounded as Christ Church.

The saint's shrine was restored under Queen Mary but destroyed once and for all in 1561, when a Calvinist divine had her relics mixed up with those of the widow of the reformer Peter Martyr Vermigli, as a deliberate attempt to end her cult. In modern times it has been possible to reconstruct part of the shrine from fragments found in a well in Christ Church, and it has become once again a place of pilgrimage. She is also venerated as St Frevisse at Borny in Artois, northern France.

AA.SS., Oct., 8, pp. 533-90, gives the early legendary Life. See also F. M. Stenton, "St Frideswide and Her Times," in D. M. Stenton (ed.), *Preparatory to Anglo-Saxon England* (1970); J. Blair, "Saint Frideswide Reconsidered," in *Oxoniensia* 52 (1987), pp. 71-127; H. M. Mayr-Harting, "Functions of a Twelfth-Century Shrine. . . ." in *Studies in Medieval History Presented to R. H. C. Davis (1985); O.D.C.C.*, pp. 537-8; *O.D.S.*, pp. 189-90, on which the above account is largely based.

Bd Thomas of Biville (*c.* 1187-1257)

Thomas Helye was born about the year 1187 at Biville in Normandy; his parents seem to have been people of local importance, and he received a good education. He decided to use his ability to teach local children, and he became a cross between a village school teacher and a catechist. When the people of Cherbourg heard how successful he was at these tasks, they invited him to do the same in their town; again, he was very successful but became ill and had to return home. His way of life with his parents was more like that of a monk than a layperson. He was ordained deacon by the bishop of Coutances and went as a pilgrim to both Rome and Compostela before going to Paris to complete his studies and be ordained priest.

He had a special ability as a preacher and was also a careful pastor; it is said that he spent a good part of the night in prayer in order to have more time during the day for his duties as a priest. When he was given charge of a parish he appointed a curate in his place and continued what he did best: preaching, catechizing, visiting the sick, and working for the conversion of sinners wherever there seemed to be a need. He was at heart a missionary and would not be tied down to one place. He led a very austere life. In 1257 he was taken ill at the castle of Vauville in La Manche and died there on 19 October. The first miracle after his death was the restoring of the withered hand of his hostess. Around his native Biville he became known as "the wonder-worker," and a widespread local cult was approved in 1859.

His shrine in the church at Biville was threatened with destruction at the time of the French Revolution, but his bones were hidden. The parish priest was arrested and imprisoned for concealing this "crime" and for not revealing the names of those involved. After the Revolution the relics were restored to the church at Biville, where they still are.

There is a valuable medieval Life by a contemporary named Clement, who had witnessed much of what he recorded of Thomas' missionary work; see *AA.SS.*, Oct., 8, pp. 592-622. See also the Life by P. Pinel, (1927). Van Ortroy, in *Anal.Boll.* 22 (1903), p. 505, throws considerable doubt on the tradition that at one time Thomas had been appointed chaplain to St Louis IX.

St Peter of Alcántara, *Founder* (1499-1562)

Pedro Garavita was born at Alcántara, a small town in the province of Estremadura in Spain, in 1499. His father was a lawyer and governor of the town. He studied at the university of Salamanca and decided to join the strict Franciscan Friars of the Observance in 1515. He practised severe bodily mortifications, sleeping little as possible and that usually in a sitting position; it is said that it was because of this that he later became the patron saint of night-watchmen. When he was still only twenty-two years old he was sent to found a new friary at Badajoz; he was ordained in 1524. He became guardian, or superior, of a number of houses, and from 1538 to 1541 was provincial of the province of St Gabriel.

His rule was noted for his attempts to impose as strict a way of life as possible on the friars. He tried to follow the evangelical counsels to the letter, having, for example, only one habit and no other clothing. He became famous for his preaching and appears to have enjoyed the gift of infused knowledge from God. His efforts to reform the Estremaduran province still further were unsuccessful, and at the end of his term of office he was allowed to retire to live almost as a hermit at Arabida, near Lisbon. Here another friar was attempting to interpret the Franciscan Rule in an eremitical sense for a small group of his brethren; Peter joined them and soon became their inspiration, leading them to adopt the extremely rigorous way of life which he had tried to impose elsewhere. In 1554 he went to Rome to obtain permission to found a Congregation of friars, and he was allowed by the pope to put himself under the direction of the Conventual branch of the Franciscans instead of the Observant branch because the minister general of the latter opposed his plans.

On his return to Spain he established a new house at Pedrosa, and this was the beginning of the Franciscans of the Observance of St Peter of Alcántara, or Alcantarines. They were formally restored to Observant control in 1561, when they were recognized as a province in their own right, and kept their separate existence until Pope Leo XIII united the different Observant traditions in 1897. Their Rule reflected Peter's desire to live as austere a religious life as possible: cells were only seven feet long, the friars went barefoot, took neither meat nor wine, and practised three hours of mental prayer every day; their communities were limited to eight friars, and they were forbidden to accept Mass stipends so that their reliance on alms would be complete.

Peter was motivated at least in part by a desire to help the reform of the Church; he saw his life of extreme penance as one way of countering the ills that were, he believed, affecting religion at the time. When people lamented the wickedness of the world and the evils of society, he would reply: "The remedy is simple. You and I must first be what we ought to be; then we shall have cured what concerns ourselves. Let each one do the same, and all will be well. The trouble is that we all talk of reforming others without ever reforming ourselves." He faced opposition from his former brethren and was at various times condemned as a hypocrite, a traitor, and an ambitious disturber of the religious peace. He urged his opponents to do all they could to stop his reform so that it could be properly tested. His sincerity and zeal won him support, and he became much sought-after as a confessor and spiritual director, but the opposition continued to the end of his life.

It is from another sixteenth-century reformer, St Teresa of Avila (15 Oct.), that we learn most about Peter's spiritual life. They met in 1560, and Teresa later described him as the person who had done most to encourage her in her reform at a time when she was facing opposition to the founding of her first convent. He was particularly supportive of her plan to have no endowments for her houses and to live in absolute poverty. She related much of what he told her about his own life, his mortifications, and his experiences in prayer: "It was usual for him to eat but once in three days. . . . One of his companions told me that sometimes he ate nothing at all for eight days. But that perhaps might be when he was in prayer, for he used to have great raptures and vehement transports of divine love, of which I was once an eyewitness. His poverty was as extreme as his mortification, even from his youth. . . . When I came to know him he was very old, and his body so shrivelled and weak that it seemed to be composed as it were of the roots and dried bark of a tree rather than flesh. . . . He spoke little unless questions were asked him; and he answered in a few words, but in these he was worth hearing, for he had an excellent understanding." Teresa admired a book on prayer which Peter had written; it is not clear whether this was his own work or whether it was a summary of Luis de Granada's work on the same subject, perhaps written with the latter's help; some scholars have claimed that it was Luis who borrowed from and expanded Peter's original writings.

Peter died in 1562 and was canonized in 1669. His cult was not widespread—as the previous editors of this work put it, his life "seems only to have aroused languid interest." This is not surprising, considering the towering reformers, founders, and mystics who were his contemporaries. Yet his life witnesses in its own way to the vitality of religious reform in sixteenth-century Spain, and if he is overshadowed by others that is only what he would have desired and thought fit.

AA.SS., Oct., 8, pp. 623-809, for the earliest Life (1615) and a later one of 1669. His book on prayer was trans. into English by D. Devas (1926). See also E. Allison Peers, *Studies of the Spanish Mystics*, 2 (1930); *Estudios sobre San Pedro . . . 1562-1962* (1962); a popular Life by J. Piat (1959); *D.T.C.*, 12, pt. 2 (1935), 1793-1800; *Bibl.SS.*, 10, 652-62; *O.D.C.C.*, p. 1070; *O.D.S.*, p. 390.

St Philip Howard, *Martyr* (1557-95)

Philip Howard was born in London in 1557, the eldest son of the fourth duke of Norfolk and heir to the premier aristocratic family in England. When Queen Elizabeth I ascended the throne in 1558 his father gave up his Catholicism, and so Philip was brought up a Protestant, with John Knox as his tutor. In 1572 the family was disgraced when the duke was executed for treason after being implicated in a plot to depose Elizabeth and marry Mary, Queen of Scots (the Ridolfi Plot). Philip became the ward of Lord Burghley, the queen's chief minister, who sent him to study at Cambridge, where he graduated as M.A. in 1576. He was presented at court and became one of Elizabeth's favourites, and succeeded to the title earl of Arundel in 1580. He gained a reputation for high and rather profligate living.

His way of life was soon to change. When only twelve years old he had been married to Anne, daughter of Thomas, Lord Dacre, but had completely neglected her for several years. They were reconciled in the early 1580s, and she was one of the influences that persuaded him to become a Catholic in 1584. The other was a debate he attended between St Edmund Campion (1 Dec.) and some Protestant theologians in 1581, in which he felt that the Jesuit had the better of all the arguments. As even more severe laws against the English Catholics were passed in 1584 and 1585, Philip and Anne decided to leave the country and live on the Continent. Just before they left, Philip wrote to the queen saying that he had come to the point "in which he must consent either to the certain destruction of his body or the manifest endangering of his soul." To leave the country without royal permission, however, was itself an offence, and Philip was arrested at sea and put in the Tower of London. Although cleared of a charge of treason, he was fined a massive ten thousand pounds and ordered to be detained at the queen's pleasure. In 1589 he was accused again of treason, this time on a charge of having prayed for the success of the Spanish Armada in the previous year and of having corresponded with Cardinal Allen in Rome. Although the judges ruled that prayer in itself could not be treasonous, he was found guilty and condemned to death. The sentence was not carried out; instead, he remained in the Tower until his death in 1595 after a protracted illness.

For a person of his rank at that time imprisonment in the Tower did not necessarily imply a life of hardship. Philip, however, imposed on himself a régime of rigorous penance and prayer, fasting three days a week on bread and water. He was forbidden to see his wife, or the son who had been born after his initial imprisonment and whom he had never seen. He wrote a number of meditations and translated some works of devotion, and he corresponded with St Robert Southwell (21 Feb.), who was also in the Tower at the time. The latter wrote to him, "The cause is God's, the conflict short, the reward eternal," while Philip himself scratched a crucifix on the wall of his room with the Latin inscription, "The more suffering for Christ in this world, so much more the glory with Christ in the next." On another occasion he wrote, "The Catholic and Roman faith which I hold is the only cause (as far as I can in any way imagine) why either I have been thus long imprisoned or why I am now ready to be executed." The decree of canonization quotes him as saying, "I regret having only one life to offer up for this noble cause."

Shortly before he died he wrote a very moving letter to his wife, asking again for her forgiveness for the ways in which he had wronged her. In it he wrote: "I call God to witness it is no small grief unto me that I cannot make you recompense in this world for the wrongs I have done you; for if it had pleased God to have granted me longer life, I doubt not but that you should have found me as good a husband ... by his grace, as you have found me bad before. . . . (God) knows that which is past is a nail in my conscience. . . . I beseech you for the love of God to comfort yourself whatever shall happen, and to be best pleased with that, which shall please God best and be his will to send."

His writing on the wall of his room can still be seen in the Beauchamp tower of the Tower of London. His relics are in Arundel Cathedral. He was beatified in 1929 and canonized as one of the Forty English and Welsh Martyrs in 1970.

A.A.S., 62 (1970), pp. 558 ff., 745-53 ; *D.N.B.*, 10, pp. 52-4; *O.D.S.*, pp. 235-6; *M.M.P.*, pp. 107-8; *C.R.S.*, 21 (1919) is wholly devoted to the saint; see also H. G. F. Howard (ed.), *The Lives of Philip Howard and of Anne Dacre, His Wife* (1857; new ed., F. W. Steer, 1971). The saint's translation of Lanspergius' *An Epistle of Jesus Christ* was ed. by a monk of Parkminster 1926; also, as *A Letter from Jesus Christ*, by J. Griffiths (1981). The quotation from the letter to his wife is from J. Cumming (ed.), *Letters from Saints to Sinners* (1996), pp. 154-5.

20

St Caprasius, *Martyr* (? Third Century)

The main evidence for the existence of Caprasius, or Caprais in French, comes from the fact that there was a church dedicated to him at Agen, in south-western France, in the sixth century. Local legend makes him the first bishop of the town, but there is no evidence to support this, and it seems to have been first mentioned in the fourteenth century. Agen was also the town with which St Faith was connected (see 6 Oct.), and a ninth-century tradition fused the stories of the two saints into one, so that it was believed they suffered at the same time under the prefect Dacian. According to this tradition, which was accepted by all later writers, when the persecution began Caprasius fled with his people to the safety of nearby Mont-Saint-Vincent to escape death; from there he could see the martyrdom of St Faith and was so moved by her heroic steadfastness that he gave himself up to the prefect, confessing he was a Christian and a bishop. He was condemned to death, and on his way to execution was joined by Alberta, Faith's sister, and by two young brothers, Primus and Felician. All four were beheaded, and this was followed by a general massacre of those pagans who had been converted by their example. While we can be sure of Caprasius' existence, that of his three companions is very doubtful. What was taken to be his body was discovered in the fifth century, and a cult developed very quickly.

One tenth-century *passio* is a straightforward copy of the Life of another local French saint, Symphorian of Autun (22 Aug.). *AA.SS.*, Oct., 8, pp. 815-29; *Bibl.SS.*, 3, 768.

St Artemius, *Martyr* (363)

Artemius is said to have been a veteran of Constantine the Great's army who was appointed as imperial prefect in Egypt. He was an Arian (the Arians denied that Christ was truly divine) and saw it as his duty to increase the power of his fellow-heretics and reduce that of the orthodox Christians. The orthodox archbishop of Alexandria, the great St Athanasius (2 May), had been driven into exile, and Artemius spent a great amount of time and energy trying to find him, hunting for him unsuccessfully among the monasteries and hermitages of the Egyptian desert. He also turned his zeal against the pagans, destroying their temples and idols and trying to force them to accept Christianity. This, in the end, proved his undoing: when the emperor Constantius, an Arian, died in 361, he was succeeded by Julian the Apostate, a pagan. Artemius was accused of attacking the emperor's religion, and after being deprived of his property he was beheaded about the year 363.

139

The Eastern Church venerated Artemius as a martyr, despite his heresy (which is denied by the Orthodox to this day). A church was built in his honour in Constantinople in the sixth century, and his relics were transferred there about the same time. There is no evidence of a cult in the West, but in the sixteenth century Cardinal Baronius, the famous ecclesiastical historian, revised the Roman Martyrology and added Artemius' name to the list of saints for 20 October, on the grounds that the saint had always been recognized in the East. Baronius was not at his strongest, however, when dealing with the Eastern Church, and some writers have suggested that he may have been confused between this Artemius and another martyr of the same name; they argue that it was to this other Artemius that the shrine belonged, and that the famous miracle cures must be attributed to him. The earliest Greek Life, however, which was written by an Arian chronicler, assumes that they were the same person, and that seems to be more likely.

The miracles worked at the shrine are interesting because they seem to have an element of what is termed "incubation." This had been a pagan practice whereby those hoping for revelations or cures from a particular god spent the night sleeping in or close to the shrine. The practice was transferred to certain Christian shrines and holy places; for example, the church of SS Cosmas and Damian in Constantinople, and those of St Andrew at Patras and of Our Lady in Athens and Notre Dame in Paris. The practice lasted a very long time, and "the beliefs associated with it are not wholly extinct" (*O.D.C.C.*).

AA.SS., Oct., 8, pp. 847-85; *Bibl.SS.*, 2, 488-9. On the practice of incubation, see *O.D.C.C.*, p. 697.

St Andrew of Crete, *Martyr* (766)

Andrew was a monk in Crete who went to Constantinople to take part in the bitter struggles over the use of images in Christian churches, the famous Iconoclast controversy, which divided the Eastern Church for more than a century and involved emperors, popes, saints, and ordinary people; indeed, the passions aroused by the controversy, and the way that people took sides and used violence to support their party, is one of the most amazing aspects of the whole affair. The emperor at the time when Andrew left Crete was Constantine V, a keen supporter of those who attacked the use of images. He waged a fierce persecution against his opponents and many of the secular clergy accepted his decrees, but a large number of monks suffered martyrdom rather than depart from traditional practice, especially with regard to icons.

Andrew was present in Constantinople when the emperor was watching the public torture and execution of a number of orthodox Christians. He made a public and passionate protest, and when he was taken before the emperor and accused of idolatry, he replied by accusing Constantine of heresy. He was attacked and badly beaten by the bystanders, who then put him in prison; as he was being carried away he shouted to the emperor, "See how powerless you are against faith!" He was brought before the emperor again the next day and again defended the use of images. He was scourged and ordered to be led through the streets as an example to the people; as he was being dragged along he was stabbed and killed by a fanatic in the crowd. His body was thrown into a cesspit but was later rescued and buried at a near-by place called Krisis, where a monastery dedicated to St Andrew was built.

Andrew is commemorated by the Orthodox Church on 17 October. He is sometimes called "the Calybite," or "in Krisi," to distinguish him from another St Andrew of Crete (4 July), also a monk, who became a bishop and died about twenty-five years earlier.

AA.SS., Oct., 8, pp. 142-9, gives two independent versions of the *passio*. See also *Bibl.SS.*, 1, 1129-30. On iconoclasm, *N.C.E.*, 7, pp. 327-9; *O.D.C.C.*, pp. 687-8.

St Acca of Hexham, *Bishop* (740)

Acca was Northumbrian by birth. He was educated in the household of St Bosa (9 Mar.) and became a disciple of St Wilfrid (12 Oct.), accompanying him on his final visit to Rome. Here, according to Bede, who knew him personally, Acca "learned many useful things about the government of Holy Church which he could not have learned in his own country." When Wilfrid was restored to the see of Hexham, he made Acca abbot of the monastery of St Andrew there; when Wilfrid died in 709, Acca succeeded him as bishop. Bede regarded him very highly: "He was a man of great energy and noble in the sight of God and man. . . . He was also most learned in the holy Scriptures, orthodox in his profession of the Catholic faith, and well acquainted with the rules of church administration."

Acca's activities as bishop were varied. He enlarged and decorated the church originally built by Wilfrid; Eddius tells us that he provided "splendid ornaments of gold, silver and precious stones, and decorated the altars with purple and silk," and asks, "who is sufficient to describe it all?" He also collected materials for a library, was an assiduous collector of relics, and a patron of scholars. He encouraged Eddius to write his Life of St Wilfrid, and he assisted Bede with information and sources for his history as well as encouraging him to write some of his theological works, most of which were dedicated to Acca. Bede wrote a number of letters to the bishop, seeking his opinion on the correct interpretation of parts of the Bible. Finally, Acca invited Maban, a famous singer of the time from Kent, to instruct himself and his clergy in the correct way of performing the chant. Bede concludes his account of Acca's work as bishop by saying, "And in all these activities he remains unflagging until the time comes for him to receive the reward of his piety and devotion."

In 732, however, for some reason unknown to us, Acca left his diocese—he may have retired or been forced into exile. He went to Galloway in Scotland, where he may have become bishop of Whitthorn. He died in Scotland in 740, and was buried in Hexham. The Acca cross at Hexham, a fine example of Anglo-Saxon art, dates from about 740 and may have marked Acca's tomb. When his relics were translated in the late eleventh century a portable altar was found in the coffin, inscribed with the words, *Almae Trinitati, agiae Sophiae, sanctae Mariae.*

Bede, *H.E.*, bks. 3, ch. 13; 4, ch. 14; 5, ch. 20; for Bede's letters to Acca see *P.L.*, 94, 684-7, 689-94, 697-710. See also *AA.SS.*, Oct., 8, pp. 965-80; J. Raine (ed.), *Memorials of Hexham*, 1 (*S.S.*, 1864), pp. 31-6; C. J. Godfrey, *The Church in Anglo-Saxon England* (1962); D. P. Kirby (ed.), *St Wilfrid at Hexham* (1974); *O.D.S.*, pp. 2-3.

Bd Mary Teresa de Soubiran, *Foundress* (1835-89)

Sophie Thérèse Augustine Marie de Soubiran La Louvière was born at Castelnaudary, near Carcassonne in south-west France, in May 1835. She was the second child of Joseph de Soubiran La Louvière, head of an ancient family related to several of the royal families of Europe. It was an intensely Catholic family, and Sophie was brought up in a pious but strict atmosphere. She decided early on that she was called to the religious life, and under the guidance of an uncle who was a canon she agreed to join a *béguinage* which he was keen to establish. This was not to her liking, for the *béguinage* was a community of laywomen who took temporary vows; they lived in some comfort and enjoyed considerable freedom. Sophie felt called rather to the austerity and hidden life of the Carmelites but was advised to follow her uncle's wishes in the matter. After a spell in Ghent in Belgium to learn the *béguine* way of life, she returned to Castelnaudary and was appointed superior of the new community in 1854-5. She took the religious name of Mary Teresa.

For eight years or so the foundation flourished, but in a way different from the original *béguine* ideal. The Sisters gave up the right to their property, began the practice of nightly adoration of the Blessed Sacrament, and established an orphanage. Mary Teresa was still not satisfied that she was following her true vocation. After making an Ignatian retreat and consulting several friends and advisors, she decided to go ahead with a plan to found a new Congregation, dedicated to living the full religious life and to the saving of souls through practical work. She named it the Society of Mary the Helper (*de Marie Auxiliatrice*) and in September 1864 left Castelnaudary with some of the Sisters to open her first convent in Toulouse. The Constitution of the new Congregation was based on the Ignatian spirit; it was approved in 1867 by the archbishop of Toulouse and in the following year by the Holy See. In 1869 two new houses were opened, in Amiens and Lyons. The Franco-Prussian War in 1870 drove the Sisters to take refuge in England for a time; they settled in London, first in Southwark, then in Brompton, and later they opened a convent and hostel in Kennington. When they returned to France they left a community in the last-named convent, and this became the Congregation's first house outside France.

In addition to its care of orphans and teaching of poor children, the community in Toulouse had established a hostel for young working women, the first of its kind. This became the principal work of the Sisters in the large industrial cities where they were established. It is from these early years in Toulouse that Mary Teresa's extant writings begin to date; they allow us to trace her inner development over the next twenty-five years, as she wrote extensively on spiritual matters and gave advice to her Sisters. They were a most remarkable twenty-five years: we are used to accounts of religious founders who faced opposition and even persecution, but no story can equal that of Mary Teresa in its bizarreness.

In 1871 the Congregation elected as assistant mother general a woman who had been a member for only three years—Mother Mary Frances. She was extremely capable and was able to convince the chapter to adopt a plan for the rapid expansion of their work; developments went ahead quickly but without sufficient resources, and in 1874 Mother Mary Frances announced that the financial position of the Congregation was desperate. She blamed Mary Teresa for this, and a number of people, who should have known better, supported her and persuaded the foundress to resign in favour of Mary Frances. Mary Teresa went to a convent of the Sisters of Charity for seven months while it was decided what should happen to her; in the end she was expelled from the Congregation altogether, forbidden to have any contact with its members, and left as a layperson. She was eventually able to make her religious profession again in 1877 in a convent of the Sisters of Our Lady of Charity in Paris.

By 1885 it was clear that her original Congregation was in a critical state—when Mary Teresa heard about this from her cousin, who had also been expelled, she wrote, "Now I am sure that this little society, which God loves so much . . . is morally dead—that is, that its aims, its form, its methods have ceased to exist. That is and always will be a very deep and very bitter grief to me. I love God's plans, and I am as nothing before his holy and incomprehensible will." In a letter written shortly after her expulsion she said that she had learned a great truth as a result of what had happened: "The great truth that God is all, and the rest is nothing . . . and upon [this] one can lean securely amid the incomprehensible mysteries of this world. And should I have learned this without such cruel anguish? I do not think so. Time passes, and it passes quickly: we shall soon know the reason of so many things that surprise and shock our feeble, short-sighted reason."

Mary Teresa contracted tuberculosis and after an illness of several months died in June 1889. She was beatified in 1946. Her Congregation did not cease to exist. Shortly after her death its chapter at last turned against Mother Mary Frances and refused to allow her to make further changes; she resigned and left the Congregation in 1890. Under a new superior it began to rebuild its life and became active again in the way its foundress would have wished. As for Mary Frances, it transpired after her death in 1921 that at the time of her entry into the Congregation she had still been married, though she had deserted her husband. She was, therefore, never validly a nun, and all her actions as mother general were likewise invalid. Presumably, then, Mary Teresa had remained, at least canonically, a member of the Congregation to the end of her life.

Mary Teresa was beatified on 20 October 1946 by Pope Pius XII, and the cause of her canonization was reopened in 1955.

A.A.S., 39 (1947), pp. 17–25, for her beatification. M-T. Delmas published an admirable Life in 1946, while in 1947 an abridged version of Mary Teresa's own writings and spiritual notes was edited in English by T. Baily as *A Study in Failure*. See also C. Hoare, *Life out of Death* (1946); *Bibl.SS.*, 11, 1329–31.

St Mary Bertilla Boscardin (1888-1922)

Anna Francesca Boscardin was born in 1888 at Brendola, near Vicenza in northern Italy. Her parents were poor peasants, and her father was a violent man, very jealous and often drunk, as he himself confessed when giving evidence for his daughter's beatification; mother and daughter sometimes had to flee for protection. Annetta, as she was called at home, had only intermittent elementary schooling, spending more time working on housework or in the fields and in service nearby. She was considered to be without much ability and was nicknamed "the goose," and she seemed to share this low opinion of herself throughout her life. Her parish priest, however, saw there was something more to her and allowed her to make her First Communion when she was only eight-and-a-half years old instead of the normal eleven. At twelve she was allowed to join the Children of Mary (the normal age was fourteen), and the priest gave her a copy of the catechism, which she apparently studied every day for the rest of her life.

He was not impressed when, at the age of fifteen, Annetta asked to be allowed to join a convent. The nuns, he told her, would not be able to make anything out of her, as she knew nothing; she agreed but still insisted that she should be allowed to consecrate herself to God by becoming a nun. Eventually she was accepted by the Sisters of St Dorothy at Vicenza—the parish priest said she could at least peel the potatoes for the community, while she told the reverend mother she just wanted to become a saint! She was given the name of Maria Bertilla, and worked for a year in the laundry and bakery, volunteering for the heaviest and most uncongenial work. Then she was moved to the hospital run by the Sisters in Treviso, but only after her profession in 1907 was she allowed to work on the wards—before that she was confined to kitchen work. When she started to look after the children in the diptheria ward she found her true vocation, to nurse the sick and especially those with little or no hope of survival. The medical staff spoke highly of her ability to deal with ill and disturbed children.

In 1915 the hospital was taken over by the military for the wounded, and in 1917 it was in the front line of the fighting. Bertilla wrote in her spiritual diary, "Here I am, Lord, to do your will whatever comes—be it life, death or terror." In the heaviest of the bombardments she stayed by the bedsides of the wounded who could not be moved, taking them marsala and coffee and praying with them. When they were evacuated to a safer hospital she went with them, taking special care of those with typhus; then she was moved to Como to look after the soldiers who had contracted tuberculosis, but her superior thought she was over-working and becoming too attached to the patients, so she was relegated once again to the laundry. She was rescued by the mother general and after the armistice returned to the hospital at Treviso, where she was given charge of the children's isolation ward. About this time she prayed to Our Lady: "Dear Mother, I do not ask you for visions, or revelations, or favours, even spiritual ones. . . . In this life I want only what you want; just to believe, without any proof or enjoyment, and to suffer joyfully without any consolation . . . to work hard for you until I die."

Her spiritual life had, indeed, developed to such an extent that she had reached the heights known only to the mystics. She wrote that all she had of her own was her will, and she was determined with the help of God's grace never to seek to follow it; she would make every effort to follow this way of self-abnegation purely for the love of Jesus, as though neither heaven nor hell existed, nor even the comfort of a clear conscience.

Mary Bertilla had been suffering for a number of years from a painful tumour. In 1922 she underwent an operation, but it was clear that she could not live much longer. She asked her Sisters not to weep for her because, as she told them, "if we wish to see Jesus, we must die. I am happy. . . . I am going into the company of my God." She died on 20 October 1922. Crowds attended her funeral in Vicenza, and cures were attributed to her intercession. A year after she died a plaque was put up in the hospital at Treviso: "To Sister Bertilla Boscardin, a chosen soul of heroic goodness, who for several years was a truly angelic alleviator of human suffering here . . . ." She was beatified in 1952 and canonized in 1961 in the presence of some of the patients whom she had nursed. At the ceremony Pope John XXIII declared: "Hers was the greatness that comes from humility, from sacrifice taken to the point of heroism, from a simplicity arising from an abundant trust in God."

A.A.S., 53 (1961), pp. 278, 289-95, for the canonization. Her spiritual diary was published in 1952 by P. G. di S. M. Maddelena. See also E. Federici, *Santa M. Bertilla Boscardin* (1961); *Bibl.SS.*, 8, 1041-2; A. Sicari, *Nuovi ritratti di santi*, 4 (1994), pp. 145-62.

21

St Hilarion (*c.* 291-371)

Hilarion was born of pagan parents in a village called Tabatha in the south of Gaza in Palestine. He was sent to Alexandria for his education and became a Christian there when he was about fifteen years old. For a short time he stayed with St Antony (17 Jan.) in the Egyptian desert, imitating his life of extreme asceticism. He found it difficult, however, to cope with the distractions created by the many people who came to visit his famous master, and he left to seek true solitude back in his native Palestine; this constant seeking after quiet and isolation became the main theme of his life.

Back in Gaza, he found that his parents had died. He divided his inheritance between his brothers and the poor and retired to a place called Majuma, between the sea and a swamp, where he lived a life of extreme hardship based on what he had learned while with St Antony in Egypt. He was reputed not to change his tunic until it was worn out and never to wash his hair shirt on the grounds that "it is idle to look for cleanliness in a hair shirt." (Alban Butler commented on this that the respect we owe our neighbours makes such practices "unseasonable in the world.") He was reputed to live for several years on only fifteen figs a day, not eaten until sunset; later he was persuaded to add vegetables, bread, and oil to his diet in order to stay alive. At first he lived in a hut made of rushes; then he built a more substantial cell measuring about four feet by five, which could still be seen in St Jerome's day. Many miracles were attributed to him while he was at Majuma, especially cures and the casting-out of evil spirits.

While in his desert retreat Hilarion suffered a great deal from dryness of spirit and temptations to despair but persevered in prayer despite these trials. St Jerome relates that though he lived for many years in Palestine he only once visited the Holy Places in Jerusalem, and then for only one day. He went once so that he would not seem to be despising what the Church honoured, but he did not go more often, according to St Jerome, lest he be thought to believe that the worship of God was confined to particular places.

One suspects that places of pilgrimage, with their crowds of people, would have been abhorrent to him as distractions from the solitude he needed for prayer. After he had been at Majuma for several years, his fame became so widespread that people flocked to see him and seek his assistance; a group of disciples had joined him against his will, and he complained, "I have returned to the world and received my reward in this life. All Palestine regards me, and I even possess a farm and household goods, under pretext of the brethren's needs." As a result he decided to leave his native country, and so he began the almost endless journeys that took up the rest of his life as he sought a place where he could live in complete solitude. He returned to Egypt for a time, then went to Sicily and from there to Dalmatia, hoping that he would remain unknown in a place where he did not speak the language. His miraculous powers, however, did not allow him to live in peace, and he finally moved to Cyprus, where he found some solitude, though he was still disturbed by visitors, among them St Epiphanius (12 May), bishop of Salamis, who wrote about him to St Jerome. When he died aged about eighty, the local people wanted to make a shrine for his relics, but his disciple St Hesychius (3 Oct.) removed the body secretly and took it back to Majuma.

Hilarion's fame is due to the Life written by St Jerome (30 Sept.) sometime between 382 and 396, only about twenty years after Hilarion's death. Some historians have been so critical of this work that they have suggested that the whole story was invented by Jerome. It is now accepted as trustworthy, if only because Jerome was writing too close in time and place to his subject to have been able to get away with a complete fabrication. Jerome's intention was to make out that Hilarion was a second St Antony and the founder of monasticism in Palestine; he may have glorified his subject to some extent, but his account is basically sound. This Life appeared in many versions throughout the Eastern Church, translated into Greek, Armenian and Coptic, itself a witness to the popularity of the cult. In the West St Bede listed Hilarion in his martyrology, and there was a legend that his body had been taken to France, where there is evidence of an ancient cult at Duravel. He is the patron of many villages in Cyprus and features in a large number of icons and mosaics.

AA.SS., Oct., 9, pp. 16-59; Jerome's Life is also in *P.L.*, 23, 29-64, and there is an Eng. trans. in *Early Christian Biographies* (Fathers of the Church, 15, 1952). See also *Bibl.SS.*, 7, 731-5; E. Coleiro, "St Jerome's Lives of the Hermits," *Vigiliae Christianae*, 11 (1957), pp. 161-78; J. N. D. Kelly, *Jerome* (1975); *O.D.C.C.*, p. 648; *O.D.S.*, p. 229.

St Fintan of Taghmon, *Abbot* (*c.* 635)

Fintan, or Munnu, was the son of Talchan of the Irish O'Neill clan. He trained as a monk under a number of leading Irish abbots of the day, including St Comgall (11 May) at Bangor, Senell on Lough Erne, and one of St Columba's (9 June) monasteries at Kilmore. The way of life at the last-named was the most attractive to him, and so he decided to go to Iona to join Columba's community there. There are two traditions about what happened next. According to Irish accounts, Columba was dead when Fintan reached Iona, and he was refused permission to stay because Columba had foretold that Fintan would found his own monastery in Ireland and become the father of many monks. Scottish tradition has it that Fintan stayed on Iona for a number of years and returned to Ireland only when Columba died in 597. Whatever the truth of the matter, Fintan did return to Ireland and founded a monastery at Taghmon in Wexford.

Irish monasticism was noted for its extreme asceticism, and Fintan gained a reputation for being one of the most austere. He was also famous for upholding the customs of the Celtic church against those who wished to introduce Roman ways, even opposing the wishes of Pope Honorius I with regard to the method of working out the date of Easter. He made his views known at a number of synods, particularly the one held in 630 at Magh Lene. The previous edition of this work quoted with approval the judgment of the editor of the Lives of the saint: "Speaking generally the historical element in this life is larger than in some others, and we get an impression of Munnu as a real man and not merely a peg to hang miracles on, a man of somewhat harsh and hasty temper, but placable and conciliatory when the momentary irritation was over." His monastery became famous and features in a number of Lives of Irish saints. These state that Fintan suffered for a time from leprosy, an affliction which he had apparently wished for so that he could emulate the merits of St Molua (4 Aug.) and be welcomed like him into heaven. He died about the year 635. He is sometimes confused with a St Mundus in Scotland, where his cult resulted in a number of church dedications.

AA.SS., Oct., 9, pp. 325-42, gives the longest of the Latin Lives; see also Plummer, *V.S.H.*, 2, pp. 226-39, from whom the quotation above is taken; A. O. & M. O. Anderson, *Adamnan's Life of Columba* (1961), pp. 206-15; *The Irish Saints*, pp. 174-7; *O.D.S.*, pp. 180-1.

St Condedus (*c.* 685)

Condedus, or Condé or Condede in French, is thought to have been an Englishman who went to France to seek solitude and holiness. He first of all settled at Fontaine-Saint-Valéry, then moved to the famous monastery at Fontenelle, where he became a monk. He still hankered after solitude, however, and after a short time he left the monastery and became a hermit on an island in the river Seine, near Caudebec. The king, Thierry III, was so impressed by Condedus that he gave him the island and other land to support the hermitage. The saint built two chapels there, one dedicated to Our Lady, the other to SS Peter and Paul, and these became popular with the local people who visited them to hear Condedus preach and receive spiritual direction from him. He is said to have worked a number of rather fanciful miracles. He died about 685 and was buried on the island. Later on his remains were moved to the monastery at Fontenelle because floods were threatening to destroy them; the island has since been totally submerged by the river.

AA.SS., Oct., 9, pp. 351-8, prints a short Life written about a century after the saint's death by a monk at Fontenelle; this has been re-edited by W. Levison in *M.G.H., Scriptores rerum Merov.*, 5, pp. 644-51. See also *Bibl.SS.*, 4, 142-4.

St John of Bridlington (1379)

John was born at Thwing, near Bridlington on the Yorkshire coast. He studied at Oxford for two years and on his return joined the monastery of the Austin canons at Bridlington. He lived an exemplary life as a religious and held a number of offices in the community, being successively precentor, cellarer, and finally prior in 1360.

He had tried to avoid the last position but was obliged by his brethren to accept it. He carried out its duties with prudence and mildness for seventeen years, at the same time developing his own spiritual life by constant prayer. He seems to have been particularly attached to St John's Gospel and urged those under his care to study it closely if they wanted to advance in holiness. By the time of his death on 10 October 1379 he had gained a strong reputation for sanctity, and miracles were soon reported at his tomb and through his intercession, including the raising of the dead. He was canonized by Pope Boniface IX in 1401, the last English saint of the Middle Ages to be formally canonized.

Richard Scrope, archbishop of York, and the bishops of Lincoln and Carlisle translated the relics of the saint to a new shrine behind the high altar in 1404. This became a popular place of pilgrimage and was visited by King Henry V, who attributed his victory over the French at Agincourt to the intercession of the two saints John of Bridlington and John of Beverley (7 May). The priory gained both wealth and spiritual privileges because of the shrine.

The nave of the priory church still stands and is the Anglican parish church of Bridlington. John is featured in fifteenth-century stained-glass windows at Morley in Derbyshire, Ludlow in Shropshire, and in the Beauchamp Chapel at Warwick, as well as on a rood-screen in a church near Norwich—witnesses to the popularity of his cult throughout England.

AA.SS., Oct., 5, pp. 135-44, prints a near-contemporary Life of little value. See J. S. Purvis, *St John of Bridlington* (1924), and an important article by P. Grosjean in *Anal.Boll.* 53 (1935), pp. 101-29. See also *D.N.B.*, 29, pp. 450-1.

Bd James Strzemie, *Bishop (c. 1340-1409)*

James Strzemie, or Strepar, was a member of a noble Polish family which had settled in Galicia and was born in the diocese of Cracow about the year 1340. He joined the Franciscan Friars Minor and was a member of the Society of Pilgrim Brothers of Christ in the Lands of the Infidels, which consisted of Franciscan and Dominican friars dedicated to missionary work in the Ukraine. He became guardian of the friary at Lvov in the Ukraine, where he played a conspicuous part in the troubled ecclesiastical affairs of the city, which had been put under interdict. There were troubles between the friars and the secular clergy and between both and the Orthodox Christians. He worked there for over ten years, and was appointed head of the Franciscan mission to western Russia and inquisitor in matters of faith in Ruthenia.

He had considerable success as a missionary preacher and in 1392 was appointed archbishop of Halicz, a diocese where he had already done a great deal of work as a missionary. He set out to consolidate this work, building churches in the more remote parts of his diocese and bringing in experienced priests from Poland to take charge of them. He also established religious houses and opened hospitals and schools. He carried out visitations, sometimes on foot, and always wore the simple habit of his Order rather than the showy robes of an archbishop. He promoted devotion to the Blessed Sacrament and to the Virgin Mary, and there appears to have been a spiritual awakening in his diocese as a result of his work. He retained his missionary instincts and was especially keen on any initiatives to convert schismatics and pagans. He died at Lvov on 1 June 1409. During his life he had been given the title "Protector of the Kingdom," and after his death he continued to be regarded as a special patron. Miracles were reported at his tomb, and a popular cult developed quickly, which was confirmed in 1790. There was a revival of his cult in 1909 to mark the fifth centenary of his death.

There are a number of biographies in Polish but little in other languages. See Léon, *Auréole séraphique* 2, pp. 312-5; *Bibl.SS.*, 6, 419-21.

Bd Matthew of Agrigento, *Bishop* (1450)

Matthew was born of a Spanish family at Agrigento in Sicily in the last years of the fourteenth century. At the age of eighteen he joined the Franciscan Conventuals. Some time after this he heard of the fame of St Bernardino of Siena (20 May) and decided to leave the Conventuals to join the Observant Friars. He became a close friend of Bernardino, travelling around Italy with him and himself gaining a reputation as an effective preacher. He returned to his native Sicily about the year 1421 to work for church reform among the clergy, many of whom were guilty of simony and most of whom were indifferent and neglectful of their duties. Matthew preached throughout the island trying to increase the fervour of both priests and people, in particular by spreading devotion to the Holy Name of Jesus. He was an effective propagandist for this devotion and was caught up in the controversies about it; Bernardino was accused of heresy and of encouraging superstition when he introduced the IHS symbol, and he and St John Capistrano (23 Oct.) had to appeal to the pope to clear themselves of the charges.

Matthew was appointed provincial of the Observants in Sicily and in 1425 was given permission by Pope Martin V to found three new Observant houses in the island. In 1427-8 he was in Spain to seek help against the opponents of the reform from the king of Aragon, Alfonso V, who ruled Sicily at the time. While he was in Spain he founded Observant houses in Barcelona and Valencia. There is a letter dated March 1427 from the queen to one of the court officials, saying how much spiritual profit she and others had gained from Matthew's Lenten sermons; he had aroused great enthusiasm among the people of Valencia as well among members of the royal household. He had attacked the fashions of the day so effectively that the queen altered her style of dress and ordered her ladies-in-waiting to do the same; these attacks on fashion were part of his general theme of the evil of luxury and the need for Christians to lead a simple life. The queen's letters also relate how Matthew had cured the sick and restored sight to a blind person as well as performing other miracles. Finally, he had spread devotion to the Holy Name and introduced the IHS symbol to Spain, uging people to display it on their houses and in public places; this met with the same fierce opposition as in Italy, especially from the

Dominicans and Augustinians. One result of his visits to Spain was a lasting friend-ship with the king and queen of Aragon, who became keen and practical supporters of the reform.

Back in Sicily he founded another house, at Syracuse, in 1429. He was also involved in reforming other religious houses in Italy and Sicily at the command of the pope. In 1442 Matthew was appointed bishop of Agrigento by Alfonso V. He accepted the new post very much against his will, and perhaps only after being ordered to do so by Pope Eugenius IV. He wished to continue his work of reform, but his efforts to get rid of simony among his clergy ran into serious opposition. He had to go to Rome to defend himself against the calumnies of his opponents; on his return to his diocese he was accused of disturbing the peace by being a firebrand and refusing to listen to those he was trying to reform. He asked the pope if he might be allowed to resign, as he seemed to be achieving nothing; he was also suffering from ill-health. In the end his resignation was accepted reluctantly, and he returned to the Observants.

Matthew's troubles were not over. When he went back to the friary he had founded, he was refused admittance on the grounds that he had accepted the bishopric out of ambition and would only bring the same dissensions into the community as he had aroused in his diocese. He went back to the Conventuals for a time, but was persuaded to rejoin the Observants by the minister provincial; when he fell ill, however, they were too poor to get him the medical help he needed, and so they returned him to the Conventuals at Palermo, where he died in 1450. His unofficial cult was confirmed in 1767. His life is evidence both of the serious efforts that individuals, fully supported by popes and rulers, were making to reform the Church in the fifteenth century and of the difficulties such reformers encountered when the majority of the clergy seemed to have lost their zeal and sense of vocation.

It is surprising that for a long time little was known in detail about Matthew's life, despite his fame and involvement in some of the main movements of his day. Research over the last fifty years, especially by the Franciscan Agostino Amore, has brought a wealth of documentation to light and done a great deal to tell us more about this important reformer, though there are still gaps in our knowledge. Two articles in the *Archivum Franc. Historicum* by Amore document Matthew's work in Spain and Sicily: see 49 (1956), pp. 255-335, and 52 (1959), pp. 12-42. Amore also published some of Matthew's sermons: *Beato Matteo Agrigentini: Sermones Varii* (1960).

22

St Abercius of Hieropolis, *Bishop* (*c.* 200)

Abercius Marcellus lived in Phrygia Salutaris during the second century. He was bishop of Hieropolis and made a journey to Rome when he was seventy-two years old. His return journey took him through Syria and Mesopotamia, and he was very struck by the many Christians he met and their devotion to the Eucharist in particular. When the bishop arrived back in Hieropolis he had an epitaph made for his future tomb; using early Christian symbolic language, this described his journey and the impressions it had made on him.

This epitaph was used later to concoct a fictitious Life of Abercius in Greek, which may have been written in Hieropolis toward the end of the fourth century. It included the inscription and attributed to the bishop a number of writings, including a letter to the emperor, Marcus Aurelius, and a "Book of Teaching." It also made out that he had made so many converts that he deserved the title, "Equal to the Apostles," and that he had made his journey to Rome at the command of the emperor, who had heard of his reputation as a miracle-worker and whose daughter was possessed by an evil spirit which Abercius successfully exorcised.

In the early 1880s much of the original inscription was discovered by the archaeologist Sir W. M. Ramsay. This discovery gave rise to considerable controversy, including whether Abercius was a pagan priest or a Christian bishop, but it is now generally believed that it was indeed the epitaph over Abercius' tomb and that he had been bishop of Hieropolis. The inscription is now in the Lateran Museum, having been presented to Leo XIII by Sultan Abdul Hamid. His cult has been popular in the Eastern Church since the tenth century, and he features in the Roman Martyrology, where his see is wrongly given as Hierapolis (an error also found in the fictitious Life).

H. Leclerq's articles in *D.A.C.L.*, 1, 66–87, and the *Catholic Encyclopedia*, 1, pp. 40-1, provide a critical introduction to Abercius and good illustrations; see also *O.D.C.C.*, pp. 4-5; E. Ferguson, *Early Christians Speak* (1987).

St Philip of Heraclea, *Bishop,* and Companions, *Martyrs* (303)

Philip, bishop of Heraclea, and Severus, a priest, and Hermes, a deacon, suffered death during the persecution of the emperor Diocletian (284-305). When the first imperial edicts against the Christians were issued, Philip was advised to leave the city but refused, preferring to stay and help his flock withstand any attacks that might come. When the church was closed by the authorities, Philip continued to hold services in the open air. When he was ordered to hand over the sacred vessels and holy books used in the services, he replied, "The vessels we will give you, for it is not by precious metal but by charity that God is honoured. But the sacred books it becomes neither you to demand nor me to surrender." Hermes added that it was not in the governor's power to destroy the word of God, even if he should take away all the manuscripts in which it was written. The church and the books were destroyed, and both Philip and Hermes were tortured in an attempt to get them to join in sacrifices to the emperor and the gods; when they refused they were put in prison. People still had access to them, however, and they continued to instruct those who wished to be baptized. Hermes' conduct in particular seemed inexplicable to the Roman authorities, since he had been greatly respected in the town and had been a member of its senate.

In the meantime, Severus, a priest, had been in hiding to avoid the attention of the authorities. He now surrendered to them and was imprisoned along with Philip and Hermes. After about seven months the three were moved to Adrianople. They were again brought to court, and this time they were badly beaten when they continued to profess their Christian faith. After further interrogations the order was given for them to be executed. Because of the beatings they had received Philip and Hermes had difficulty in walking to the stake, but Hermes encouraged Philip by saying, "Master, let us hasten to go to the Lord. Why should we be concerned about our feet, since we shall have no more use for them?" After they had been burned their bodies were thrown into the river, but some Christians rescued them. Severus suffered martyrdom the next day.

The burning of the holy books and the destruction of Philip's church fits in with the edicts issued by Diocletian and allows the martyrdoms to be dated to his reign; the most likely year is 303, though some have argued for 305. The former Roman Martyrology was mistaken in placing them in the reign of Julian the Apostate (332-63) and also in adding a St Eusebius to the group. The execution of Philip and his companions is among the best attested of the events of Diocletian's persecution, and the Latin *acta*, based on an earlier Greek original, are fundamentally trustworthy.

AA.SS., Oct., 9, 523-5 and 537-53; *Bibl.SS.*, 5, 756-8; A. Hamman, *Le Gesta dei martiri* (1959), pp. 265-83.

SS Nunilo and Alodia, *Martyrs* (851)

Nunilo, or Nunilone, and Alodia were sisters who lived at Huesca in Spain in the first half of the ninth century. Their mother was a Christian, their father a Muslim. When he died, their mother married another Muslim, a person of some importance in the town, who treated his step-daughters badly and objected to their practice of the Christian religion. They came under pressure to marry but had decided to devote themselves to a life of virginity in God's service, and so they left home and went to live with a Christian aunt.

Persecution of the Christians in Spain began in 850 with the publication of the laws of Abd-er-Rahman II against them; in particular, it was decreed that children of Muslim fathers had to follow Islam and not Christianity. The two sisters were too well known in the town to escape the attentions of the authorities for long and were arrested. The judge tried to win them over by a mixture of threats and flattery, and when they still refused to renounce their faith he handed them over to a group of disreputable women to see if they could shake their resolution. When this also failed, the judge ordered the sisters to be beheaded. They suffered death in 851; for a time the authorities guarded the bodies to prevent the development of a cult, but eventually they were transferred to a Christian shrine. There is an ancient liturgical tradition in the Rioja region of Spain that the two martyrs died there at Nájera, but the account by Eulogius is largely trustworthy, and Huesca is the much more likely place.

The source of our information about the two saints is the *Memoriale Sanctorum* of St Eulogius of Córdoba (11 Mar.), who was himself martyred in the same persecution in 859; extracts from his work are given, with a critical commentary, in *AA.SS.*, Oct., 9, pp. 626–47; see also *Bibl.SS.*, 9, 1081-2.

St Donatus of Fiesole, *Bishop* (*c.* 876)

Donatus, also called Donat and Dino, was an Irish monk who in the early ninth century went on pilgrimage to Rome. On his way back he stopped at Fiesole, near Florence, just at the time when the clergy and people of the city were gathered in the cathedral to elect a new bishop. Legend has it that as Donatus entered the cathedral, the bells began to ring of their own accord and candles in the cathedral were suddenly alight. This was taken as a divine sign that Donatus should be bishop, and he was unanimously and immediately elected, about the year 829. Whatever actually happened, there is no doubt that Donatus was bishop of Fiesole for many years. He was in Rome in 850 for the coronation of Louis II by the pope and sat in judgment alongside pope and king in a dispute between the bishops of Arezzo and Siena. He was back in Rome in 861 to attend a council, and a few years later went to Capua to receive confirmation of the rights of his diocese from Lothair II. It is clear he was a trusted courtier; he was given the right to hold his own court and to levy taxes, and on one occasion led an army of his subjects into battle against the Saracens in southern Italy on behalf of the king.

He had a reputation for learning; he wrote poetry (one of his poems described the beauty of the Irish scenery) and was, according to the epitaph that he wrote about himself, an enthusiastic teacher of grammar and prose-writing. His works included a Life of St Brigid of Ireland (1 Feb.), and he seems to have had a particular devotion to her: when he founded a hospice in Piacenza for Irish pilgrims, he dedicated it to her.   He died about 876 and was buried at Fiesole in the original cathedral; his relics were translated to the present cathedral in 1817. As well as a local cult in and around Fiesole, his feast-day is observed in Ireland.

AA.SS., Oct., 9, pp. 648–62, and *Propylaeum*, p. 470; *D.N.B.*, 15, p. 216; A. M. Tommasini, *Irish Saints in Italy* (1937), pp. 383–94; *O.D.S.*, pp. 135–6; *Bibl.SS.*, 4, 787-91.

23

ST JOHN OF CAPISTRANO (1386-1456)

John was born at Capistrano in the Abruzzi in 1386. He went to Perugia to study law and was so successful that he became governor of the city in 1412 and married the daughter of one of the leading families. During a civil war he was imprisoned for a time, and as the result of a vision of St Francis (4 Oct.) he underwent a spiritual conversion, for, on his release, he was determined to become a religious. It is not clear what happened to his wife, but it is assumed that his decision to enter a monastery was by mutual consent; he obtained a dispensation from the impediment of matrimony. Before he entered he paraded through the streets, sitting backwards on a donkey and wearing a paper which listed his worst sins. He was pelted with dirt by the children, and covered in filth presented himself to the Friars Minor, asking to be admitted as a novice; this was in 1416. He was ordained four years later.

He led a life of extreme austerity, always going about barefoot, wearing a hair shirt, and taking very little sleep. He studied theology under St Bernardino of Siena (20 May) and developed into an outstanding preacher, basing himself on the saint as a model both in his way of life and in his preaching. He also worked with Bernardino in the reform of the Franciscan Observant Friars and with St Colette (6 Mar.) in the reform of the Franciscan nuns. For a time his extreme poverty, and that of the Observants, was looked on with suspicion, and in 1429 he and they were accused of preaching heresy about the poverty of Christ but were acquitted. He was appointed vicar general of the Order on several occasions. He wrote a treatise called "A Mirror for the Clergy," in which he attacked clergy who led immoral lives; in contrast, "the life of good and upright clergy is a light which casts its rays with the brightness of holiness upon all who see them. . . . And so if the clergy exist to take care of others, they should themselves be a living demonstration of how the rest of men should live in the house of the Lord."

In 1451 he was appointed by Pope Nicholas V as commissary and inquisitor general in Hungary and Bohemia to bring about the conversion or subjection of the Hussites and other heretical groups. He was assisted by twelve of his Franciscan brethren in this. His way of dealing with the heretics has been severely criticized; as the previous edition of this work put it, "his zeal was of the kind that scars and consumes, though he was merciful to the submissive and repentant." He may have been ahead of his time in his more humane attitude to witchcraft and the use of torture. Contemporaries, however, greeted him with great enthusiasm and claimed that he could work miracles. They described his physical appearance as small, withered, and emaciated but his manner as cheerful and energetic.

The capture of Constantinople by the Turks in 1453 ended his campaign in Hungary. He was asked to preach a crusade and rally the Christian leaders against the threat from Islam. There was little effective response in Bavaria and Austria, despite his strenuous preaching. He was more successful in Hungary, and himself led some troops to defend Belgrade. It was claimed that it was his prayers and exhortations, linked to the skill of the Hungarian general, Hunyady, that led to a decisive victory against the Turks, who were besieging the city. Unfortunately, after the battle thousands of bodies were left unburied for too long, and there was an outbreak of disease. John succumbed to this (as also did Hunyady) and died at Villach on 23 October 1456. He was canonized in 1724. His feast was formerly celebrated on 28 March, having been extended to the Universal Church in 1890.

AA.SS., Oct., 10, pp. 269-552, prints a number of contemporary Lives and seven of his letters. See also J. Hofer, *St John Capistran, Reformer* (1943); *Bibl.SS.*, 6, 646-54; *O.D.S.*, p. 260; *O.D.C.C.*, p. 569; *Dict.Sp.*, 8 (1972), 316-23. Extracts above are from *The Office of Readings*, 3, pp. 353-4.

St Severinus of Bordeaux, *Bishop* (*c.* 420)

There are difficulties in unravelling two saints called Severinus (in French, Seurin), both of whom have been venerated today. First was Severinus, bishop of Cologne in Germany, who was distinguished for his zeal in defending orthodox belief against the Arians, who denied that Christ was truly divine. Second was Severinus, bishop of Bordeaux in France, who was reputed to have been bishop of Trier or Cologne in Germany before he was directed by a heavenly voice to move to Bordeaux. When he arrived the sitting bishop, St Amand (18 June), conveniently resigned in the face of Severinus' obvious virtues and venerable age. Not surprisingly, some accounts have conflated the two saints. St Gregory of Tours (17 Nov.) tells us that Severinus of Bordeaux had been bishop of Cologne, and the Roman Martyrology followed him in making the same attribution. A Life by Venantius Fortunatus, however, written a little after 587, is the most reliable of the ancient sources and says quite definitely that Severinus was bishop of Trier before he moved westward.

No credible reason is given in any of the sources for Severinus' move from Germany to Bordeaux. It could be that the people of Bordeaux, having made him one of their principal patrons, needed to explain how an "outsider" had been chosen as bishop and replaced their own Amand; a heavenly voice, and a bishop from a distinguished German see, would have made the choice more acceptable. There might also be something in the fact that the Franks invaded the area around Trier in 407, and this led to a serious decline in the religious life of the region. Did Severinus for some reason throw in his lot with the invaders and move back with them to France? Gregory of Tours got his information from Bordeaux pilgrims, and the interval of 150 years might well have led to confusion between the two German cities.

Severinus died in Bordeaux about the year 420. As has been said, he became a principal patron of the city, and a number of miracles in its favour and defence are attributed to him. He was buried in the crypt of the cathedral, but his relics were later stolen.

The Life by Venantius Fortunatus was edited by W. Levison in *M.G.H., Scriptores rerum Merov.*, 7, pp. 205-24. See also *Bibl.SS.*, 11, pp. 961-3; *N.C.E.*, 13, p. 143.

St Severinus Boethius (*c.* 480-524)

Anicius Manlius Torquatus Severinus Boethius was born about the year 480, a member of the one of the most illustrious Roman families. His father was consul in 487, an office Boethius occupied in 510. By the time he was thirty he had a reputation for learning, especially in philosophy. He married Rusticiana, the daughter of his legal guardian and friend who had cared for him when he had been left an orphan. He entered public life, according to his own account, in response to Plato's maxim "states would be happy either if philsophers ruled them, or if it chanced that their rulers turned philosophers," though it seems that he would have preferred the quieter life of the scholar. Twelve years after having been consul he reached what he calls "the highest point of his good fortune," when his two sons became consuls. Later the king, Theodoric the Ostrogoth, appointed him "master of the offices," a post of the highest responsibility. He interceded with the king to avert a forced requisition of grain in southern Italy and in general was a humane and practical official.

The reasons for his fall from grace are not altogether clear but seem to be linked to divisions between the eastern and western parts of the Roman Empire and Theodoric's desire for a practical independence from the emperor; Boethius and his circle upheld the ideal of a united empire and the old culture. When he defended an ex-consul, Albinus, against a charge of treason against the king, he was himself arrested and imprisoned at Ticinium (present-day Pavia); after about nine months he was executed, probably after being tortured. Throughout the Middle Ages he was regarded as a martyr, but his execution seems to have been a purely political act. The king was an Arian heretic, and Boethius was condemned unjustly, but neither of these facts are sufficient to support the claim that he was a martyr for the Catholic faith. He died about 524, and his tomb is honoured at San Pietro in Pavia. His cult as St Severinus Boethius, which goes back at least to the ninth century but only became popular from the thirteenth, was confirmed by Pope Leo XIII in 1883.

Boethius was famous above all else for his writings. He translated a number of important classical Greek authors into Latin, including works by Plato, Aristotle, Pythagoras, Ptolemy, Euclid, and Archimedes, and it was through his translations and commentaries that these authors were known in the Middle Ages in western Europe. He also wrote treatises on logic, mathematics, and music as well as on theological subjects, including one on the Trinity. He has been called "the last of the Roman philosophers, and the first of the scholastic theologians."

His best-known work is the *Consolation of Philosophy*, written while he was in prison. It is in the form of a dialogue between the author and Philosophy, with metrical interludes. It contains Boethius' defence of himself and his actions against the unjust charges and then goes on to examine the broader issues of human life and happiness. Philosophy seeks to comfort him in his misfortune by pointing out the transitory nature and vanity of earthly success—it is only things of the mind that have eternal value, and it is through knowledge that the soul reaches God; moreover, the way the world is governed is ultimately just, despite appearances and events to the contrary.

It became one of the most popular books of the Middle Ages and was translated into a number of languages, including into Anglo-Saxon by King Alfred (who added some more explicitly Christian sentiment to it) and into Middle English by Chaucer. Because it contains nothing that can be called specifically Christian, the work has been used to prove that Boethius was no longer a Christian by the time of his death. The previous edition of this work quotes Dr Johnson as saying in 1770 that it was very surprising that, upon such a subject and in a situation where he was facing death, Boethius should have been more of a philosopher than a Christian. Present-day scholars reject such a view, stressing the undoubted orthodoxy of Boethius' theological writings and making the point that the *Consolation* was written as a philosophical dialogue in the ancient Greek tradition, not a theological exercise. In Boethius' mind there could not be any contradiction between the truth discovered by reason and the truth revealed through Christianity.

AA.SS., May, 6, pp. 47-54; works in *P.L.*, 63 and 64; V. E. Watts (ed.), *The Consolation of Philosophy* (with Introduction, 1969). See also *D.H.G.E.*, 9, 348-80; *Bibl.SS.*, 3, 218-27; H. M. Barrett, *Boethius: Some Aspects of His Times and Work* (1940); M. Gibson (ed.), *Boethius. His Life, Thought and Influence* (1981); *O.D.C.C.*, p. 183.

St Ignatius of Constantinople, *Patriarch* (877)

Ignatius, whose baptismal name was Nicetas, was the younger son of the eastern emperor, Michael I; his mother was daughter of another emperor, Nicephorus I. When his father was deposed in 813 he and his brother were mutilated and shut up in a monastery. Nicetas became a monk and changed his name to Ignatius. He was later elected abbot of the monastery and in 846 was made patriarch of Constantinople. He was rather autocratic by temperament, and in his zeal to reform the Church made a number of enemies. He deposed an archbishop but failed to get Rome's support for his actions, and found that an anti-Ignatian party was forming at court. Eventually, in 857, he publicly refused Communion to Bardas, uncle of the young emperor Michael III and regent, who was generally thought to be guilty of incest. The regent, or *caesar* as he was called, persuaded the emperor that Ignatius should be dismissed; trumped-up charges were brought against him and he was deposed and exiled. He seems to have resigned from his see, though the details of this are unclear, and it may have been meant to be a temporary measure. Whatever the truth of the matter, it was enough for Bardas, and he chose another patriarch, his secretary Photius, to replace Ignatius; the new patriarch was consecrated by the bishop whom Ignatius had deposed some years before. Photius was in many ways an ideal candidate, very learned, religious, and capable as an administrator. He was, though, being used by the court party not just to get back at Ignatius but to assert their authority over the Church and, in particular, to weaken the position of the rigorists who wanted the Church to be wholly independent of the State. This was the beginning of the so-called Photian Schism between Constantinople and Rome; traditionally this has been seen in the West as an attempt on the part of the patriarch to maintain complete independence of the pope, but it is truer to see in it a power struggle within the Eastern Church itself.

Both sides appealed to Pope Nicholas I, and he sent envoys to investigate the whole affair. They exceeded their mandate by taking part in a synod in Constantinople which condemned and deposed Ignatius; the pope declared the findings of the synod to be null, re-instated Ignatius, and deposed Photius and all those he had appointed. Another quarrel concerned the missionaries who were then converting Bulgaria: Should they be under Rome or Constantinople? In 867, a council in Constantinople deposed and excommunicated the pope. Then there was a new emperor, Basil (he had become emperor by murdering Michael III), who re-instated Ignatius and deposed Photius. Finally, at least as far as concerns us here, the Fourth Council of Constantinople (869-70; the eighth ecumenical council of the Church) excommunicated Photius and officially restored Ignatius as patriarch.

Ignatius resumed his duties with his former zeal and energy but not always with prudence. He encouraged the Bulgarian prince, Boris, to expel the Latin bishops and priests from his territories and to accept Ignatius' Greek replacements; when he consecrated an archbishop and bishops for Bulgaria in 870, the pope, John VIII, threatened to excommunicate him. When papal legates arrived in the imperial city in 877 with an ultimatum, they found that Ignatius had already died, on 23 October, in the Monastery of The Holy Archangels that he had built as patriarch. He was succeeded by Photius, and another Council of Constantinople in 879-80, with papal legates in attendance, seems to have revoked the sentence of the previous one.

Ignatius' undoubted personal holiness, his fearlessness in rebuking immorality in high places, and his patience under persecution were what made him a saint. In the Eastern Church he is venerated alongside Photius, even though the two men had opposed each other while alive on matters of deeply-held principle. Former accounts that looked at this opposition from the point of view of a simplistic East/West controversy are no longer valid.

AA.SS., Oct., 10, pp. 167-205, gives a Life by Nicetas, which Dvornik calls "little better than a political tract"; Dvornik's own *The Photian Schism, History and Legend* (1948), developed the more modern approach adopted above. See also his article in *N.C.E.*, 11 (1967), pp. 326-9, with a good bibliography, and *O.D.C.C.*, pp. 1087-8.

Bd John Buoni, *Founder* (*c.* 1168-1249)

We know very little about John's early life; he lived at Mantua and may have belonged to the famous Buonomini family. The name "Buoni" may relate to this, but is more likely to have been an epithet given because of his later holiness—"John the Good." His father died when he was fifteen; he then left home and made his living as an entertainer or clown in various princely courts and the houses of the wealthy, leading a licentious and debauched life, "though ever pursued by the prayers of his devoted mother," according to the previous edition of this work. When he was about forty years old, in 1208, he had a near-fatal illness, and on his recovery decided to change his way of life, in line with a resolution he had made while he had been ill. He consulted the bishop of Mantua and was given permission to become a hermit, which he did at a place near Cesena. He developed a life of prayer and overcame the temptations to return to his former life of sexual pleasure so successfully that he gained a reputation for holiness and attracted a number of disciples who wished to share his way of life. For a time they lived according to regulations that John made on the spot as need arose, but when they had built a church and their community had become more settled, John applied to Pope Inno- cent IV for a definite rule and was told to follow that of St Augustine.

Despite his advancing age John did not lessen his austerities. He is reputed to have observed three Lents each year and to have worn only one light garment in even the coldest weather. A number of miracles were attributed to him—he was able, for example, to stand in red-hot ashes without getting burnt. One of these cases is particularly well authenticated in the papers prepared for John's canoniza- tion only two years after his death. He was giving a lesson to some of his disciples, telling them they should fear nothing, neither cold, nor heat, nor hardships, nor tribulations, for God would always come to their aid. As he was talking he stepped into the fire and began to shuffle the embers about with his feet, and remained standing there "for as long a time as it would take to say the *Miserere* half way through." Independent witnesses were closely cross-examined about this incident and gave substantially the same detailed account.

At the same time he was maliciously accused of serious wrong-doing by some of his former companions; he never defended himself against these calumnies except by a simple denial. So many people went to see him either out of curiosity or to confess their sins to him that he decided to leave secretly and live out the rest of his life in the solitude he had always wanted. Having walked all night, however, he found himself back at his own cell and concluded that it was God's will that he should stay there. He died at Mantua in 1249, and his tomb became famous for the miracles worked there. A canonization process was begun as early as 1251; his name was added to the Roman Martyrology in 1672 as a *beatus*.

His Congregation, called the Boniti, did not survive very long as an independent body. Soon after John's death they had eleven houses, but in 1256 they were united by Pope Alexander IV with a number of other Congregations to form the Order of Hermit-Friars of St Augustine.

AA.SS., Oct., 9, has nearly two hundred folio pages of documents relating to Bd John, made up of a sixteenth-century biography and the depositions of witnesses who on three occasions in the 1250s gave evidence for his canonization. See also *Bibl.SS.*, 6, 629-31, and H. Thurston in *The Month* 159 (Feb. 1932), pp. 146-7, about the miracle story related above.

Bd Bartholomew of Vicenza, *Bishop* (*c.* 1200-71)

Bartholomew Breganza was a native of Vicenza in Italy. He studied at Padua and about the year 1220 joined the Dominicans, receiving the habit from St Dominic (8 Aug.) himself. He was appointed prior of a number of houses and directed them well and prudently. In 1233, while preaching in Bologna, he established a military Order called the *Militia Christi*, otherwise known as the *Fratres Gaudentes* ("Joyful Brethren"); this had been founded in Languedoc in France a few years earlier, and its role was to preserve public order and peace; it spread to other Italian towns and lasted down to the eighteenth century.

Bartholomew's fame spread, and he was called to Rome by Pope Gregory IX to become apostolic penitentiary, a post which put him in charge of the theologians in the Curia. In 1244 he accompanied Pope Innocent IV to the council at Lyons as his official theologian. At the time it was felt that a particular need of the Church was to appoint suitable bishops in the Near East, partly to remedy the abuses of the Crusaders and partly to ensure that the Latin form of Christianity would at least hold its own against the Orthodox. As a result, Bartholomew was consecrated bishop of Limassol in Cyprus. From there he visited Palestine, where he met St Louis, king of France (25 Aug.), who was leading a Crusade to recapture Jerusalem, and the two became close friends. In 1255 or 1256 the pope appointed Bartholomew bishop of his native Vicenza, and a few years later he was able to take up the king's invitation to visit France, as he was appointed papal legate to the English king, Henry III, who was in Aquitaine at the time.

The new bishop quarrelled with Ezzelino da Romano, a violent and evil ruler who supported the Ghibelline faction against the pope, and was forced into exile. On his return he worked to restore the churches ruined by Ezzelino and to establish peace among the towns and cities of the Veneto region; he also combatted the Albigensian heretics who had been able to settle in the area while he had been away. His last recorded public act was to preach at the second translation of the relics of St Dominic. He died on 1 July 1271. A local cult developed immediately after his death, and he was usually referred to as Blessed Bartholomew; numerous miracles were reported at his shrine. There was no formal beatification but the cult was officially confirmed in 1793.

Among Bartholomew's writings that have survived (most have been lost) are one called "The Hunting of Divine Love" and an "Exposition of the Canticle of Canticles"; in addition there are three cycles of sermons: on Our Lady, the feasts of Christ, and the Epistles and Gospels of the Sundays after Trinity.

AA.SS., July, 1, p. 246; *Bibl.SS.*, 2, 880-1; J. Procter (ed.), *Short Lives of the Dominican Saints* (1901), pp. 297-301.

Bd Arnold Rèche (1838-90)

Nicholas-Jules Rèche was born at Landroff, about thirty miles south-east of Metz in Lorraine, on 12 September 1838, the eldest of eight children. His parents were Claude Rèche and Anne Clausset. Their marriage was not a very happy one. Anne was subject to fits of depression and reacted badly to the privations brought about by their poverty. At one stage she took to wandering about the village, and she was all the time pushing her husband to find her somewhere better to live. He was nicknamed "the zealot" because of his religious fervour. Nicholas-Jules seemed to take after his father; the parish priest described him as the "only serious pupil" in the catechism class, and it was not long before the young man was giving the lessons himself. He was serious and hard-working, a good communicator, and a devout follower of the traditional religious practices of his day.

When he was twenty-one he became a coachman to a wealthy family, and then worked as a mule driver for the builder of a church at Charleville. He began to devote more time to prayer and practised quite severe bodily austerities; he was also to be seen saying the rosary as he led the waggons to and from the building site. His fellow-workers called him "the bigot" or "the fanatic." He also began to help with the special Sunday evening classes put on by the Brothers of the Christian Schools for local teenagers; it seems to have been this that decided him he had a vocation to devote his life to religious education and training. He entered the novitiate of the Brothers in November 1862, and on Christmas Day of the same year received the religious habit, taking the name of Brother Arnold. He made his simple vows the following year, and renewed them annually until 1868; he was then allowed to take them for three years at once and in 1871 finally made his solemn profession.

Arnold spent fourteen years teaching in the Brothers' boarding school in Reims, from 1863 to 1877; during this time he gained his teaching diploma in Paris and was awarded a bronze cross by the International Red Cross for his work in nursing wounded French and German soldiers during the Franco-Prussian War. He was not a good classroom teacher, however, finding it very difficult to keep his pupils in order; he worked hard to remedy this but is said to have been successful only when he was teaching Christian doctrine. He often described himself as a timid person, not fit even to control himself, and his teaching experiences gave him a deep sense of failure. He wrote to a relative: "Pray for me that I may not be altogether useless, that I may accomplish all the good that God expects of me, that I won't be an obstacle to the good work that the Brothers around me are trying to do." He began to improve slowly, and then in 1877 was given a job more suited to his abilities when he was appointed director of novices in the novitiate at nearby Thillois. He proved to be a skilled and successful spiritual director and instilled in his charges strict adherence to the Rule and the need for humility and daily humiliations.

In his own spiritual life Arnold had a strong devotion to the Holy Eucharist, the passion and the Sacred Heart. He lived a life of deep interior prayer, while at the same time being strongly attached to the liturgy of the Mass and to community prayer. He read the scriptures assiduously and recited the rosary every day. In

March 1890 he was asked to take on the responsibilities of director general of the house at Courlancy to fill the vacancy created by the sudden death of the previous incumbent; despite his ill health he accepted out of obedience, but on 23 October he suffered a cerebral hemorrhage and died after receiving the last sacraments. He was buried in the public cemetery in Reims, and several cures were reported; the formal process for his canonization was opened in 1938, and he was beatified by Pope John Paul II in November 1987. The prayers approved at the time of the beatification refer to him as "an admirable guide for the young in the ways of prayer and charity." He had indeed been "an ambassador and minister of Jesus Christ," as St John Baptist De La Salle (7 Apr.) had wanted all his disciples to become.

G. Rigault, *Un ascèt lasallien: Le Frère Arnould* (1956); Luke Salm, F.S.C., *Brother Arnold Rèche F.S.C., Apostolic Ascetic* (1986); *Notitiae*, 23 (1987), pp. 1278-80.

ST ANTONY MARY CLARET
His episcopal coat of arms, designed by him in January 1850. The lower part of the shield refers to his earthly origins: the bridge of Sallent and on one side of it the moon (his mother) and on the other side the sun (his father). This symbolism is apt enough, not only because his parents were born on opposite sides of the river Llobregat, but also because of the images of light (Claret i Clará) in their names. The upper part of the shield refers to heavenly "relations." In the centre is a monogram of Mary, his mother and protectress, flanked on one side by the palm of St Stephen, patron saint of his town, and on the other by the lily that symbolized both St Anthony of Padua, whose name he bore, and of St Aloysius, patron of the Congregation he had belonged to in the seminary. He had also been ordained to the diaconate on the feast of St Stephen and to the priesthood on the feast of St Anthony. Below the shield is a ribbon bearing the motto: "The charity of Christ impels us."

24

ST ANTONY MARY CLARET, *Founder and Bishop* (1807-70)

Antonio Juan Claret i Clará was born at Sallent in Catalonia in 1807. He followed his father's trade as a weaver before entering the seminary at Vic when he was twenty-two. He was ordained a secular priest in 1835 but was strongly attracted by the idea of joining a religious Order. He had already thought of becoming a Carthusian, but his health was against his adopting such a strict régime, and so he went to Rome to offer his services as a missionary to Propaganda. He became a Jesuit novice, but when his health broke down he was advised by his superiors to return to Spain to work for the evangelization of his own country. To enable him to do this he was given the title of Apostolic Missionary.

For ten years he was engaged in giving retreats and missions in Catalonia; he also worked in the Canaries for about fifteen months. He was dedicated to spreading devotion to the heart of Mary and set up a number of parish groups for women which gave them a role in spreading this devotion and in the general work of evangelization. He was involved with St Joachima de Mas (22 May) in setting up the Carmelites of Charity, who were devoted to looking after the sick and teaching. He inspired other priests to take up the work of evangelization and in 1849 founded the Congregation of Missionary Sons of the Immaculate Heart of Mary, more often called the Claretians. He wrote, "That man is a son of the Immaculate Heart of Mary who is aflame with charity and who spreads the flame wherever he goes . . . and brings all his resources to bear on his efforts to enkindle all men with the fire of divine love."

Antony attached a special importance to the apostolate of the printed word and is credited with the publication of over two hundred books and pamphlets, including catechisms, works of devotion, and an important series of books of spiritual advice to priests and laypeople. He was particularly concerned about the proper instruction of boys and girls and about developing a genuine lay spirituality. In 1847 he was the main inspiration behind the foundation of the famous Religious Library, a publishing venture that met with remarkable success. Between 1848 and 1866, for example, it produced over five million books and booklets and a further four million leaflets. Antony was not content with suggesting ideas and titles; he had learned printing before entering the seminary and took a keen interest in the technical side of the business, correcting galley proofs, designing layouts, and advising on bindings. In all this he showed himself to be a modern apostle, using whatever means the times provided to spread the gospel.

In 1850, much against his will, he was appointed archbishop of Santiago in Cuba.

It was at his consecration that he took the name Mary, because, he wrote, "she is my Mother, my Protector, my Teacher, my all, after Jesus." The task of reforming his diocese was extremely difficult, as it had been leaderless for about fourteen years, and he was opposed by powerful groups, some of whom were openly anti-Christian. Attempts were even made on his life, and on one occasion he was seriously wounded by an assassin whose mistress had been converted by the archbishop's efforts. Antony interceded for his would-be killer and had the death sentence against him remitted. He visited every part of his diocese three times in six years, set up fifty-three new parishes, restored the seminary and established bursaries to help poor seminary students, and set up the Confraternity of Christian Doctrine, specifying that men and women as well as priests should join it. He made a great impression by involving himself in pastoral work of every kind; in 1852, for example, he was to be found visiting the hospitals and ministering to the sick and dying at a time of earthquakes and epidemics. In describing the ideal "son of the Immaculate Heart of Mary" he had written: "Nothing deters him; privations only bring him joy; he does not flinch from heavy tasks; he embraces hardships . . . he rejoices in the midst of suffering"—a suitable description of his own work as bishop in Cuba.

Yet he was not satisfied and wondered about resigning as archbishop; he even wrote to the pope asking to be allowed to do so. Here we get a glimpse of something fundamental in his character: he was a man of action, driven to spread the gospel, full of initiatives and ready to tackle any problems he came up against. But he was not one for the slow consolidation of what he had started: as his most recent biographer has said, it was a case of the prophet prevailing over the administrator (Lozano). In Cuba he had started the work of re-evangelizing the island; others could carry it forward. While he directed all his activity toward advancing the glory of God, there is no doubt that on the human level the expenditure of great amounts of energy was very satisfying to him; perhaps it was to cure him of this that God allowed the next stage of his life to be a particularly frustrating one.

He left Cuba in 1857: in the end he was ordered to resign his see and return to Spain to become the confessor of Queen Isabella II. He had to spend almost all his time at court; the only breaks came when he accompanied the royal family on its travels around Spain, which gave him an opportunity to preach throughout the country. In Andalusia, for example, which they visited in 1862, he preached 205 times in the space of about forty days. He also founded the Congregation of Catholic Mothers, and established religious libraries for the people to meet the needs of what was becoming an increasingly literate population. It was, however, a very trying time for him, and not only because of the sometimes scandalous conduct of the queen, which forced him to refuse to continue as her confessor on a number of occasions. As we have seen, he was almost by nature a missionary and found being tied to one place a severe trial. He wrote, "Living at court and being constantly in the palace is a continuous martyrdom for me. . . . Every day at prayer I have to make acts of resignation to God's will. Day and night and always I have to offer up the sacrifice of staying in Madrid." It was not just the court ceremonial and the holding of daily audiences that irked him—he wanted to be off, "running" as he put it, to preach the word of God.

He would not have been the person he was, however, if he had not used his new position, with the undoubted influence it gave him, to launch new projects. He had wide cultural interests, and while he was rector of the Royal Monastery of the Escorial he set up a science laboratory, a museum of natural history, and schools of music and languages. He established the Academy of St Michael, a learned and cultural association of writers and artists who should take part in an active apostolate by writing books and setting up libraries as well as forming a Christian élite in society. The Academy had branches throughout the country. He was also engaged in these years in re-orienting his original Congregation toward a more modern apostolate, with a second set of Constitutions which emphasized catechetical work, spiritual direction, and the training of seminarians. Meanwhile, the Claretian Sisters, co-founded by Mother Antonia Paris and himself in Cuba and dedicated to providing Christian education for girls, involved considerable work and negotiations with local bishops and the Roman authorities.

At the same time his own spiritual life developed to such a high degree that he experienced ecstasies, had the gift of prophecy, and was responsible for a number of miraculous cures. The comparative inactivity of life at court allowed him to develop a life of almost monastic regularity. He set aside a maximum of six hours for sleep and spent the first two hours of the day in prayer and reading the Bible. This was followed by an hour of prayer with his household, then Mass, after which he heard confessions from after breakfast until 11 o'clock or noon. From noon until half-past one he held audience, and the afternoon was spent either visiting hospitals and prisons, preaching in local schools and convents, or writing. Every day included prayer before the Blessed Sacrament exposed, the rosary, and of course, the divine office. He fasted on three days each week, took the discipline on two, and wore a hair shirt on Tuesdays, Thursdays, and Saturdays. He regarded all this as no more than a step toward "being always in the presence of God," his ultimate earthly aim.

His position at Court meant that he was inevitably involved in politics. He had already run into anti-clerical opposition to the work he was doing to restore the Escorial, and after the liberal revolution of 1868 he went into exile with the queen. He eventually went to Rome, where he was an active supporter of the definition of papal infallibility at the First Vatican Council in 1870. While in Rome he suffered a stroke, and although he made a good recovery, his general health was giving cause for concern. The Revolution in Spain had forced the Claretians to close their houses there and move to France. At first Antony stayed with them, but even there his political opponents tried to have him arrested, and so he took refuge in the Cistercian monastery of Fontfroide, near Narbonne in southern France. Here he was accused of collecting weapons for use against the Spanish government, but before any further action could be taken against him, he died on 24 October 1870. He was beatified in 1934 and canonized in 1950. His tomb is in Vic, near Barcelona. His feast-day was on 23 October until the Calendar reform of 1969.

There are numerous photographs of him; they show a small, stocky figure. At the time of his canonization Pius XII contrasted Antony's ordinary appearance with the respect he was able to win from the highest in the land; he also contrasted his humble origins with the worldly positions of honour he held for much of his life and the fact that he was always in the presence of God despite his life of busy external activity. Antony himself wrote of how the love of Christ "goads us to run, and even, so to speak, to fly, propelled on the wings of a holy zeal," so that we do everything in our power "that God may be better known, loved and served in this life." This was the motivation for his lifelong interest in evangelization, whether at home or abroad. His own summary of his life, made in Rome in 1870, was, "I have fulfilled my mission, I have preached the gospel, I have kept holy poverty."

The Claretians continue his mission of evangelization through publishing on a large scale. Their editions of the *Christian Community Bible*, published in Quezon City in the Philippines, in Spanish, English, Tagalog, and Chinese have sold millions of copies all over the world in recent years.

A.A.S., 42 (1950), pp. 369-72, 479-81; and 44 (1952), pp. 345-58, give a sketch of St Antony's life along with the decree of canonization. For his writings, see A. M. Claret, *Escritos autobiográficos y espirituales* (1959). There are many biographies in Spanish and Catalan; in English, the best Life by far is by J. M. Lozano, C.M.F., *Anthony Claret, A Life at the Service of the Gospel* (1985), on which the above account is heavily dependent. See also *Bibl.SS.*, 2, 205-10. Some of the extracts above are from *The Office of Readings*, 3, p. 355-6.

St Proclus of Constantinople, *Patriarch* (*c.* 390-446)

Proclus was a native of Constantinople, born not later than 390-5. Some accounts say he was a disciple of St John Chrysostom (13 Sept.), but he may just have excelled in the study of rhetoric like the saint and shared his ideas. He entered the service of Patriarch Atticus and became his secretary, even though St John and Atticus were opponents in the ecclesiastical politics of the day. Atticus was so impressed with him that he ordained him deacon and, after an interval, priest. When the patriarch died in 425, many thought Proclus should succeed him, but this did not happen, and instead, in the following year, he was consecrated archbishop of Cyzicus. The people of that city refused to accept him, and so he had to remain in Constantinople, where he became famous as a preacher. In 428 the see became vacant again, and again Proclus seemed to be the obvious candidate to become patriarch; the emperor, however, intervened and insisted that Nestorius be chosen.

The new patriarch began to put forward the doctrines which were later condemned as the Nestorian heresy. These concerned the nature of the Incarnation. Nestorius taught that in the incarnate Christ there were two persons, one human and one divine; one result of this was that Mary should be regarded only as the mother of Christ the man and not as the mother of God, and so Nestorius and his followers refused to use the term *Theotokos* ("God-bearer"), which had been traditionally applied to Mary. In 429 Proclus preached a famous sermon attacking these views, upholding the use of the title *Theotokos* and claiming, "We do not proclaim a deified man, but we confess an incarnate God." He does not, however, seem to have taken much part in the subsequent controversy nor in the important Council of Ephesus in 431, which condemned the heresy and deposed Nestorius. A new patriarch was chosen; when he died in 434 Proclus at last became patriarch.

He was noted for his moderation at a time when accusation and counter-accusation were the order of the ecclesiastical day and when some orthodox believers wanted to hound the heretics to physical destruction. He was asked by the Armenian bishops to pass judgment on the writings of their hero, Theodore of Mopsuestia, and produced his best-known work, the so-called "Tome of St Proclus to the Armenians," in which he defended the orthodox view of the Incarnation and criticized the writings of Theodore, but without naming him lest he offend those who revered him as a saint. He won public favour by assisting at the translation of the remains of St John Chrysostom to Constantinople, and he healed the long-standing rift which had alienated the saint's followers. He is said to have been responsible for the addition to the Eastern liturgy of the famous *Trisagion* ("thrice-holy")—"Holy God, Holy Mighty, Holy Immortal, have mercy on us"—as a result of its efficacy in ending a serious earthquake in the city.

St Cyril of Alexandria (27 June) referred to Proclus as "a man full of religion, perfectly instructed in the discipline of the Church, and a careful observer of the canons." The Greek historian Socrates, who knew him personally, wrote: "In moral excellence he had few equals. He was always gentle to everyone, for he was convinced that kindness advances the cause of truth better than severity. He therefore determined not to irritate and harass heretics, and so restored to the Church in his own person that mild and benignant dignity of character which had so often been unhappily violated. . . . He was a pattern for all true prelates."

It should be added, however, that Proclus could stand up for his rights as keenly as any others in that quarrelsome age. He had a major difference of opinion with the pope on the issue of episcopal jurisdiction: the patriarchs had claimed authority over Thessalonika, which was also claimed by the pope. There was also trouble over the Illyrian bishops' claim to have the right of appeal to Constantinople rather than Rome. In these quarrels Proclus defended the position of the patriarchs with a great deal more than mildness and moderation.

Proclus died on 24 July 446. In addition to the "Tome" already mentioned we have a number of his sermons (there are questions about the attribution of some of these) and letters, mainly to do with doctrinal differences between the orthodox view and the Nestorians. Alban Butler described his style as "concise, sententious and full of lively witty turns, more proper to please and delight than to move the heart . . . and (requiring) much pains and study . . . not to be compared to the easy natural gravity of St Basil or the sweet style of St Chrysostom," a judgment which does not, perhaps, fit the image of the gentle, patient, and moderate patriarch described by others. The Orthodox keep his feast on 20 November.

AA.SS., Oct., 10, pp. 637-49; *Bibl.SS.*, 10, 1141-50; *O.D.C.C.*, pp. 1129-30 (on Proclus), and 961-3 (on Nestorius).

SS Aretas and the Martyrs of Najran, and St Elsebaan (523)

Aksum was the ancient religious and political capital of Ethiopia, converted to Christianity by St Frumentius (27 Oct.). Early in the sixth century Ethiopians from this area crossed the Red Sea and imposed their rule on the Jews and Arabs of what is present-day Yemen. A member of the deposed ruling family named Dunaan, a former convert to Judaism, led a revolt against the Ethiopians, took the town of Zafar, and massacred the garrison and clergy. He turned the church into a synagogue and then laid siege to the town of Najran, one of the principal Christian strongholds in the country. Resistance was fierce, and in the end Dunaan was successful only because he promised an amnesty to the inhabitants if they surrendered; when they did, he had his soldiers sack the place and condemned all the Christians to death if they did not give up their religion. The leader of the resistance had been a certain Banu Harith (his name was transposed into Aretas); he and the members of his tribe who had supported him were beheaded, while the priests, deacons, and consecrated virgins were burned to death. Dunaan tried to get Aretas' wife to agree to live with him; when she refused, he had her four daughters executed before her eyes and then had her beheaded. The number of those killed was four thousand.

Refugees from Najran spread word of the massacre throughout the Middle East. There was universal condemnation of what had happened, and the impression created by it lasted for many years. Mohammed mentioned the massacre in the Qur'an and condemned those who had been guilty of it to hell (see *Sura* 85). The patriarch of Alexandria wrote to the Eastern bishops recommending that the slain should be commemorated as martyrs, and he and the emperor urged the Aksumite king, Elesbaan, to revenge their killing. He did so by re-invading the Yemen, killing Dunaan and occupying his main stronghold. Alban Butler claimed that the king, "having by the divine blessing defeated the tyrant, made use of his victory with great clemency and moderation," but as the previous edition of this work pointed out, this is not true. Both in battle and later in his dealings with the Jews he showed great ferocity and cruelty. It is said that at the end of his life he abdicated in favour of his son, gave his crown to the church of the Holy Sepulchre in Jerusalem, and lived an exemplary life as a hermit.

It was the sixteenth-century ecclesiastical historian Cardinal Baronius who added Aretas and the Najran martyrs and St Elsebaan to the Roman Martyrology. There is no doubt that the martyrs suffered for upholding the Christian faith, and Elsebaan may well have repented of his cruelty and died a good death. All of them, however, were almost certainly Monophysite heretics, believing that in Christ there was only one—divine—nature, since the Ethiopian church was largely Monophysite in its official doctrine. Baronius was either ignorant of this (his knowledge of the Eastern churches was sketchy) or decided that the palm of martyrdom excused what was probably no more than technical heresy anyway.

AA.SS., Oct., 10, pp. 661-762, gives the Greek text of the *passio*; there is also a Syriac account written by a contemporary, Bishop Simeon, one of the first to hear of the massacre. See also *Bibl.SS.*, 2, 401-3.

St Senoch, *Abbot* (576)

Senoch, or Senou, was born of pagan parents in Poitou in the kingdom of the Franks. He was converted to Christianity and left home to become a hermit; he settled in Touraine at a place where there is now a village called Saint-Senou. He found some ruins to live in, using the stone to build himself a cell and a chapel. He was joined by three disciples but preferred to be alone and spent most of his time shut up in his own cell. He practised severe austerities and gained a considerable reputation for sanctity; this led to his being visited by a large number of people who insisted on giving him money and goods, which Senoch used to relieve the poor of the area.

He left his cell in 573 to visit the town of Tours, where a new bishop, St Gregory of Tours (17 Nov.), had been installed. The two men exchanged the kiss of peace and Senoch returned to his hermitage. Shortly after this he made another journey to visit some friends and his relatives at home. He met with such respect and even veneration because of his reputation for holiness that he was rather proud of himself when he got back to his cell. St Gregory got to hear of this and rebuked him rather severely, reminding him of the words of St Paul that we should glory in nothing but our infirmities so that the power of Christ might dwell in us. Senoch accepted the rebuke humbly and decided that he had dwelt too long alone as a hermit; in future he would spend more time with his brethren, who would ensure that he did not think too highly of himself.

St Gregory, who is our principal source of information about Senoch, gives an account of various miracles of healing worked at his intercession. The two obviously became close friends, and Senoch died in 576 in the arms of the bishop. A huge crowd gathered for the funeral Mass, said by St Gregory, and again for the Mass of the "month's mind," at which a paralytic was cured at Senoch's grave. His cult became widespread in France, where he was sometimes venerated under the name Enoch. His relics are claimed by the church of Sassenay (possibly a corruption of St Senoch), near Chalon-sur-Saône. Senoch is sometimes regarded as the patron saint of bridge builders because he is said to have repaired a number of ruined bridges.

All the relevant material about the life of Senoch is printed in *AA.SS.*, Oct., 10, pp. 764-71. See also *Bibl.SS.*, 11, 845-6.

St Maglorius (Sixth Century)

Apparently of Irish origin, Maelor, or Maglorius, was educated by St Illtyd (6 Nov.) at Llanilltyd Fawr in Wales. He became a monk, was ordained deacon, and taken to Brittany by St Samson (28 July), who may have been his cousin. There he was put in charge of the monastery at Kerfunt and shared in the missionary labours of his master. Tradition says that when the latter died, Maelor succeeded him as abbot of the monastery at Dol and bishop of the same place, but this now seems to be untrue. Eventually Maelor retired to a solitary spot on the coast of Brittany, but even there he was visited by large numbers of people wanting advice or hoping to see a miracle. He healed the chieftain of Sark, one of the Channel Islands, of a skin disorder and was given a piece of land on the island; he retired there with some of his monks and built a monastery. He organized the local people to defend themselves against raiders and may have visited another of the islands, Jersey, to drive away what is described as a dragon; as a result, he was given some land there as well. Back on Sark he laboured for the people during an epidemic and famine, without any thought of danger to himself.

We do not know the date of his death. According to a late Life he interpreted the words of the psalmist literally, "This I will seek after, to dwell in the house of the Lord all the days of my life," and refused to move from the church during the last months of his life. His relics were moved first of all to Lehon, near Dinant, in 857, and then to Paris, to avoid destruction during the Viking raids; they are still claimed by the church of Saint-Jacques. His name features in a number of martyrologies and Breton calendars, and there can be no doubt about his cult, whatever truth may be in the legendary Lives. The English mystic Richard Rolle refers to him in his book, *The Fire of Love* (ch. 13).

AA.SS., Oct., 10, pp. 772-93; *D.N.B.*, 35, pp. 323-4; *O.D.S.*, p. 313.

Bd John-Angelo Porro (*c*. 1451-1506)

Giovannangelo was born in the duchy of Milan about the year 1451. In his early twenties he joined the Order of the Servants of Mary, or Servites, as they are better known, and after his ordination was sent to Monte Senario, where the Order had originated. His superiors felt that he was more suited to a life of contemplation than to the active pastoral life, and he remained there on and off for twenty years, gaining a reputation for great holiness. He then moved to Florence, where he became master of novices, an office he fulfilled so well that he is regarded in the Order as the patron of novice-masters. At various times he was stationed in other Servite houses, and in all of them he developed a special mission to the poor and uneducated of the locality, paying particular attention to instructing them in Christian doctrine. While he was stationed in Milan he went about the streets gathering together groups of children so that they could be taught at least the rudiments of their religion properly. He was also involved in the reform of the Order's house in Milan, which seems to have been experiencing some sort of crisis with regard to strict observance of the Rule. He himself tried to continue living as a hermit even when officially he was living in community.

The previous edition of this work described him as "an ornament of the Order of the Servants of Mary" but claimed that his career and personality "remain veiled in great obscurity." We know much more about him now, thanks to new sources coming to light, and can obtain a reasonably clear picture of him and his spirituality. He seems to have been fairly delicate in health, with a sensitive and refined mind. His spiritual ideals were simplicity, poverty, austerity, and perseverance in prayer. When an inventory of the monastery's goods was made in 1474, there was nothing to list in his cell except for a pair of torn sheets; it seems to have been his practice to sleep on the ground. His approach to prayer was in line with the best traditions of the Servite Order, and he was deeply contemplative.

He was staying in the monastery at Cavacurta when he had a vision telling him of his sister's death and warning him that he should return home as his own death was imminent. He returned to Milan, worn out with work and the austerities he had practised, and died in the Servite house in 1505. A cult developed very quickly after his death and was approved officially in 1737. His relics are preserved in the Servite church in Milan.

AA.SS., Oct., 10, pp. 883-908, gives a Life by Philip Albericius. See also F. M. Berlasso, *Il b. Giovannangelo Porro* (1964); *Bibl.SS.*, 10, 1046-51.

Bd Louis Guanella, *Founder* (1842-1915)

Luigi Guanella was born in 1842 at Franciscio di Campodolcino, near Lake Como in northern Italy, the ninth of thirteen children. When he was twelve years old he went to the college run by the Somaschi fathers in Como, where he studied for six years before entering the seminary to study for the priesthood. He was ordained in 1866 and was given charge of the parish of Savogno; here he built an elementary school and started to teach. He organized various kinds of assistance for the poor people of the parish and set up a branch of Young Catholic Action, a movement founded in 1867. His activities and writings made him the enemy of anti-clerical politicians and the local Freemasons; he had to give up his school and his name was black-listed by the government so that he could not be a parish priest. As a result of this opposition he decided to give up ordinary parish work, and in 1875 he went off to Turin to join St John Bosco (31 Jan.), whose work he had admired for a long time. He entered the new Congregation of the Salesians and took triennial vows; he was appointed to be director of one of their oratories and began to write for the *Catholic Reader*.

In 1878 he was faced with a difficult choice when his former bishop recalled him to the diocese; despite the opposition of John Bosco he obeyed the bishop and returned to parish work. Again he opened a school for poor children, at Traona, and once again he had to close it because of Masonic opposition. He was forced to move to a tiny parish in the mountains, where the civil authorities thought he would be out of the way and could do no harm. It turned out to be a providential move: there were in the area an orphanage and a hospice for the elderly and sick run by a religious community which had just been founded by Don Coppini (1827-81) in 1878. Coppini himself had been a revolutionary in 1848 and secretary to the legendary Mazzini before becoming a priest. Luigi was very impressed by the work of the Congregation and felt he should do all he could to cultivate "this grain of mustard." An invaluable collaborator in this enterprise was a Sister Marcellina Bosatta, one of the nuns of Coppini's original foundation.

In 1886 they transferred the operation to Como, where they found more spacious accommodation, and named it "The Little House of Divine Providence," after the example of St Joseph Benedict Cottolengo (29 Apr.), who had opened a similar house in Turin in 1828 and who was one of Louis' main inspirations in his dedication to the sick and disadvantaged. By 1890 the house was caring for over two hundred people, and a Congregation named the Daughters of Mary of Providence was established to carry on the work; they were approved by the Holy See in 1917. By 1895 Louis had also accepted a number of men who had vocations to join him in his work. He sent them to various seminaries for their training and eventually set up another Congregation, the Servants of Charity; he made his own religious vows with the first members in 1908. This Congregation received approval in 1928 and 1935. Louis insisted that assistance must be given to the disadvantaged "without any exceptions"; in 1905 and 1908 he offered shelter to those who had been made homeless by earthquakes, and in 1915 he went personally to help those affected by the earthquake in Marsica, even though he was seventy-three years old, and provided help for the orphaned and the injured in the Congregation's house in Rome. In 1913 he decided to organize a worldwide crusade of prayer for the dying and so established the Archconfraternity of St Joseph for the Dying, which in the 1960s claimed to have ten million members across the world.

In addition to his charitable work Louis kept up his interest in education, opening day, evening, and vocational schools. He had a special devotion to Mary, to whom he gave the title "Our Lady of Work"; he was particularly interested in working conditions and in preparing young people for the world of work. He was, indeed, a person full of ideas and initiatives. He was involved in the plan to reclaim part of the Spagna Plain, an area that had been badly affected by malaria, and established an institute for the disabled there. Another initiative was the sending of some of his Congregation into the parts of Switzerland bordering on Italy to see what could be done to re-establish a Catholic presence in the Protestant valleys. He was friendly with Fr Scalabrini and impressed by the work he was doing for the spiritual care of the many thousands of Italians who were emigrating for economic reasons in these years; he sent one of his first priests to America to help with the work, after going there himself in 1912 to see what the situation was like. He wrote over fifty short works, some of them devotional, others on history, social matters, and the defence of the Church against anti-clericalism. He was a friend of all those at the time who were developing a social Catholicism through movements such as the *Opera dei Congressi* and various forms of Catholic Action.

In 1915 he was awarded a gold medal by the civil authorities in Como for his work with the war-wounded. He suffered an apoplectic attack in September of the same year and died on 24 October at Como. Pope Pius XI called him the "Garibaldi of Charity," and his cause was introduced at Rome in 1939; he was beatified by Paul VI in 1964.

Both his Congregations flourished and opened a large number of hospitals and homes. These are the lasting legacy of a person who lived the precepts of the gospel to the full and gave an outstanding example of personal holiness and involvement in the problems of the modern world, despite living in a society when opposition to religion and particularly to the Church was very strong and when many Catholics preferred to keep their heads down and wait for better times.

There are a number of biographies of Louis Guanella; see, for example, A. Tamborini and G. Preatoni, *Il Servo della Carità, Beato Luigi Guanella* (1964). *Bibl.SS.*, 6, 430-2.

Bd Joseph Baldo, *Founder* (1843-1915)

Giuseppe Baldo was born in Puegnago, near Brescia in the diocese of Verona, on 19 February 1843. His father, Angelo, was a farmer, his mother, Hippolita Casa, a midwife. He had a deeply religious upbringing, and when he was sixteen he entered the seminary at Verona to study for the priesthood. His progress was such that he was ordained by papal indult at the very early age of twenty-two. He served as a curate for a time in a country parish but was soon recalled to the seminary to become its vice rector. He proved to be both a first-rate teacher and an excellent spiritual director and published a manual of prayers, a book of homilies, and works on seminary discipline. After having been at the seminary for about eleven years he requested a move back to parish work, for he felt called to a wider apostolate; he was appointed parish priest of Ronco all'Adige in 1877.

He had to enter the parish almost in disguise, for a group of anti-clerical Freemasons had threatened him with death if he dared enter openly with the usual ceremony. This anti-clerical opposition was very similar to that faced by Bd Louis Guanella (previous entry), his exact contemporary, who also worked in northern Italy. But Joseph Baldo was not one to be frightened: on his first Sunday in the parish he announced openly to the people, "I am your parish priest. From now on you will have a new owner, a new heart to which you have the right to appeal, a new soul which must do nothing else but pray, suffer and agonize for you." Nor did he believe that the priest should stay in his sacristy and be seen only on religious occasions: his concerns must include whatever would help to increase the dignity of his people and meet their material as well as their spiritual needs. He launched a social and charitable programme that was revolutionary in its impact. Between 1882 and 1885 he set up schools for men and women and a Workers' Mutual Assistance Society; later on he opened a rural savings bank to take the poor out of the power of the moneylenders, vocational schools for boys and girls, and a nursery. In addition, he formed a sodality of women called the Servants of Charity of our Lady of Succour to look after the sick in their homes. In 1888 he was able to open a small hospital and refuge for the sick poor and elderly who lived alone. Five years later he laid the foundations for a new Congregation, the Little Daughters of St Joseph, composed of nurses dedicated to the work of the hospital. The early years of the Congregation were difficult because money which had been promised did not materialize, and its members lived in considerable poverty. It survived because of its founder's prudence and vision.

On the spiritual side, he established a Society of the Forty Hours, an Association of Christian Mothers, a Confraternity of the Blessed Sacrament, and a parish committee to which he gave a practical role in the evangelization of the parish. For himself, he prayed for a long and painful illness before he died, to "purify him of any possible dregs of human weakness." For twenty-two months he suffered a terminal illness which caused him great pain; he bore this with patience and seemed to be in almost continual prayer. He died in the parish he had served for thirty-eight years, on 24 October 1915. His remains were moved in 1950 to the chapel of the motherhouse of his Congregation, and he was beatified in 1989.

A number of studies have appeared along with the publication of sets of documents connected with his cause. See E. Valentini, *Il messagio pedagogico sociale del servo di Dio d. G. B.* (1956), and *Il pensiero e l'azione del servo di Dio d. G. B.* (1977); T. Taddei, *Don G. B. "o buono o nulla"* (1985); *Bibl.SS.*, Suppl. 1 (1987), 115-8, with photograph.

MARTYRS' PALMS
representing spiritual victory over death.

25

THE FORTY MARTYRS OF ENGLAND AND WALES

There are two feast-days in the year when groups of English and Welsh martyrs are honoured, 4 May and 25 October. The first of these is dedicated to a large number of martyrs beatified over the years by various popes, the last group by Pope John Paul II in 1987. Today's feast is more specific and is dedicated to the forty martyrs canonized in 1970 by Pope Paul VI. The group comprises thirteen secular priests, ten Jesuits, three Benedictines, three Carthusians, two Franciscans, a Brigettine, an Austin Friar, three laywomen, and four laymen. As well as being honoured today as a group, each of them has a separate feast-day as well, and an account of their lives will be found under those dates. The following list gives their names, the place and year of their martyrdom and date of their individual feast-day:

John Almond	Tyburn	1612	3 Dec.
Edmund Arrowsmith	Lancaster	1628	28 Aug.
Ambrose Barlow	Lancaster	1641	10 Sept.
John Boste	Durham	1594	24 July
Alexander Briant	Tyburn	1581	1 Dec.
Edmund Campion	Tyburn	1581	1 Dec.
Margaret Clitherow	York	1586	25 Mar.
Philip Evans	Cardiff	1679	22 July
Thomas Garnet	Tyburn	1608	23 June
Edmund Gennings	London	1591	10 Dec.
Richard Gwyn	Wrexham	1584	15 Oct.
John Houghton	Tyburn	1535	4 May
Philip Howard	died in prison	1595	19 Oct.
John Jones	London	1598	12 July
John Kemble	Hereford	1679	22 Aug.
Luke Kirby	Tyburn	1582	30 May
Robert Lawrence	Tyburn	1535	4 May
David Lewis	Usk	1679	27 Aug.
Anne Line	Tyburn	1601	27 Feb.
John Lloyd	Cardiff	1679	22 July
Cuthbert Mayne	Launceston	1577	30 Nov.
Henry Morse	Tyburn	1645	1 Feb.
Nicholas Owen	London	1606	22 Mar.
John Paine	Chelmsford	1582	2 Apr.

Polydore Plasden	Tyburn	1591	10 Dec.
John Plessington	Chester	1679	19 July
Richard Reynolds	Tyburn	1535	11 May
John Rigby	Southwark	1600	21 June
John Roberts	Tyburn	1610	10 Dec.
Alban Roe	Tyburn	1642	21 Jan.
Ralph Sherwin	Tyburn	1581	1 Dec.
Robert Southwell	Tyburn	1595	21 Feb.
John Southworth	Tyburn	1654	28 June
John Stone	Canterbury	1539	12 May
John Wall	Worcester	1679	26 Aug.
Henry Walpole	York	1595	7 Apr.
Margaret Ward	Tyburn	1588	30 Aug.
Augustine Webster	Tyburn	1535	4 May
Swithun Wells	London	1591	10 Dec.
Eustace White	Tyburn	1591	10 Dec.

The first of these martyrs were executed in 1535 for refusing to recognize Henry VIII as supreme head of the Church in England, the last in 1679 as a result of the so-called Popish Plot. The charges against them ranged from denial of the royal supremacy, being a priest in England who had been ordained abroad, reconciling people to the Catholic faith, and sheltering priests who were on the run from the authorities. Legislation changed over the period, as did official attitudes to Catholics; there were periods of relative calm and periods of intense anti-Catholic activity. A brief historical outline is given here, followed by an indication of some features of the devotion to the Forty Martyrs.

It was in 1534 that the Act of Supremacy, declaring Henry VIII to be the "Supreme Head of the Church in England," was passed, which led to the death of the earliest of the above martyrs in the following year. There were no executions of those loyal to the old religion in Edward VI's reign (1547-53), and in Mary I's reign (1553-8) it was the turn of the Reformers to be persecuted as the queen restored Catholicism and tried to rid the country of heresy. Between January 1555 and her death in November 1558 about two hundred and eighty Protestants, the great majority of them ordinary laypeople, suffered martyrdom for their beliefs, a rate of religious executions not matched in England before or since.

The succession of Elizabeth I in 1558 brought a return to Protestantism, with the first acts of Parliament of 1559 restoring the royal supremacy over the Church in England and making it a crime to uphold the authority of the pope or to refuse to attend the new religious services. There was little active persecution of Catholics, however, for the first twelve years of the reign, when the government probably hoped that the old religion would slowly die out once it was deprived of bishops and priests. The change to a much more severe anti-Catholicism came after the Northern Rebellion of 1569, one of whose aims was to restore Catholicism, the

Ridolfi Plot of 1571 to depose the queen (unwisely supported by the pope), and the unfortunate excommunication of Elizabeth by Pope St Pius V (30 Apr.) in 1570—unfortunate because technically it made all English Catholics traitors by removing them from their allegiance to the queen and ordering them to take action to depose her. While attempts were made later to reduce the impact of the papal Bull and to claim it was not operative in England, a great deal of damage had been done. Subsequent legislation in 1571, 1581, and 1585 made it increasingly difficult to practise the old religion and, among other things, made it treason to deny any of the queen's titles, to reconcile people to Catholicism, or even just to be a priest in England if one had been ordained abroad since 1559, or to shelter or help such a priest. Twenty of the Forty Martyrs suffered under this legislation in Elizabeth's reign; altogether about 190 people suffered martyrdom between 1570 and Elizabeth's death in 1603.

A further reason why the years after 1570 saw a much more active anti-Catholicism lay in the setting-up of colleges on the Continent to provide priests to work in England and Wales. The first of these was established in 1568 by Cardinal Allen at Douai in Flanders. His initial intention was to provide a Catholic education for young men so that they would be better able to defend and speak for the old religion as laypeople. But the college (and others like it founded in Rome, Valladolid, and Seville) became best known for the priests they trained—known as the "seminary priests." The first of these arrived in England in 1574, and there followed a steady stream: by the end of Elizabeth's reign something like eight hundred had been ordained, and about four hundred of these had served at one time or another on what became known as the "English mission." In addition, from 1580, a new source of priests began to appear, the Jesuits. While there were never more than about a dozen of these at any one time in England in Elizabeth's reign, they and the seminary priests put to rest any hopes that the government might have had that Catholicism would simply fade away. One of the first of the Douai priests, Fr Henry Shaw, wrote to Cardinal Allen from England in 1575: "The number of Catholics increases so abundantly on all sides that [Lord Burghley] has privately admitted to one of his friends that for one staunch Catholic at the beginning of the reign, there were now, he knew for certain, ten" (McGrath). Even allowing for exaggeration on both sides, the contribution of the new clergy was beginning to be impressive and was going to be essential to the survival of the old religion.

Most of the seminary priests who suffered martyrdom were condemned under an act of 1585, called "An Act against Jesuits, Seminary Priests and other such like disobedient persons." This ordered any priests who had been ordained abroad after 1559 to leave England and Wales within forty days or to suffer the penalty for high treason. In addition, any person who sheltered or helped such a priest after that period was liable to the death penalty. The act was particularly severe in that the priests did not have to take part in treasonable activities to be condemned; their existence in the country was sufficient to warrant condemnation, even though they were careful not to get involved in politics and avoided any connection with plots against the queen. Of the 146 people put to death for their religion between 1585 and 1603, 123 were condemned under this act.

It is only fair to look at the government's view of the situation as well. No doubt some ministers were motivated by a straightforward hatred of Catholicism and were happy to be able to use any pretext to prevent Catholic priests from strengthening its presence; there was, however, another view as well. While individual priests and the vast majority of Catholics were loyal to the queen, there were those on the Continent who actively plotted against her, including the pope, Philip II of Spain, and a small number of Catholic exiles. We have mentioned already that Pope St Pius V supported the Ridolfi Plot; his successor, Gregory XIII, supported a Spanish expedition which invaded Ireland in 1579, and Sixtus V encouraged Philip II in his plans for the Armada in 1588. Cardinal Allen urged his countrymen to forsake the queen and join up with the Spanish invaders. The Catholic Reformation was on the move in Europe and fighting back, often literally, against Protestantism. The English government was dishonest and unjust in treating the missionary priests as traitors in any ordinary sense of that term, but as McGrath argues, "it is surely unreasonable to expect it to behave as though the activities of the priests could be considered in isolation and without reference to the general political situation . . . there was always the possibility that if an invasion met with initial success, then the priests might be called upon to urge all Catholics to support the invader."

The legislation of Elizabeth's reign remained in force throughout the reigns of her Stuart successors, but active persecution leading to martyrdom became more sporadic. While there were twenty-four executions between 1604 and 1618, there were only two between then and 1641; nine people were martyred in 1642 but only two in the Commonwealth period from 1649 to 1660. Finally, eighteen died for their Catholicism in 1679 and three more in the following year, all because of the Popish Plot, invented maliciously by Titus Oates and the cause of one of those outbursts of national anti-Catholic feeling that were to erupt occasionally in England until well into the nineteenth century. They were the last people to be martyred in England and Wales, with the exception of the Irish bishop, St Oliver Plunket (11 July), executed at Tyburn in 1681. Persecution continued but took the form of extra taxation, exclusion from public office and the universities, and a range of other legal disabilities. The more punitive laws were not always enforced in full, and Catholicism survived sufficiently strongly to form a basis for growth in the late eighteenth century. The Continental colleges continued to send priests to work in England and Wales and to educate the sons of well-to-do Catholics; Douai lasted until the French Revolution forced it to close and transfer its activities to two colleges in England, at Ushaw near Durham and at Ware in Hertfordshire.

Veneration of the martyrs of the Reformation period began early. Pope Gregory XIII (1572-85) allowed those who had already been executed to be depicted in murals on the walls of the English College in Rome, alongside the likes of St Alban and St Thomas of Canterbury, while in 1642 Pope Urban VIII launched an official inquiry with a view to canonizing some of the English and Welsh martyrs. The English Civil War prevented the inquiry from getting anywhere, and nothing more was done officially until 1874, when Cardinal Manning sent a list to Rome of 360 names for possible beatification. By 1895 Pope Leo XIII had confirmed the cult of sixty-three *beati* from the list, and in 1929 a further 136 were beatified. It was from these that the Forty were chosen for canonization in 1970, the criteria being that they should be beatified, well-known, and already the object of devotion on the part of English Catholics. A further eighty-five from Manning's list were beatified in 1987. Devotion to the martyrs increased in popularity in the 1960s and 1970s, and a substantial number of churches and schools were named after them, particularly in the northern dioceses where the recusant traditions had been strongest.

Today that devotion appears to be on the wane, despite the additional beatifications of 1987. This may be due in part to the changes in liturgical outlook and practice that followed Vatican II; it may also be the result of a change in Catholic historical inquiry, which has moved from a concentration on the martyrs to a study of those priests and laypeople who kept Catholicism alive in a less heroic but equally important way, in the face of persecution and persistent discrimination that called for patience and perseverance of a high order. The decline in devotion to the martyrs could also be the result of the welcome growth in ecumenism; if so, this would be a pity, for true ecumenism must recognize the factors that have shaped each of the Christian bodies in the country and be willing to celebrate, as well as to forgive, the past. The comment of the British Council of Churches at the time of the canonization of the Forty in 1970 is relevant here: "The martyr tradition is one in which all have shared and from which all may draw strength, even across ecumenical boundaries." In 1987, when the pope beatified eighty-seven of the martyrs, the archbishop of Canterbury, Dr Runcie, said, "these beatifications will indeed prompt all the Christians of England, Wales and Scotland to pursue the path of reconciliation and reunion with greater understanding and effectiveness. . . . Today we can celebrate their heroic Christian witness and deplore the intolerance of the age which flawed Christian convictions."

The martyr tradition celebrated on this feast-day is a rich one. As well as the heroism of the individuals who accepted death rather than give up their beliefs, it has its stories of chases and narrow escapes, safe houses and priests' hiding holes, Masses celebrated in secret with the ever-present fear of the knock on the door followed by torture and perhaps death; it had its betrayals as well as its intense loyalties. There is also the tradition of the English colleges abroad, kept alive today in Rome and Valladolid. The veneration of Douai itself was a key element in the tradition, the *alma mater* of so many of the martyrs and so important in keeping English Catholicism alive. Its memory was so strong that it coloured the development of seminary training in England long after Catholic Emancipation in 1829 had repealed most of the legal disabilities affecting Catholics. Finally, mention must be made of Tyburn, London's place of execution close by present-day Marble Arch, where nineteen of the Forty died. In 1901 Cardinal Vaughan, himself a member of one of the families that had been part of the recusant tradition, set up a convent nearby to house a group of exiled French nuns, The Adorers of the Sacred Heart of Montmartre. The chapel became a shrine to the martyrs and there was an annual Tyburn Walk to commemorate them and pray for their canonization. The convent was destroyed by bombing in 1944. A public appeal for funds to build a fitting martyrs' memorial as part of the restored convent was launched in 1959, and the present Martyrs' Crypt has become a place of pilgrimage again. The nuns' hidden life of prayer and adoration is a fitting tribute to the essential Catholicism for which the Forty Martyrs died.

R. Challoner, *Memoirs of Missionary Priests* (1741; ed. J. H. Pollen 1924); B. Camm (ed.), *Lives of the English Martyrs*, 1 (1904), vol. 2, ed. E. H. Burton and J. H. Pollen (1914); C. Tigar, *The Forty Martyrs of England and Wales* (1961); P. Caraman, S.J., in *N.C.E.*, 9, pp. 319-32, gives a full chronological list. For the general history, see P. McGrath, *Papists and Puritans Under Elizabeth I* (1967); J. Bossy, *The English Catholic Community 1570-1850* (1975); the annual volumes of the Catholic Record Society contain valuable source material, and the *Recusant History* journal useful articles. On the early years of Douai and the other colleges, P. Hughes, *The Reformation in England*, 3 (1954), ch. 2. See also T. P. Ellis, *The Catholic Martyrs of Wales* (1933); P. Caraman, S.J., *Henry Morse, Priest of the Plague* (1957), and (ed.), *John Gerard, The Autobiography of an Elizabethan* (2d ed., 1956).

SS Crispin and Crispinian, *Martyrs* (*c.* 285)

The names of these two martyrs were famous throughout northern Europe in the Middle Ages, and according to Shakespeare, that of Crispin was invoked by King Henry V before the battle of Agincourt, fought on 25 October. We know very little indeed about them, however, as their late *passio* is wholly unreliable, and even the place of their martyrdom is uncertain. It is most likely that they suffered in Rome during the persecution of the emperor Diocletian (284-305). There is no reason to doubt their existence or martyrdom, which is attested by the *Hieronymianum*.

Legend has it that they were Roman brothers of noble birth, who travelled to Gaul as missionaries. They set themselves up in Soissons and worked as shoemakers to avoid having to rely on alms from their converts. They were successful and won over many by their exemplary lives and teaching. After living and working in this fashion for a number of years they were reported to the authorities for being Christians, tortured, and finally put to death; this was during the reign of the emperor Maximian (285-305). Later a church was built over their tomb at Soissons, which St Gregory of Tours (17 Nov.) mentions several times in his writings, and their shrine was decorated by St Eligius (1 Dec.), who died in 660. The two saints are the patrons of shoemakers and, by extension, all leather workers.

The Roman Martyrology declares that their relics were transferred to the church of St Laurence in Rome, but it seems much more likely that the process was exactly the reverse of this: that is, they were martyred in Rome and their relics transferred later to Soissons, where a local cult grew up as a result and the above legend developed to link them with the area.

There is also a tradition linking them to England. According to this they fled from the persecution in Gaul and took refuge in Faversham in Kent, where they carried on their trade as shoemakers in a house on the site of the Swan Inn at the bottom of Preston Street. A certain Mr Southouse, writing about the year 1670, says that the house was visited by a considerable number of foreigners. There is an altar in their honour in the local parish church.

The previous edition of this work used the example of Crispin and Crispinian to show, rather sententiously it must be said, that a holy life was possible no matter how busy one might have to be in pursuit of one's calling: "opportunities for every kind of good work never fail in any circumstances, and the means of sanctification may be practised in every state of life."

AA.SS., Oct., 11, pp. 495-540; *O.D.S.*, p. 114. See also M. I. Allen in *Anal.Boll.* 108 (1990), pp. 357-86, on a metrical version of their *passio*.

St Gaudentius of Brescia, *Bishop* (*c.* 410)

Gaudentius seems to have been educated under St Philastrius, bishop of Brescia (8 July), and to have gained a considerable reputation while still young. In order to avoid publicity he decided to go on pilgrimage to Jerusalem about the year 386. While he was at Caesarea in Cappadocia he met the aged nieces of St Basil (2 Jan.), who entrusted him with the relics of the Forty Martyrs of Sebaste (whose feast-day was formerly celebrated on 10 Mar.). He continued his journey to Jerusalem, but then St Philastrius died, and the people of Brescia demanded that Gaudentius should become their bishop. He refused at first but was then threatened with excommunication by the other bishops of the region if he did not obey what was obviously a divine call; this threat seems to have been instigated by St Ambrose (7 Dec.). In the end he agreed and was consecrated by St Ambrose, probably in 390; the sermon he preached on the occasion expresses his humility and his feelings of inadequacy at being so young and inexperienced. He appears to have been both a cultured and a very religious person.

In 406 he was chosen by Pope Innocent I and the emperor, Honorius, to lead a deputation to the Eastern Church to defend the cause of St John Chrysostom (13 Sept.), who had been exiled from Constantinople for his attempts at reform. Its members were ill-treated and imprisoned, and efforts were made to bribe them to support the other side. They were eventually sent back to Italy in an unseaworthy ship, with the hope, it seems, that they would be drowned on the way. They survived, and Gaudentius returned to his diocese, where he died about 410. The writer Rufinus called him "the glory of the doctors of the age."

Twenty-one of his sermons, or treatises, as he preferred to call them, have survived and are the main source for what we know about his life and teachings. Ten of them relate to Holy Week and Easter and have many references to the Eucharist. Gaudentius wrote these down only because he was entreated to do so by a leading citizen, Benevolus, who in 404 was too ill to attend the Easter ceremonies. In one of them, preached on Holy Saturday as the neophytes were being baptized, the bishop explained the mysteries that had been kept hidden from them when they were only catechumens; with regard to the Eucharist he says, "The Creator and Lord of Nature, who brings the bread out of the ground, makes also of bread his own body; because he has promised and is able to perform it. And he who made wine out of water, converts wine into his own blood."

Other themes in these writings are the divinity of Christ, the perpetual virginity of Mary, the Church, and the importance of faith. Christians, according to Gaudentius, are called by Christ in baptism and must respond freely by engaging in two battles, an internal one against concupiscence and evil desires and an external one against the world and the devil. They must also live in this world as strangers and pilgrims, holding on to nothing; Gaudentius insists that Christians have to distance themselves from material goods. Finally, he praises those who dedicate their lives to virginity, while also allowing that matrimony is a holy state. His writings were much referred to and very influential.

He built a church at Brescia, which he called the "Assembly of the Saints," and at its opening claimed to have deposited in it relics of the apostles and other martyrs, stating that a mere portion of a martyr's relics had the same efficacy as the whole body would have. "Therefore," he continued, "that we may be helped by the patronage of so many saints, let us come and pray with full confidence and earnestness, that by their intercession we may deserve to obtain everything we ask for, and glorify Christ our Lord, the giver of so much grace." In 1602 Gaudentius' own relics were moved to this church, now called St John's, where they are still venerated.

AA.SS., Oct., 11, pp. 587-604, pieces together details of his life from various sources. The sermons are in *P.L.*, 20, 827-1002. See also *Bibl.SS.*, 6, 47-54, with full bibliography, and *Dict.Sp.*, 5 (1967), 139-43; F. Trisoglio, *San Gaudenzio da Brescia scrittore* (1960); *O.D.C.C.*, pp. 550-1.

Bd Christopher of Romagna (1272)

Christopher was a parish priest who, when he was about forty years old, gave up his work as a secular priest and joined the newly-formed Order of Friars Minor, becoming a personal disciple of St Francis (4 Oct.) himself. He built up a reputation for his work among the lepers and for his austerities. Eventually he was sent into France to preach against the Albigensians and establish Franciscan houses. The first of these was opened at Cahors, in the Guyenne area of southern France; because of this Christopher is sometimes said to be "of Cahors." It was here that he died at a great age (his biographer says he was 100) in 1272, having been successful in establishing the Friars Minor throughout the region.

There is considerable debate about where he worked as a parish priest before becoming a friar. It is usually said that it was in the town of Cesena in the Romagna, but there is no early evidence to support this, and his cult seems to have been introduced there only in the eighteenth century. His relics had been destroyed in

1580 when the Huguenots burned down the monastery in Cahors, and the Bollandists thought there was not enough evidence of a continuing cult to continue to regard him as Blessed; but a process of investigation set up in 1902 resulted in his cult receiving official approval in 1905.

Anal.Eccles., 1905, p. 206, gives the decree of confirmation and some biographical details. See also the Life written shortly after Christopher's death by Bernardo da Bessa, a fellow-member of the house in Cahors, in *Anal. Franc.* 3 (1897), pp. 161–73; *Bibl.SS.*, 3, 366–7.

Bd Thomas of Florence (*c.* 1369-1447)

Tomaso Bellacci was a native of Florence. As a young man he led so wild and dissipated a life that when a friend persuaded him to change his ways and he tried to join a religious Order, there was some reluctance to accept him. He joined a lay Confraternity to begin with and finally was allowed to become a lay brother in the house of the Observant Friars at Fiesole, just outside the city. Here he led a life as edifying as his previous one had been notorious and became master of novices despite remaining a lay brother. He insisted on his charges following the Franciscan Rule in the strictest ways possible and was himself noted for his penances and austerities.

In 1414 a certain Friar John went to Naples to spread the Observant reform in the Franciscan houses there and took Thomas with him as his assistant. He spent six years there, working by word and example to implement the reform, and his efforts were supported by a number of miracles. His reputation was spreading throughout Italy, and he was asked by Pope Martin V to return to Tuscany to work with Bd Antony of Stroncone (7 Feb.) in combatting the Fraticelli, a branch of the Franciscan Order which had been condemned as heretical because of their extreme views on poverty. Thomas founded a number of new houses, and St Bernardino (20 May), the leader of the Observants, gave him full authority over them. His headquarters were at Scarlino, and here he established the custom of the friars' going in procession after the night office to a nearby wood, where each friar had a rough shelter of boughs in which he remained for a time in private prayer.

The Council of Florence in 1439 brought about a short-lived reunion between the Eastern and Western Churches. As a result, Friar Albert of Sarzana was sent as papal legate to the Syrian Jacobites; again Thomas was taken along as assistant even though he was in his seventieth year. Albert commissioned him and three other friars to go to Ethiopia; on the way they were seized by the Turks and ill-treated. Thomas insisted on preaching to his captors and was saved from execution only by the intervention of Pope Eugene IV, who paid the Turks a ransom to release the delegation. Thomas was disappointed to be deprived of martyrdom and set off for Rome to ask permission to work amongst the Turks again. He was taken ill at Rieti and died there on 31 October 1447. He was buried in the church of St Francis, where his relics are still venerated, and a very large number of miracles was reported at his tomb.

There was a movement to have Thomas canonized along with St Bernardino, whose cause was then in progress. As this would have delayed the canonization of the great reformer, it was decided to put off Thomas' until that had been completed. It is said that St John of Capistrano (23 Oct.) went to Thomas' grave and ordered him under obedience to stop working miracles until his master had been made a saint; the miracles ceased for three years. Thomas' cause, however, was never proceeded with, but his cult as a *beatus* was approved in 1771.

AA.SS., Oct., 13, pp. 860-82, prints the second of the three late medieval Lives. See also *Bibl.SS.*, 12, 580-2.

Bd Balthasar of Chiavari (1419-92)

Balthasar Ravaschieri was born at Chiavari on the Gulf of Genoa in the year 1419. He joined the Friars Minor of the Observance, was professed, and then ordained priest; he became a doctor of theology later. He was a friend of St Bernardino of Feltre (28 Sept.) and joined enthusiastically and successfully in his preaching campaigns. He went on to become guardian of the house in Chiavari and provincial of the Genoa province of the Order. Unfortunately, this work was cut short by Balthasar's increasing ill health caused by gout, but this did not stop his pastoral activity altogether. When he was too ill to walk he had himself carried into church so that he could assist at Mass and the divine office, and he developed a special ministry of the confessional; crowds flocked to the town to confess to him and receive spiritual direction. To get some time and peace for his own spiritual needs he used to be carried into the nearby woods, where he stayed for periods of meditation and reading. During one of these periods he had a vision of Our Lady and was said to have been miraculously sheltered from a dangerous fall of snow. Balthasar died on 17 October 1492 at Binasco, between Milan and Pavia; his remains were moved from there to Pavia in 1805. A local cult developed very quickly and has been continuous ever since; it was officially approved in 1930.

We do not know very much about the details of Balthasar's life, but his cult is very well attested. See P. da Carasco, O.F.M., *Il Beato Baldassare Ravaschieri ed il suo cultu* (1908); *A.A.S.* 22 (1930), pp. 171-4; *Bibl.SS.*, 2, 717.

Bd Thaddeus MacCarthy, *Bishop* (*c.* 1455-97)

We know very little of the early life of Thaddeus MacCarthy (Tadhg Machar). He belonged to the royal family of that name in Munster in Ireland; his father was lord of Muskerry, his mother a daughter of FitzMaurice, lord of Kerry. He is said to have begun his ecclesiastical studies with the Friars Minor at Kilcrea and then to have gone abroad; he seems to have been in Rome when Pope Sixtus IV appointed him bishop of the Irish diocese of Ross in 1482, when he was about twenty-seven years old.

He was not left in peace for long. When Henry Tudor became king in 1485 his Yorkist opponents in Ireland tried to ensure their dominance by taking control of as much of the Church as possible. There was already a rival claimant to the diocese of

Ross in the person of Hugh O'Driscoll, who had been auxiliary bishop there before Thaddeus' appointment, and he was now put forward by the Yorkists as the rightful bishop; charges were laid against Thaddeus in Rome that he had obtained the see under false pretences, and in 1488 he was suspended by the pope. Meanwhile he had been forced to leave his diocese when its lands had been seized by his opponents and had taken up residence in a Cistercian abbey given to him *in commendam* by the bishop of Clogher. He decided to go to Rome to plead his case in person; after two years Pope Innocent VIII confirmed Hugh as bishop of Ross but made Thaddeus bishop of the joint diocese of Cork and Cloyne.

When he arrived in his new diocese he found his cathedral closed against him and all the endowments in the hands of his former opponents. Having failed to assert his rights as bishop he set off again to Rome. This time he was fully supported and given papal letters to the powerful earl of Kildare, the lord deputy of Ireland, and to other leading figures, ordering them to assist him in his efforts to gain possession of his diocese. He set off back to Ireland on foot as a simple pilgrim; when he reached Ivrea at the foot of the Alps he stayed at a hospice run by the Canons Regular of St Bernard. He died there peacefully on 24 October 1497. The story of the bishop travelling home incognito as a pilgrim caught the imagination of the local people, and Thaddeus was buried with great solemnity in the cathedral. His tomb became a place of pilgrimage and many miracles were reported. He was never formally beatified, but in the nineteenth century the bishops of Cork and Ivrea co-operated in putting forward his cause in Rome, and his cult was confirmed by Pope Leo XIII in 1895.

The decree confirming the cult is given in *Anal. Eccles.*, 3 (1895), p. 456; it gives little biographical detail, dwelling instead on the miracles said to have been worked at the shrine at Ivrea.

26

St Rusticus of Narbonne, *Bishop* (*c.* 461)

Rusticus was born in southern Gaul, the son of a bishop named Bonosus. He finished his studies in Rome and returned home with the intention of becoming a monk. A long letter by St Jerome (30 Sept.), written about 411, was probably addressed to him under the name of Rusticus of Marsiglia; it gives the recipient wise advice about the solitary life, mixing doctrinal points with practical hints and urging a study of the scriptures and the acceptance of poverty.

About the year 427 Rusticus was made bishop of Narbonne. His diocese was in a very unsatisfactory state due to the invasions of the Goths, who had introduced Arianism; in addition, the orthodox Christians were divided by feuds. These issues seem to have come to a head at a synod held by Rusticus in 458. In the end he was so discouraged by his task that he wrote to Pope St Leo the Great (10 Nov.), setting out his difficulties in the form of questions about discipline, and asking to be allowed to resign. The pope refused, sending him instead an important letter about how he should govern his diocese and appealing to his sense of pastoral responsibility; he should not be frightened by his difficulties, wrote the pope, "since Christ is both our counsel and our strength, without whom we can do nothing, but with whom we can do everything."

Rusticus built a new cathedral in Narbonne to replace an earlier one destroyed by fire; the inscription he erected to mark its foundation is still extant. About ten years later he built a basilica outside the town dedicated to the martyr St Felix of Gerona. We know very little else about him, except that he was held in high esteem by the other bishops in Gaul. A letter from the bishop of Arles, written about the year 452, refers to him as being "one of the most skilful doctors of the Church," because of what he had done to heal its problems. We know he attended the synod at Arles which approved St Leo's "Dogmatic Letter," or "Tome," condemning the Monophysite heresy (the belief that there was only one nature in Christ). He died about 461.

There is an unusual amount of archaeological evidence about Rusticus and his cult. In addition to the foundation inscription already referred to, we have four other inscriptions from Narbonne or the surrounding neighbourhood. The most complete of these tells us not only that his father was a bishop but that a maternal uncle was as well, a man named Arator. Another of the inscriptions carries the words, "*Orate pro me Rustico vestro*" (Pray for me your Rusticus).

We do not have any formal Life of Rusticus, but scattered references have been gathered together in *AA.SS.*, Oct., 11, pp. 860-83. On the inscriptions see Leclercq, *D.A.C.*, 12, 828, 847-54. See also *Bibl.SS.*, 11, 513-4.

St Cedd, *Bishop* (664)

Cedd was a brother of St Chad (2 Mar.) and a monk at Lindisfarne for a number of years. When Peada, king of the Middle Angles, became a Christian in 653, Cedd was one of the four priests sent from Lindisfarne to evangelize his people. After some time, when King Sigebert of the East Saxons also became a Christian, Cedd was sent with another priest into what is now the county of Essex to preach and baptize the people there. The two priests travelled about the area to get an idea of what it and its people were like, and then Cedd returned to Lindisfarne to consult with his former superior, St Finan (17 Feb.). The latter was so impressed by what Cedd had to say that he consecrated him bishop of the East Saxons.

Cedd returned to Essex and continued the work of evangelization. He ordained priests and deacons to help him to teach and baptize the people, and he built a number of churches. He also established two monasteries, later destroyed at the time of the Danish invasions and not rebuilt. One of these was at present-day Bradwell-on-Sea, where the church remains largely intact; the other was at Tilbury, on the Thames. Bede tells us that Cedd established "communities of the servants of Christ and taught them to maintain the discipline of the regular life, so far as these untutored folk were then capable of doing." Bede also tells the story of how the bishop excommunicated one of the nobles because of an illicit marriage and forbade anyone to enter his house. The king disobeyed this prohibition, and Cedd, meeting him coming out of the house, warned: "Since you have refused to avoid the house of a man who is lost and damned, this very house will be the place of your death." Not long afterwards the king was murdered by his own kinsmen.

Cedd made a number of visits to Lindisfarne, and on one of these the king, knowing him to be, in Bede's phrase, "a wise, holy and virtuous man," gave him land to found a monastery in the wilds of North Yorkshire. He consecrated the site by fasting on it for forty days—a Lindisfarne custom, apparently, dating from the time of St Columba (9 June). The monastery, founded in 658, has been identified with Lastingham, also destroyed by the Danish invaders. In 664 Cedd attended the Synod of Whitby and acted as interpreter between the two sides—the Scots/Irish and the so-called Roman party—in their dispute over the fixing of the date of Easter. Cedd himself was in the Celtic tradition but accepted the Roman calendar as a result of the synod—something which an Irish synod had already done several years before. He returned to Lastingham and died there on 26 October 664 from an epidemic which was sweeping the north country at the time. Bede tells us that thirty of Cedd's brethren from Essex, on hearing of his death, travelled north "either, God willing, to live near the body of their Father, or else to die and be laid to rest at his side." They suffered in the same epidemic and died at Lastingham.

Cedd was buried at first in the grounds of the monastery, but his body was later moved to the sanctuary of a stone church dedicated to St Mary. By the eleventh century his relics were being venerated at Lichfield along with those of his brother St Chad. The church at Bradwell-on-Sea is interesting in that it was built on the Roman plan and not the Celtic, despite Cedd's Lindisfarne training.

Almost all we know about St Cedd is to be found in Bede, *H.E.*, bk.3: 22 and 23. See also H. M. and J. Taylor, *Anglo-Saxon Architecture* (1965).

St Eata of Hexham, *Abbot and Bishop* (686)

Eata was one of the twelve English young men whom St Aidan (31 Aug.) chose to train as his fellow workers on his arrival from Iona to start preaching in Northumbria. Eata became abbot of the abbey of Melrose, in present-day southern Scotland, and received the great St Cuthbert (20 Mar.) as a novice there. Bede says that as an abbot he was "the gentlest and simplest" of men. Some years later Alcfrith, sub-king of Deira, gave Eata land at Ripon for a monastery, and he went there with Cuthbert and others to start the foundation. They left, however, rather than accept the Roman method of establishing the date of Easter, an issue which had divided the Irish and English monks for many years, although the Church in Ireland had accepted the Roman practice some years earlier. When the Synod of Whitby in 664 finally decided the question, Eata accepted its findings. A number of monks, led by St Colman (18 Feb.), refused to do so and left Lindisfarne. Eata was then chosen to rule those who remained; it seems that he was recommended by St Colman himself for the post because he had been a personal disciple of St Aidan.

In 678 St Wilfrid (12 Oct.), bishop of Northumbria, was driven from his see and his diocese divided. Eata became bishop of Bernicia in the north; this was further divided in 681, and Eata became bishop of Lindisfarne. He later exchanged this for Hexham so that St Cuthbert could be bishop at Lindisfarne. He worked there as bishop for only about a year before his death from dysentery in 686. He had helped to bring peace to the church in Northumbria through his acceptance of Whitby and of the decisions of St Theodore of Canterbury (19 Sept.). He seems to have been venerated as a saint very soon after he died. He was buried to the south of St Wilfrid's church at Hexham; a chapel was later built over his tomb, but in the eleventh century his remains were moved inside the main church. There is a story in a late Life of the saint that in 1113 the archbishop of York tried to have the relics moved to the minster because he was disappointed that York had no local saint; he was dissuaded when Eata appeared in a vision and belaboured him with his crozier.

AA.SS., Oct., 11, pp. 922-31; Bede, *H.E.*, bk.3, 26, and 4, 12, 26, 28; J. Raine, *S.S.*, 8 (1838), pp. 121-5, and 44 (1864), pp. 211-5; *Bibl.SS.*, 4, 883-4; *O.D.S.*, pp. 142-3.

Bd Damian of Finale Borgo (1484)

Damiano Furcheri was born about the beginning of the fifteenth century at Perti, near Finario (present-day Finale Borgo), not far from Genoa. As a young man he joined the Dominicans and became well known throughout Lombardy and Liguria. Contemporaries speak of him as a cultured and effective preacher, zealous for the conversion of souls. He belonged to the reformed branch of the Order, inspired by the master general, Martial Auribelli, which was particularly active in Lombardy. It met with strong opposition and was eventually disbanded in 1529, but while it was active it was a force for the restoration of religion and reform. For this reason the pope, Pius II, ordered that it be introduced into the convent in Reggio Emilia, and Damian was given the task of carrying this out. It was there that he died in 1484, and his shrine became popular for the miracles attributed to his intercession. His cult was widespread and was officially approved in 1848. Among his writings that have survived are a set of sermons on the seasons of the year and the feasts of the saints, and a book of pious meditations.

AA.SS., Oct., 13, pp. 102-5; *Bibl.SS.*, 5, 1320-1. An article in *Archiv. Fratrum Praed.*, 31 (1961), pp. 213-306, deals with the reform and its history.

Bd Bonaventure of Potenza (1651-1711)

Carlo Antonio Lavagna was born at Potenza in the then kingdom of Naples in 1651; his parents were Lelio Lavagna and Caterina Pica. He joined the Conventual Friars Minor in the town of Nocera, taking the name Bonaventure in religion. He was noted for his exact obedience of the Rule, and there are rather far-fetched accounts of what he is said to have done under obedience; some of these actions were later claimed as miracles. He spent eight years at Amalfi, and these were the most fruitful of his career both in terms of his own spiritual development and in his pastoral work among the local people, including the education of the young. He was proposed as guardian (superior) on a a number of occasions, but his humility made him ask to be excused from any position of authority, and so the only office he was given was that of master of novices. He was especially devoted to the Immaculate Conception of Our Lady and often expressed the wish to have the skill of the medieval theologian, Duns Scotus (8 Nov.), to be able to defend the doctrine against those who questioned it.

Bonaventure died at Ravello on 26 October 1711, with the name of Mary on his lips. He is one of those saints and holy people in the Naples region noted for the fact that their blood liquified after their death. There is a gruesome story of how, long after he had expired, the local vicar general ordered a surgeon to take some blood from Bonaventure's arm; to enable this to be done, the guardian ordered the dead man to raise his arm for the surgeon and, out of obedience, Bonaventure did so. When the story got out it naturally created a sensation and added to the reputation he already had for holiness. It now seems, from the evidence collected and analyzed by the Bollandists, that Bonaventure was probably still alive when the blood was taken by the surgeon. It is worth noting that the town of Ravello, where Bonaventure died, is the place where the annual liquefaction of the blood of St Pantaleon (27 July) can be observed. Bonaventure was formally beatified in 1775.

AA.SS., Oct., 12, pp. 108-69; *Bibl.SS.*, 3, 300-1. A popular account of his life was published at Ravello in 1930 by G. Dal Gal. See also A. Gallo, *Il Martire dell'obbedienza* (1956).

27

SS Frumentius, *Bishop*, and Aedesius (*c.* 380)

Around the year 330 a philosopher named Meropius went on a voyage of discovery to Arabia. He had been entrusted with the education of two young people, Frumentius and Aedesius, from his home town of Tyre in Palestine, and these accompanied him on the journey. On their way home they put in at a port on the Ethiopian coast; a quarrel broke out between the local inhabitants and the ship's crew, and the latter, along with most of the passengers, were killed. Frumentius and Aedesius survived and were taken to the king's court at Aksum, the capital of the region. They entered the royal household, one as a cupbearer and the other as secretary; when the king died they were given their liberty but remained in the capital at the request of the queen regent.

Frumentius seems to have held a position of some importance, and he began using it to increase the Christian presence in the country. He persuaded a number of Christian merchants to settle there and obtained special trading privileges for them and the right for them to worship as Christians. When the new king came of age the two Tyrians left; Aedesius went back to his home in Palestine and was ordained priest, but Frumentius went to Alexandria to report on the progress of Christianity in Ethiopia. He wanted to persuade the bishop, St Athanasius (2 May), to send missionaries to develop what had been started, but Athanasius was so impressed that he made Frumentius himself a bishop and sent him back to continue his missionary work. This was sometime in the mid fourth century, between 340 and 356.

Frumentius, now known in Ethiopia as Bishop Salama ("Bishop of Peace") began a successful preaching campaign in Aksum, making many converts, including two of the royal princes. The Eastern emperor at the time, however, was Constantius (337-61), an Arian. He was strongly opposed to St Athanasius, the great upholder of orthodox teaching about Christ, and so was naturally suspicious of the activities of his protégé Frumentius. He tried to turn the king against the bishop and have the latter deported to Alexandria, where Athanasius had been driven into exile and replaced by an Arian. Frumentius, however, was able to stay and continue his work of converting the country; his preaching was supported by a number of miracles. He died about the year 380. Much of the country had still to be Christianized, but he is regarded as the "Apostle of the Ethiopians." He was given the titles "Abuna," "Our Father," and "Aba salama," "Father of peace"; the primate of the Ethiopian church is still given the title "Abuna."

We know very little about what happened to Aedesius, whose feast-day is also on

27 October, though their cult does not seem to have been a joint one. He supplied the writer Rufinus with a full account of their first stay in Aksum, and this is our main source of information about Frumentius. Perhaps he was given the title of saint simply because of his association with the latter.

AA.SS., Oct., 12, pp. 257-70, gives Rufinus' account as in his *Historia Ecclesiastica*. There is also some inscription evidence, and Athanasius gives us the emperor's letter against Frumentius; see *P.G.*, 25, 656-7. See also *Bibl.SS.*, 5, 1292-4; *O.D.C.C.*, p. 540; *The Coptic Encyclopedia*, 3 (1991), pp. 999-1000, under Salama. The old diocese of Louisiana (erected in 1787) observed the feast of St Frumentius, but the comment in the previous edition of this work that this may have been a "gesture towards the slaves of African origin in America" is surely fanciful.

Bd Contardo Ferrini (1859-1902)

Contardo Ferrini was born in Milan on 4 April 1859. His father, Rinaldo, was a teacher of mathematics and physics who had also graduated in civil engineering and architecture, and it was from him that Contardo inherited an intellectual curiosity and a scientific spirit. His mother, Luigia, appears to have been less than happy with the time her husband and eldest son devoted to study, expecting more help about the house and with the other children from them. Contardo was a precocious child with a deep love of learning and an equally strong religious devotion nourished by prayer and frequent Communion—from the age of fourteen he was a daily communicant. In his teens, however, he experienced the usual adolescent emotional disturbances but was helped through them by a learned priest, Don Adalberto Catena. At the same time he was being introduced to serious scholarship by another priest, Mgr Antonio Ceriani, prefect of the great Ambrosian Library in Milan, who taught him Hebrew so that he could read the Bible in its original languages. Ceriani also advised him not to place too much trust in second-hand information, even from the learned, but to "go directly to the sources of the truth." A third priest also influenced Contardo at this time, Don Antonio Stoppani, a geologist who encouraged in him a lasting love of the natural world as God's creation.

In 1876 Contardo won a scholarship to study law at the Borromeo College in Pavia. Here he pursued his studies with great success and also developed his life of prayer. He was not very popular with most of his fellow-students; they nicknamed him "St Aloysius of the Borromeo" more in derision than respect, and he does seem to have been affected by a certain priggishness at this time. He was throughout his life rather over-sensitive to the views of others and usually rose too readily to the teasing bait. He wanted to set up a society for the students that would be a cross between a learned debating society, a social club, and a religious confraternity; it was established under the patronage of St Severinus Boethius (23 Oct.) just as he was about to leave Pavia, and lasted well into the present century. On the whole, however, his youthful apostolic ideals seem to have borne no discernible fruit, although some lifelong friends who first came to know him in these years spoke in later life of the influence he had had on them. Among these was Count Victor Mapelli, and Contardo's letters to him are one of our primary sources for his life and ideas. From these years also one can date his love of poetry, especially nature poetry, and his interest in walking in the Alps; he was to become a keen and able mountaineer.

He graduated in 1880 with an outstanding thesis on the penal law in the works of Homer and Hesiod and was awarded a bursary to study at the University of Berlin for two years. He was nervous about going to what he regarded as the centre of Protestantism and drew up a spiritual "Programme of Life" to help him face its temptations. When he arrived he was impressed by the keenness of the Catholic students but "nauseated by the sad sight of so corrupt a city." He joined the local conference of the St Vincent de Paul Society and so became involved in social and charitable work; he admired how well this was organized in Berlin and how active Catholics were in social and political movements. He remained active in these areas for the rest of his life and was later to become a city councillor in Milan. But when the time came for him to leave Berlin for Italy, he still had no clear idea of what he should do with his life; he felt no particular vocation to either the priesthood or marriage. Toward the end of 1881 he made a private vow of lifelong celibacy and in practice devoted himself to a life of scholarship and prayer.

In 1883 he was back in Pavia, teaching Roman law at the university. His reputation as a scholar was already established—when he had left Berlin the great historian Mommsen had said that he was taking the primacy in the study of that subject from Germany to Italy. He researched in libraries in Paris, Copenhagen, Rome, and Florence and developed a notable knowledge of languages. He spoke German fluently and knew French, English, Spanish, and Dutch well, along with the ancient languages of Latin, Greek, Hebrew, and Syriac, with a smattering of Coptic and Sanscrit. As a teacher his students found him strict but friendly and encouraging; in private conversation he was witty and never sarcastic at the expense of others. He held a number of chairs before returning to Pavia in 1894 as Professor of Roman Law. His scholarly output was amazing: he published over two hundred articles, several textbooks, and a large number of learned notes, appendices, and other contributions to encyclopedias and editions of ancient texts. He was without doubt the world's leading expert on all aspects of Roman law, with a special interest in its Byzantine aspects. His work, as he used to tell his friends, was his wife, his passion, and he made of it "a hymn of praise to the Lord of all learning."

His spiritual life was based on devotion to the Blessed Sacrament, prayer, and meditation. He joined the Third Order of St Francis and found in the Franciscan way a simple approach to God that appealed to him. He was fond of finding God in the natural world and, despite his own great learning, did not believe that study was necessary to become holy. In his book, *Un po' d'Infinito* (*A Touch of the Infinite*), he set out how modern people can best become intimate with God; in it he wrote, "If any of our great men have known and felt God, ask yourself whether this came to them in the hard study of difficult problems, or not rather in the morning before the altar, or when they watched the last rays of the sun tinting the hills, or as the moon in its rising let its light fall on a statue of the Virgin Mother and a man knelt in sweet and pure prayer." His appreciation of the beauty of creation was very strong, even though the language he used to express it may seem exaggerated to modern ears: "Nature lives by the breath of God's omnipotence, smiles in its joy of him, hides from his wrath—yet greets him, eternally young, with the smile of its own youth. For the spirit of God by which nature lives is a spirit forever young, incessantly renewing itself, happy in its snow and rain and mist, for out of these come birth and life, spring ever renewed and undaunted hope."

As we have seen, he involved himself in social work, and in 1895 he was elected to the city council in Milan. He regretted the papal prohibition on Italian Catholics taking part in national politics, arguing that this abstention from the legislature left it unprotected "from the most deplorable influences." He spoke against the evils of socialism and defended the Christian religion strongly and openly at a time when it was coming under attack; in particular, he spoke out in favour of the indissolubility of Christian marriage and in support of religious education in primary schools. Another of his favoured projects was the establishment of a specifically Catholic university in Italy, to help bring together religion and science; this did not come about until some years after his death, but the University of the Sacred Heart in Milan, which opened in 1920, regarded him as one of its principal founding fathers.

Contardo died of typhoid fever at Suna, on Lake Maggiore, on 17 October 1902; he was only forty-three years of age. He was declared Venerable in 1931 and beatified in 1947; his remains lie in the chapel of the University of the Sacred Heart. Pope Pius XII, on the occasion of the beatification, declared that Contardo had given an emphatic "Yes!" to the possibility of holiness in our times, and held him up as a model of the Catholic layperson. One may, perhaps, be permitted to regret that his cause has not progressed to canonization: what better ideal for present-day Christians than a person who was devoted to his work and recognized as expert at it, who was involved in social work and public service, while all the time focussing his whole life on God?

The standard Life is by Mgr C. Pellegrini, *La vita del prof. Contardo Ferrini* (1928). Bd Contardo's religious writings have been published as *Scritti religiosi*, ed. by C. Pellegrini (1912 and 1926) and Mgr Minoretti (1931 and 1947) . See also G. Anichini, *Un astro di santità e di scienza* (1947); in English, Bede Jarrett, *Contardo Ferrini* (1933); *Vies des Saints*, 10, pp. 587-94, has a full bibliography; *Dict.Sp.*, 5 (1964), 199-200; *Bibl.SS.*, 5, 656-8.

ST JUDE
Gold ship, silver sail, on red field.

ST SIMON
Gold book, silver fish, on red field.

28

SS SIMON AND JUDE, *Apostles* (First Century)

These two apostles have traditionally been venerated together in the Western Church, but in the East they have had separate feast-days. We know nothing for certain about either of them after they disappear from the pages of the New Testament, and even there their presence is little more than just mentioned. Simon is sur-named "the Canaanite" by Matthew and Mark, and "the Zealot" by Luke. Both terms represent the same Aramaic word and may mean that he was a member of the Zealots, a fanatical Jewish sect which was later responsible for the revolt against the Romans that eventually led to the destruction of Jerusalem, or just that he was zealous by nature or in his religious adherence. He is also called "Simon the Less," to distinguish him from Simon Peter.

Jude is referred to as "Judas of James" by Luke (6:16; Acts 1:13) and as "Judas not Iscariot" by John (14:22). He is normally identified with the Thaddeus men-tioned in the lists of apostles given by Matthew (10:3) and Mark (3:18). The phrase "Judas of James" would normally mean that he was the son of James, but he has also been taken to be his brother, in line with the opening of the Epistle of Jude, where the author identifies himself as "the brother of James" (but see what is said below about this Epistle and its authorship). In the discourse after the Last Supper when Jesus promised to manifest himself to his followers, Jude asked why he would not show himself to the whole world; Jesus replied that he and the Father would visit all those who love him (John 14:22-3).

Both apostles disappear from the New Testament after Pentecost. There are various traditions about them, but these cannot be reconciled with each other and have to be treated with great caution. The Eastern Menology of St Basil says that Simon died in peace at Edessa, but the Western tradition is that, after preaching in Egypt, he joined Jude, who had been working in Mesopotamia, and together they went to Persia, where they were martyred on the same day. This second tradition dates from the sixth century, but the veneration of the two apostles together is older than that. Their relics were said to have been transferred to St Peter's, Rome, in the seventh or eighth century, but both Reims and Toulouse in France claim to have substantial parts of them. There are a few ancient church dedications to their joint names in England. In art Simon is normally depicted holding a fish, perhaps because he was presumed to be a fisherman; Jude usually holds a club, presumably the instrument of his death, or sometimes a ship, again, perhaps, linking him with the fishermen of the Sea of Galilee.

The historian Eusebius (*c.* 275-340) tells a story about two grandsons of Jude,

Zoker and James, who were brought before the emperor Domitian (81-96) to be interrogated, because he had heard that they claimed to be of the royal house of David. When he saw that they were poor peasants, interested in a kingdom "not of this world," he dismissed them with contempt.

Jude is probably best known nowadays as the saint to pray to in hopeless or desperate cases. The origin of this rather peculiar but popular practice is not known and does not relate to anything in the various traditions about the saint. It may be that no one wanted to pray to him in normal circumstances because his name was the same as that of Judas Iscariot; only when every other saint had proved unable to help would desperate Christians turn to Jude.

As has been said above, the author of the Epistle of Jude calls himself the "brother of James" and has traditionally been assumed to be St Jude the apostle. Most scholars now regard this as unlikely, since the author refers to the apostolic times as being in the past (verse 17) and seems to separate himself from the apostles; it would have helped his case greatly if he had been able to claim direct apostolic authority, since he was concerned to attack the teachers of false doctrines who were putting the faith of Christians at risk and causing immorality. The Epistle may have been written about 70-80 A.D. or as late as the 90s. It has affinities with the second letter of St Peter in its use of Jewish myths. Since it was not directed at any particular church or group of Christians, it is known as one of the Catholic Epistles.

Both saints have been featured frequently in art. Mention may be made here of the mosaics of St Jude in St Mark's, Venice, and the separate paintings of them by Rubens in the Prado, Madrid.

AA.SS., Oct., 12, pp. 421-36; *O.D.C.C.*, pp. 764, 1276-7; *Bibl.SS.*, 11, 1169-74, on Simon, and 7, 1152-7, on Jude; *O.D.S.*, pp. 271, 437-8. See also J. H. Neyrey, S.J., "The Epistle of Jude," in *N.J.B.C.*, 59.

St Fidelis of Como, *Martyr* (? 303)

The cult of Fidelis at Como in northern Italy is an ancient one, and a tomb said to be that of the martyr was known to St Ennodius (17 July), writing in the early sixth century. There were reports of miracles at the tomb, and sometime before the year 1000 a very fine church was built on the site of a much earlier simple chapel, which dated, perhaps, from the fourth century; the church is known as Sanfedelino. There are several references to the martyr from the early ninth century onward. We know nothing for certain, however, about the person of the martyr or how he died.

There are two legends: one says he was one of three Christian soldiers (the others were Carpophorus and Exanthus) in the Roman army who tried to escape from the persecution of Maximian by deserting from duty; they got as far as Como, where they were caught and executed. The other legend says Fidelis was an army officer who looked after some Christian prisoners in Milan during the same persecution. He was able to procure the freedom of five of them, and with two more soldiers, Carpophorus and Exanthus, they tried to make their way to the Alps for safety. All but Fidelis were caught and executed on the spot, near Como; he was caught on the other side of the lake, scourged, and beheaded.

There is considerable controversy between Milan and Como over the ownership of the martyr's relics. The claims of Como rest principally on a reasonably trust-worthy account of a translation of the relics from the spot where Fidelis was murdered to Como in 964; those of Milan on a supposed earlier translation from Como to Arona, whence they were moved by St Charles Borromeo (4 Nov.). There is no historical evidence, however, to support this earlier translation. Both places have churches dedicated to St Fidelis where he is still venerated.

AA.SS., Oct., 12, pp. 543-69; *Bibl.SS.*, 5, 517-521, with a full bibliography.

St Faro of Meaux, *Bishop (c. 672)*

We know very little about the early life of Faro except that he was the brother of St Chainoaldus (6 Sept.), bishop of Laon in France, and of St Burgundofara or Fare (3 Apr.), first abbess of Faremoutier. He spent some of his youth at the court of King Theodebert II of Austrasia (the Frankish kingdom which embraced eastern France and much of western Germany). He married Blidechild and went to work at the court of Clotaire II, king of the other Frankish kingdom, Neustria. We are told that, while there, Faro intervened successfully to save the lives of some Saxon diplomats whom the king had sentenced to death for their insolence. He also developed something of a reputation for holiness, and at the age of thirty-five decided to become a cleric, if his wife would agree. Blidechild was apparently of the same mind, and retired to her estates; Faro later wanted to return to her, but she persuaded him to persevere in his new vocation. She died some years later.

Eventually Faro received the tonsure and, when the see of Meaux became vacant about the year 628, was chosen as its bishop. He also became chancellor to the new king, Dagobert, and used his influence to protect the poor and innocent in the almost constant warfare the king waged. He was noted for his zeal for souls, work-ing hard to convert those who had not yet become Christians. He also had a reputation as a miracle-worker; on one occasion he is said to have cured a blind man by conferring on him the sacrament of Confirmation. Shortly after he became bishop he was visited by St Fiacre (1 Sept.), the Irish monk who became famous as a hermit in that part of France; it was Faro who gave him the land at Breuil for a hermitage. He also founded a monastery in the suburbs of Meaux, which he dedi-cated to the Holy Cross and in which he settled some of the monks who had had to leave Luxeuil with St Columban (21 Nov.).

His was a long episcopate; we have his name on a number of charters from the 660s, and according to Bede, in 668 he gave hospitality to St Theodore (19 Sept.), archbishop of Canterbury, and to St Adrian (9 Jan.), later abbot of St Augustine's, Canterbury, as they made their way from Rome to England. Faro died about 672. The previous edition of this work claimed that his reputation for sanctity was so great that he was the most illustrious of the bishops of Meaux mentioned in the calendars of the Church.

AA.SS., Oct., 12, pp. 593-623, gives a Life by a later bishop of Meaux, written about two centuries after Faro's death and of limited historical value; see also *M.G.H.*, *Scriptores rerum Merov.*, 5, pp. 171-206; *Vies des Saints*, 10, pp. 941-5; H. M. Delsart, *Saint Fare* (1911).

ST COLMAN OF KILMACDUAGH (p. 200)
The legend of the cock, the mouse and the fly.
Wood engraving by Robert Gibbings,
from Beasts and Saints *(1934, 1995).*

29

St Evaristus, *Pope* (*c.* 105)

We know very little about Pope Evaristus except that he succeeded St Clement (23 Nov.), in the reign of the emperor Trajan, and so was the fourth successor of St Peter. There are ancient sources which make two popes of Cletus and Anacletus, and this would make Evaristus the sixth pope. He reigned for eight or nine years. The *Liber Pontificalis* says he was the son of a Hellenic Jew from Bethlehem and that he was responsible for dividing Rome into districts or parishes, assigning a priest to look after each one. This must be incorrect, however, as his reign was far too early in the history of the Church for such organization to have taken place. He is also reputed to have appointed seven deacons to look after the city. He has been given the title "martyr," but we have no knowledge of how he died. He may have been buried on the Vatican hill near the tomb of St Peter. His feast-day was formerly 26 October. He is featured in the Sistine Chapel.

AA.SS., Oct., 11, pp. 799-804; *Bibl.SS.*, 5, 372-3; *Catholicisme*, 4, 772.

St Narcissus of Jerusalem, *Bishop* (*c.* 215)

Narcissus was already a very old man when he became bishop of Jerusalem about the year 190. Eusebius devotes a whole chapter to telling us about the miracles for which he was remembered, one of which was turning water into oil for the church lamps on Holy Saturday when the deacons had forgotten to provide any. He attended a council held in Palestine to decide the question of the proper way to decide on the date of Easter. Despite his reputation for holiness, he was attacked maliciously by some people who objected to the rigour with which he imposed church discipline. Eusebius does not tell us what crime they accused him of, just saying it was a "horrendous calumny"; despite their oaths the charge was not believed, but Narcissus took advantage of the incident to retire to lead a life of solitude, something he had apparently always been attracted to.

Several bishops in succession were appointed in his place, as his retreat could not be found and many assumed he had died. When he eventually reappeared, he was persuaded against his will to resume the administration of the diocese. To help him in his advanced old age St Alexander (18 Mar.) was moved from his diocese in Cappadocia to become coadjutor bishop in Jerusalem—the first recorded instance of a bishop being translated from a diocese and of the idea of a coadjutor bishop. In a letter Alexander wrote soon after 212 he refers to Narcissus as still alive at the age of 116. We have no details of his death.

AA.SS., Oct., 12, pp. 782-90, brings together from Eusebius and other sources all we know, or are likely to know, about Narcissus. See also *Bibl.SS.*, 9, 719-21.

St Theuderius, *Abbot* (*c.* 575)

Theuderius was born at Arcisse near Vienne, in south-eastern France; his name is also given as Chef and features in the modern version of the name of his native town, Saint-Chef-d'Arcisse. He became a monk at the monastery of Lérins but was then ordained priest by St Caesarius (27 Aug.) at Arles. He returned to his native country and built a hermitage dedicated to St Eusebius of Vercelli (2 Aug.); then he built a basilica in honour of St Symphorian (22 Aug.) near the city of Vienne and handed it over to a group of monks. When he was joined by his brother and other disciples, he built a new monastery for them, dedicated this time to St Peter. Finally he settled near his home town of Arcisse, built a church in honour of Our Lady, Mother of God, and set up a small monastery to serve it, where he lived for a time.

Not long afterwards, he was called to Vienne and appointed as priest-penitentiary; he led an austere life in a cell attached to the church of St Laurence, receiving a large number of people at its grille and giving them advice and absolution. The priest or monk who carried out this role was regarded as the surrogate of the people of the area: his prayers and fasting were intended to gain God's forgiveness for their sins and to make up for any deficiencies in their own penances. Theuderius was reputed to have worked many miracles by the time of his death about 575. He was buried in the church of Our Lady, which he had built.

AA.SS., Oct., 12, pp. 832-43; B. Krusch, *M.G.H., Scriptores rerum merov.*, 3, pp. 526-30, edits a late, ninth-century Life. See also *Bibl.SS.*, 12, 442-3.

St Colman of Kilmacduagh, *Bishop* (*c.* 550-632)

Colman was born at Corker in Kiltartan about the middle of the sixth century. He lived as a hermit on the island of Aranmore for a time and then, in search of greater solitude, moved to Burren among the mountains of County Clare. He is said to have hidden himself away because he had been made a bishop against his will. He had just one disciple with him, and they lived for many years on a simple diet of vegetables and water. After this he founded a monastery at a place subsequently called Kilmacduagh after him (the cell or chapel of the son of Dui) and became its first bishop—in the early Celtic church bishops were attached to monastic settlements and not to dioceses. The land for the monastery had been given to him by one of his relations, King Guaire of Connacht. Colman was reputed to have a special relationship with wild animals, the result, perhaps, of his long years in the countryside of County Clare, and a characteristic noted of a number of Irish monks. According to legend, a cock woke him up for the night office, a mouse made sure he did not go back to sleep after it, and a fly marked the line on the page while he was reading. He died about the year 632. The National Museum of Ireland in

Dublin has part of his crozier. In the Irish martyrology of Tallaght he is one of twelve saints with the name Colman listed for the month of October.

AA.SS., Oct., 12, pp. 880-92; *O.D.S.*, p. 106; *Bibl.SS.*, 4, 92-3.

St Abraham of Rostov, *Abbot* (Twelfth Century)

Abraham was born of non-Christian parents near Galich in the south-west part of the Ukraine, sometime early in the twelfth century. As a young man he suffered from a chronic disease but was cured when, in desperation, he called on the God of the Christians for help. He was baptized and left home to become a monk. He received a divine call to go to Rostov to spread the gospel to the many people who were still pagan, and he worked with great zeal for many years among them. He built two churches for the converts he made—the first was dedicated to St John the Evangelist, who had appeared to him in a vision; the second was dedicated to the Epiphany and built on the spot where a famous pagan idol had stood. Near this second church he established a monastery and became its first abbot, while at the same time continuing his preaching and missionary work in the area.

We do not know when Abraham died, but he was the object of popular veneration before the end of the twelfth century. His relics are venerated in the church of the Epiphany in Rostov. The previous edition of this work said he was a "very uncertain figure"; it seems he was sometimes placed much earlier, in the tenth or eleventh century, and known as "the apostle of Rostov." The story of his life and work as a missionary is clear enough, however, and without the usual embellishments of fabricated accounts; we can at least admire his zealous dedication to the spreading of the gospel.

AA.SS., Oct., 11, p. 265 ; *Bibl.SS.*, 1, 119.

St Merewenna, *Abbess* (Tenth Century)

When King Edgar (959-75), a keen supporter of ecclesiastical reform, refounded the convent at Romsey in Hampshire, Merewenna, or Merwenna, became its abbess. We know nothing about her prior to this appointment, which was probably made by the king himself. It was an age of monastic revival, and the house prospered and attracted a number of noblewomen and princesses to become members of its community. One of Merewenna's better-known disciples was St Ethelfleda (23 Oct.), who later became abbess of Romsey herself; one account says she was the daughter of Count Ethelwold, who had founded the abbey in the first place, but this would seem to make her far too old. The two saints were buried side by side in the abbey church. Merewenna's original feast-day was 10 February, while Ethelfleda's was 23 October; their joint feast-day on 29 October probably marks the translation of the two bodies to a new resting place, which may have taken place about the year 1000. The cult of the two saints is well attested for the south of England at the beginning of the eleventh century.

AA.SS., Oct., 12, p. 918; Stanton, p. 209; *Bibl.SS.*, 4, pp. 1019-20, under Elfleda.

30

St Serapion of Antioch, *Bishop* (211)

Serapion became bishop of Antioch in 199; one account says he was consecrated by Pope Zephyrinus, but the dates do not tally and this is now thought to be unlikely. We know very little about him, despite the fact that he was said by some to have been one of the most important theologians of the day, and the Roman Martyrology claimed he was famous for his learning. It could be, however, that these attributes originated in the ninth-century martyrology of the monk Ado, which has to be treated with great care. Eusebius (*c.* 275-340) mentions Serapion several times in his *Ecclesiastical History* and does refer to his literary activity; he gives an extract from one of his letters condemning Montanism, an apocalyptic movement of the second century which preached the imminent coming of the Paraclete and the heavenly Jerusalem. Serapion also wrote a work against a certain Domninus, who had apostatized under persecution. But most of his writings are known only through a few fragments.

While he was bishop of Antioch there was a controversy over the use in church of the so-called Gospel of Peter, an apocryphal work which had its origins in Docetism, which taught that Christ only seemed to suffer and die. At first Serapion allowed the reading of this work in the church at Rhossos in Cilicia, apparently thinking it was orthodox; when he had read it himself, however, he wrote forbidding its use on the grounds that he found in it "some additions to the true teaching of the Saviour." He added that he would soon be visiting them to expound the true faith they were to believe.

Rather surprisingly, there was no general cult of Serapion in the Eastern Church, though there is mention in the Syriac martyrology of "Serapion, bishop of Antioch, martyr," under 14 May; there is no evidence at all that he was martyred. Equally surprisingly, according to the previous edition of this work, his feast was celebrated by the Carmelites on the grounds that he had been a member of their Order.

AA.SS., Oct. 13, pp. 248-52; *Bibl.SS.*, 11, 856-7; *O.D.C.C.*, p. 1261.

St Germanus of Capua, *Bishop* (*c.* 540)

We first hear of Germanus as one of the legates sent by Pope St Hormisdas (6 Aug.) in 519 to try to settle the Acacian Schism. This had divided the Church for thirty-five years and had begun with the formulation of a doctrinal statement which itself had sought to heal a schism over the question of the human and divine natures of Christ. This doctrinal formula had become known as the *Henoticon* and had been the work in part of Acacius, the patriarch of Constantinople in 482. The delegation was successful, and the Eastern bishops accepted the "Formula of Hormisdas" as the orthodox view. The details of the mission and the negotiations are well documented, but doubts exist about whether the Germanus involved in them was the same person as the Germanus venerated in today's feast. The *Liber Pontificalis* tells us about the former without linking him to Capua; it was Cardinal Baronius in the sixteenth century who seems to have been the first to say definitely that they were the same person.

According to a ninth-century Life, Germanus came from a wealthy family, and on his father's death sold all his property and gave the proceeds to the poor. He became bishop of Capua about the year 520. He was a personal friend of St Benedict (11 July), who was said by St Gregory the Great (3 Sept.) to have seen the soul of Germanus being carried up to heaven by angels. The *Dialogues* of St Gregory is the main source of our knowledge about Germanus. It includes an unlikely story of how he freed a Roman deacon from purgatory by his prayers when the deacon appeared to him in the guise of an attendant at the hot springs where the bishop had been sent for his health; St Gregory says he had the story on the authority of "his elders." Germanus died about the year 540 and was buried in the old city of Capua. Louis II removed the body and gave it to the town below Monte Cassino; the shrine and relics were completely destroyed in the bombardment of 1944.

AA.SS., Oct., 13, pp. 363-6, prints an eleventh-century Life from Monte Cassino. See also *Bibl.SS.*, 6, 237-9. On Hormisdas and the schism, see *O.D.C.C.*, pp. 8, 632, 666.

St Ethelnoth of Canterbury, *Bishop* (1038)

Etholnoth, or Aethelnoth, was the son of a thegn called Ethelmaer, the founder of the monastery of Cerne Abbas in Dorset, where Ethelnoth was probably a pupil of Aelfric. He later became a monk at Glastonbury and then dean of Christ Church, Canterbury. King Cnut (1016-35) followed a policy of appointing monks as bishops whenever possible, and in 1020 Ethelnoth succeeded Lyfing as archbishop of Canterbury, one of the very few occasions when a member of the chapter was chosen as archbishop. Two years later he went to Rome to receive the *pallium* (the special papal insignia granted to archbishops as a sign of favour and a symbol of delegated jurisdiction) from Pope Benedict VIII, who is said to have received him with great honour and praise. The *Anglo-Saxon Chronicle* gives a description of the ceremony in Rome: first of all the pope laid his own *pallium* on the archbishop's shoulders; the archbishop then celebrated Mass and afterwards lunched with the pope. Later he took a second *pallium* from St Peter's altar and took it back to England with him. He had probably already submitted the profession of faith required from those seeking the *pallium*. English bishops accepted that the possession of the *pallium* gave a bishop metropolitan jurisdiction, allowing him to govern a whole province and consecrate other diocesan bishops.

Ethelnoth was close to the king and won praise from chroniclers of the time for the way he guided him; it was probably when he went to Rome that he took a gift of money from the king to help toward the rebuilding of the cathedral at Chartres, which had been burned down in 1020. On another occasion he is reported to have rebuked Cnut for expressing doubt and for profanity in public. He persuaded the king to make some important donations to his former monastery at Glastonbury. The two also took part in some holy body-snatching, a disreputable but common enough practice at the time to enable churches and monasteries to build up their collections of important relics. In 1023 the archbishop, with the full approval of the king, removed the body of St Alphege, or Aelfheah (19 Apr.), from St Paul's in London, while members of the royal bodyguard stood at strategic points along the route to prevent a counter-attack from the outraged citizens of London. The tomb was broken into by two monks from Canterbury, who used an iron candlestick as a crowbar; the body was then carried on a plank covered by a cloth stolen from the high altar. It was taken across the river in a royal barge and on to its new resting place, while the guards lined up near Woolwich to cover the retreat. The story comes from Godric, one of the two monks involved, and includes a dramatic account of how the king rushed half-dressed from his bath to help in the raid. The king was persuaded by Ethelnoth to pay for an elaborate shrine to be erected at Canterbury to St Alphege, who had been martyred by soldiers belonging to Cnut's father.

We know very little about Ethelnoth's rule as archbishop. He seems to have been well regarded as an experienced ruler and to have tried to implement the general reforms of the tenth century; he and his immediate predecessors "kept Canterbury at least respectable" (Barlow), in marked distinction from some of those who succeeded him. He died on 30 October 1038. There is no evidence of a cult at Canterbury, and the previous edition of this work said he was "one of those Anglo-Saxon ecclesiastics whose claim to saintship is very contestable."

AA.SS., Oct., 13, pp. 451-6, under "Aedelnodus"; *Bibl.SS.*, 5, 123; *O.D.S.*, p. 166. See also F. Barlow, *The English Church 1000-1066* (1963), for excellent coverage of the context, and especially pp. 72, 176, 209, 298.

Bd Benvenuta of Cividale (1254-92)

Benvenuta Boiani was born in 1254 at Cividale in Friuli, the youngest of seven daughters of Corrado and Albertina da Buttinico, a well-to-do couple with noble connections. It is said that her name came from her father, who had been hoping for a son; when he was told he had another daughter he said, "She is welcome (*benvenuta*) all the same!" Her devotion to Our Lady was noticeable from an early age, and she would repeat the short form of the "Hail Mary" (what is today the first half) many times during the day. Her family seems to have been a very religious one; it supported her in her devotions and in her decision to take a vow of lifelong chastity. She joined the Third Order of St Dominic. She seems to have lived most of her life at home.

She was drawn much more to a contemplative than to an active spiritual life. She inflicted severe austerities on herself, sometimes using the discipline three times a night. When she was still young she tied a rope around her waist so tightly that as she grew up it bit into her flesh and caused a great deal of pain. It seemed that an operation would be required to remove it, but she asked God for his help and the rope was reported to have fallen unbroken from her body. Her confessor ordered her to mitigate her austerities and not to practise any new ones without his permission. For five years she suffered from asthma and was almost completely paralyzed so that she was hardly able to leave her room; during this time she was tempted to despair, mainly, it seems, because she could not attend Mass or join in singing the "Salve Regina" at Compline. She was suddenly cured on the feast of the Annunciation after making a vow to visit the shrine of St Dominic at Bologna if she recovered.

Benvenuta frequently experienced visions and fell into raptures at prayer. She was generally a model of cheerfulness and trust in God but was again seriously tempted to despair as she was dying. In the end she died peacefully on 30 October 1292. She was buried in the church of St Dominic, but her exact burial place could not be found when searches were made in the fifteenth century; the church was demolished in 1807. Miracles were soon attributed to her intercession, and a popular cult developed quickly; it was approved in 1765. It has been said that her life "was a poem of praise to Our Lady, a hymn of light, purity and joy, which was lived rather than sung in her honour."

AA.SS., Oct., 13, pp. 145-85, under 29 Oct., gives a Life written shortly after her death. See also J. Procter (ed.), *Short Lives of the Dominican Saints* (1901), pp. 302-6; *Bibl.SS.* 3, 230-1.

Bd John Slade, *Martyr* (1583)

Little is known about the early life of John Slade, one of the English martyrs beatified in 1929. Challoner, in his *Memoirs of Missionary Priests*, says that he was born in Dorset, and this has generally been accepted; Caraman, however, says that he was born in Milton, Hampshire. He studied at New College, Oxford, and then became a school teacher. He was open in his support for the old religion and was arrested on a charge of denying the royal supremacy; he was brought to trial at Winchester in April 1583, along with Bd John Bodey (2 Nov.). They were both found guilty and condemned to be hanged, drawn, and quartered. For some reason there was a retrial at Andover four months later—Cardinal Allen claimed that this was because the prosecutors realized that the first sentence had been unjust and illegal. Whatever the truth of this, the same verdict was brought in, and the sentence was carried out on John Slade at Winchester on 30 October 1583.

M.M.P., pp. 83-5; *L.E.M.*, 1, pp. 1-7; P. Caraman, S.J., *N.C.E.*, 9, p. 324.

St Alphonsus Rodríguez (*c.* 1533-1617)

Alfonso was the third child of Diego Rodríguez, a well-to-do wool merchant in Segovia, Spain. When he was about ten years old, Bd Peter Favre (1 Aug.) and another Jesuit stayed at his father's house while they were preaching a mission in the city, and it was Peter Favre who prepared the boy for his First Communion. A few years after this Alphonsus and an older brother were sent to be educated by the Jesuits at Alcalá, but their father died before they had been there a year, and it was decided that Alphonsus should return to Segovia to help his mother run the family business. When he was twenty-three, his mother retired and left him in sole charge; three years later he married María Suarez.

The business was not a success, either because of Alphonsus' lack of skill or, more probably, because it was a bad time for the textile business in Spain. Then, within a space of three years, his young daughter, wife, and mother all died, and he began to think about what God wanted from him; he was already devout and honest, but perhaps he should be something more. He sold the business and retired with his young son to live with his two unmarried sisters, who taught him more systematic ways of prayer and introduced him to the practice of daily meditation. He began to go to Confession and Communion every week and lived a life of considerable austerity. When his son died some years later, he decided to join the Jesuits and applied to be admitted to their house in Segovia. They rejected him, partly because of his age (he was nearly forty) and partly because he lacked sufficient education. A friend advised him to learn Latin, and so, like St Ignatius Loyola himself, he went to school—and met with similar derision and humiliation. He toyed with the idea of becoming a hermit but decided this was a temptation to give up his true vocation, and so he tried the Jesuits again. The provincial overruled his advisors and admitted Alphonsus as a temporal coadjutor, or lay brother, in 1571. After six months he was sent to work at the College of Montesión in Majorca, where he became door keeper. He stayed there until his death forty-five years later.

Alphonsus spent whatever time he had free from his duties in prayer and achieved an almost habitual recollection and union with God. His spiritual life was not easy, however, as he suffered long periods of desolation and dryness and was beset by violent temptations; the greater the austerities he practised, the more severe seemed to be the temptations. Throughout these difficult periods he adhered to a regular programme of prayer and spiritual exercises, trusting that eventually God would reward his constancy with some spiritual comfort and consolation. He was allowed to take his final vows in 1585, at the age of fifty-four. His life of prayer and self-sacrifice became so well known that he was used as a spiritual counsellor by priests and laypeople; among those he advised was St Peter Claver (9 Sept.), who was a student at the college and came under Alfonso's direction for three years. It was at least partly due to Alphonsus that St Peter undertook his work in the Americas and became known as the "apostle of the Negroes."

Alphonsus had a deep devotion to the Immaculate Conception and was thought for a long time to have composed the Little Office of the Immaculate Conception. It is true that he did all he could to popularize the office, but he was not its author. He was also thought to have been the author of a well-known spiritual treatise, *The Practice of Perfection and Christian Virtues*, but this had been written by another Jesuit of the same name. He did leave a few spiritual writings, which are full of simple but solid spiritual advice and exhortation and which tell us a good deal about his own spiritual progress.

Toward the end of his life he suffered from ill health and considerable physical pain. By October 1617 he felt he had not long to live, and after receiving Communion on the 29th he was at peace in mind and body. Just after midnight on the 31st, after a brief agony, he kissed the crucifix, uttered the Holy Name in a loud voice, and died. His funeral was attended by the poor and the great, and his reputation for sanctity was such that in 1633 he was declared patron of Majorca. He was canonized in 1888 in the same ceremony as St Peter Claver.

Alphonsus led a life of intense prayer and humdrum activity. Gerard Manley Hopkins caught its spirit in a poem about the saint; after describing the outward heroism of the martyrs, he talks of the hidden war which saints must wage within themselves, and ends:

> Yet God (that hews mountain and continent,
> Earth, all, out; who, with trickling increment,
> Veins violets and tall trees makes more and more)
> Could crowd career with conquest while there went
> Those years and years by without event
> That in Majorca Alfonso watched the door.

AA.SS., Oct., 13, pp. 585-657; J. Nonell, *Obras espirituales del beato Alfonso Rodríguez* (1885-7); *Dict.Sp.*, 1, pp. 512-5. See also M. Farnum, *The Wool Merchant of Segovia* (1945); W. Yeomans (trans.), *Autobiography of Alphonsus Rodriguez* (1964); *Bibl.SS.*, 1, 861-3. Hopkins extract from W. H. Gardner, *Gerard Manley Hopkins, Poems and Prose* (1963), p. 67.

Bd Angelo of Acri (1669-1739)

Angelo was born at Acri in southern Italy in 1669. When he was eighteen he thought he might have a vocation to the religious life, and so he offered himself to the Capuchins as a postulant. He found the rigours of their way of life too much to bear and so left to return to the world. He was still not sure, however, that he did not have a religious vocation, and so he asked to re-enter the Order and after a time was allowed to do so. Again he found the life too hard, and again he left. He was advised by an uncle who was a priest that it was obvious that God did not want him to be a religious and was telling him to take up some secular occupation and marry. Angelo was still unconvinced, and in 1690 he made a third attempt to join the Capuchins. We can only assume that the superiors saw something worthwhile in him and were impressed by his perseverance, for they readmitted him. After what the previous edition of this work described as a "rather stormy novitiate," he was professed and began his studies for the priesthood.

He was treated severely by his superiors, who thought he needed strict discipline, and was also subject to strong temptations against chastity. He persevered, however, and was ordained; it is said that during his first Mass he was rapt in ecstasy. In 1702 he was sent to preach the Lenten series of sermons at San Giorgio. He had prepared with great care, but when he got up in the pulpit his confidence and memory failed him to such an extent that he returned to his friary before Lent was over. He was praying about this failure and asking for guidance when he heard a voice reassuring him that he would be able to preach. On asking who was speaking, the voice continued, "I am who I am. For the future preach simply and colloquially, so that all may understand you." Angelo accepted the advice: he put aside the books of oratory which he had used to prepare his Lenten sermons, forgot about the flowery speech and flights of fancy which marked, and marred, so much early eighteenth-century preaching, and from then on used only the Bible and his crucifix as his aids.

His new approach was immediately successful with the ordinary people but was ridiculed and scorned by the more refined, who looked down on the simple phrases and familiarity of his style. In 1711 he was invited by Cardinal Pignatelli to give the Lenten sermons in Naples. His first sermon provoked mirth among the gentry, and the church was almost deserted for his second and third attempts. The cardinal insisted that he should continue the course, despite the pleas of the parish priest that he be replaced by someone more suited to the tastes of the congregation. This support caused the congregation to return, perhaps out of curiosity about what the cardinal could possibly see in him. At the end of his next sermon Angelo asked them to pray for someone in the church who was about to die; as they left the church a well-known lawyer, who had led the opposition to Angelo, collapsed and died from a stroke. This, and other later remarkable happenings, made Angelo's reputation; the church was not large enough to hold all who came to hear him.

For the next twenty-eight years Angelo worked as a missionary preacher throughout the kingdom of Naples, and especially in the poorer regions of his native Calabria. He was extremely successful, bringing thousands to the sacraments and revitalizing the religious life of the area. He cured many sick people, and miracles of various sorts were attributed to him, including bilocation. He could read people's minds and on a number of occasions foretold the future in accurate detail. He continued his work until six months before his death, when he became blind. He died in the friary at Acri on 30 October 1739. There were reports of a flow of blood and movement of his arm after death, suspiciously similar to those reported of Bd Bonaventure of Potenza (26 Oct.). Angelo was beatified in 1825 and provides an encouraging example of perseverance in one's vocation as well as dedication to a life of straightforward missionary labour. He anticipated some of the popular methods of preaching used by St Alphonsus Liguori (1 Aug.) and his Redemptorists; for example, he used to set up large crosses in imitation of Calvary to mark the holding of a parish mission. A book he wrote survives; it calls on the Christian to remember and watch through the passion with Our Lord and has something of a revivalist air to it; it went through a number of editions.

AA.SS., Oct., 13, pp. 658-82, gives the full documentation used for the beatification. See also *Bibl.SS.*, 1, 1234-5.

31

St Quentin, *Martyr* (? Late Third Century)

We can be sure that there was an early martyr with the name Quentin or Quintin, and that he suffered at or near the modern town of Saint-Quentin, in north-eastern France. St Gregory of Tours (17 Nov.), who died in 594, mentioned that there was a church dedicated to St Quentin, while Bede lists him among the martyrs. There is some evidence for accepting the tradition that Quentin was the son of a Roman senator named Zeno and that he went into Gaul during the reign of Maximian (286–305) as one of the missionaries sent to evangelize the Belgic peoples. He worked in the area around Amiens with St Lucian of Beauvais (8 Jan.).

After that all is legend. There is a *passio*, but the previous edition of this work condemned it as "a worthless recital of tortures and marvels." According to this he was arrested, tortured, and eventually beheaded, and his body was thrown into the Somme. The terrible tortures he is supposed to have undergone are depicted in a medieval illustrated Life which can be seen at Saint-Quentin. His body was recovered somewhat miraculously a long time afterwards and was given a simple burial; when miracles began to occur at the tomb the remains were translated to a more fitting resting place, and in 641 St Eligius (1 Dec.) rediscovered them and built an ornate shrine to house them. They were moved again in the ninth century to avoid destruction during the Norman invasions, and in subsequent centuries the relics were attested as authentic on several occasions, even as late as 1950. His cult was popular in England as well as in France and Belgium.

The legend has survived in a surprisingly large variety of forms; see *AA.SS.*, Oct., 13, pp. 725-820, with *Propylaeum*, p. 487. A number of Carolingian metrical versions were edited in *Anal.Boll.*, 20, (1901), pp. 1-44. See also *O.D.S.*, p. 411; *Bibl.SS.*, 10, 1313-15.

St Foillan, *Abbot* (*c.* 655)

Foillan (or Feuillen), Fursey (16 Jan.), and Ultan (2 May) were brothers who left their native Ireland to preach the gospel in England; all three of them are venerated as saints. Bede tells us they came from a noble Irish family. They arrived in England sometime after 630 and were given land in East Anglia by King Sigbert, on which they built a monastery. The site was at Burgh Castle, near Yarmouth in modern Suffolk, and it provided an excellent base for them in their missionary work among the East Angles.

After a time Fursey crossed over into Gaul, where he died about 648. When East Anglia was overrun by the pagan Mercians, the monastery at Burgh Castle was destroyed, and Foillan and Ultan decided to follow their brother's example and move to Gaul. They arrived in Neustria, the western part of the Frankish kingdom, and were well received by Clovis II. Foillan moved on to Nivelles, in modern Belgium, where he was given land by Bd Itta, the widow of Bd Pepin of Landen (21 Feb.), who had founded the monastery at Nivelles of which his daughter St Gertrude (17 Mar.) was abbess. Foillan founded another monastery nearby at Fosses. He is said to have been very influential in the development of Nivelles, and also to have worked as a missionary in Brabant, on the borders of Belgium and the Netherlands.

About the year 655 he set out with some companions from Nivelles, where he had been saying Mass, to continue a visitation of various monasteries founded by Irish monks. They were set upon by outlaws and murdered in the forest of Seneffe. Their bodies were not found until the following January, when St Gertrude ordered them to be buried at Foillan's own monastery. Because he was killed while on church business he is venerated rather dubiously as a martyr in a number of places in Belgium; he is also referred to as a bishop in some calendars but without any obvious justification. It would seem better to regard him as an abbot and missionary in the true Irish tradition: the previous edition of this work called him "one of the best remembered of the lesser Irish missionary monks on the continent."

AA.SS., Oct., 13, pp. 370-445. B. Krusch, in *M.G.H., Scriptores rerum merov.*, 4, pp. 449-51, prints a valuable Life which may have been written by a contemporary at Nivelles. See also P. Grosjean, in *Anal.Boll.* 85 (1957), pp. 379-419. Bede, *H.E.*, bk. 3, 19, devotes a chapter to Fursey but only a mention to Foillan.

St Begu (Late Seventh Century)

Begu was an Anglo-Saxon nun from Hackness in North Yorkshire. Bede tells us that she had a vision of the death of St Hilda (17 Nov.), the foundress of the convent at Hackness. He adds that Begu was a devout woman who had pledged herself to God in the religious life over thirty years previously; since we know Hilda died in 680 this gives us some idea of Begu's dates; she cannot have died in 660, as sometimes stated (this may be due to her being confused with Bega—see below).

Around 1125 the monks at Whitby, having lost the relics of St Hilda to Glastonbury and looking for a replacement, found a tomb at Hackness which conveniently bore the inscription, *"Hoc est sepulchrum Begu"* ("This is the grave of Begu"). They moved the relics to their monastery, where a number of miracles were immediately reported. We know about this translation through an account written by a monk of the monastery at St Bees, in modern Cumbria, which also claimed a set of miracles worked at the same time.

Now, the name St Bees is said to have come from an Irish nun of the seventh century, whose name is normally given as Bega and who was reputed to have built a monastery on the headland now called St Bees Head, after fleeing from Ireland to avoid being forced to marry. She had herself been a hermit, and in the shrine attached to her cell there was a bracelet which was venerated as having been hers, supposedly a gift from heaven to mark her marriage to Christ alone. The Old English name for bracelet is "*beag*," and this could have given rise to the cult of a St Bega. After the translation of Begu's relics, and the account of the two sets of simultaneous miracles associated with it, it became customary to identify the two saints as the same person. But there remains a considerable amount of confusion, and a separate feast-day of St Bega is celebrated in some places on 6 September. Farmer says that the absence of literary references to the Whitby cult is unusual.

A Life of Bega is printed in *Registrum Prioratus de sancta Bega, S.S.* (1915), pp. 497-520. For Begu, see Bede, *H.E.*, bk. 4, 23. See also *O.D.S.*, p. 44; *Bibl.SS.*, 2, 1075-9, which comes down firmly on the side of there being two different saints.

St Wolfgang of Regensburg, *Bishop* (*c.* 924-94)

Wolfgang was born in Swabia (part of Germany to the north of Lake Constance) about 924. He was sent to the abbey of Reichenau, which was on an island in Lake Constance and which had a flourishing school. He became friendly with a young noble called Henry, who had just established a school in Würzburg. Wolfgang was persuaded to leave Reichenau and accompany Henry to the new school, where his ability soon aroused admiration and, apparently, not a little jealousy. Then Henry became archbishop of Trier, and again Wolfgang went with him, this time to become a teacher in the cathedral school. While he was there he came under the influence of a reforming monk called Ramould and became a keen supporter of Archbishop Henry's plans to reform the clergy.

Wolfgang's life changed on the death of the archbishop. Instead of remaining as a teacher, he moved to the Benedictine abbey of Einsiedeln (in modern Switzerland), which at the time was ruled by an English monk named Gregory, and became a monk. The bishop of Augsburg, St Ulric (4 July), ordained him priest and sent him off to evangelize the Magyars. Although he carried out the duties of a missionary with his customary zeal, his labours met with little success. He was recommended to the emperor, Otto II, as a person fitted for episcopal office and in 972 was consecrated bishop of Regensburg, despite his appeals to be allowed to return to his monastery.

As a bishop he continued to wear the monastic habit and practise as much of the monastic life as possible, including its austerities. He was a keen reformer of the clergy, both religious and secular; he encouraged the regular canons to live a communal life and appointed Ramould of Trier to be abbot of the abbey of St Emmeram, which traditionally the bishops of Regensburg had held *in commendam* so that they could enjoy its income. He intervened personally to reform two convents which had become a scandal because of their disorderliness. He was a frequent and very effective preacher, and the assistance he gave to the poor became legendary. He still hankered after a life of greater solitude and on one occasion left his diocese and retired to a secret place where he could devote himself to prayer; it is said he was found by some hunters and taken back to Regensburg. He was a model of the zealous, reforming bishop, and his work for the restoration of the religious life was very much in keeping with the great monastic reforms of the tenth century emanating from Cluny and elsewhere.

As bishop he had a number of political duties to fulfill in addition to his epsicopal ones; he attended several imperial diets and accompanied the emperor on a campaign into France. He was entrusted with the education of the young son of the duke of Bavaria, who later became emperor and a canonized saint, St Henry the Good (13 July). In 994 Wolfgang was taken ill while on a journey down the Danube and died near the Austrian town of Linz. He was canonized in 1052, and his feast-day is celebrated widely in central Europe. His relics are in the cathedral in Regensburg.

The life of St Wolfgang is well documented; see *AA.SS.*, Nov., 2, pp. 527-97; *Bibl.SS.*, 12, 1334-42; *O.D.C.C.*, p. 1496, for bibliography.

DAVID HUGH FARMER. Former Reader in history at the University of Reading. Author of *St Hugh of Lincoln* and other biographical studies of saints. Author of *The Oxford Dictionary of Saints*. General consultant editor.

REV. PHILIP CARAMAN, S.J. Author of numerous biographies of saints and chief promoter of the cause of the Forty English Martyrs (canonized in 1970). Consultant on English Martyrs.

JOHN HARWOOD. Librarian of the Missionary Institute in London and course lecturer on the Orthodox churches. Consultant on Eastern and Orthodox saints.

DOM ERIC HOLLAS, O.S.B. Monk of St John's Abbey, Collegeville, Minnesota and director of the Hill Monastic Manuscript Library in Collegeville, where he also teaches theology at St John's University. General consultant, U.S.A.

PROF. KATHLEEN JONES. Emeritus Professor of Social Policy at the University of York. Author of many books and articles on social policy and mental illness. Honorary Fellow of the Royal College of Psychiatrists. Translator of *The Poems of St John of the Cross* (1993). Consultant on social history and abnormal behaviour.

DOM DANIEL REES, O.S.B. Monk of Downside Abbey and librarian of the monastery library. Bibliographical consultant.

DR RICHARD SHARPE. Reader in diplomatic history at the University of Oxford. Author of *Medieval Irish Saints' Lives* (1991), *Adomnán of Iona. Life of St Columba* (1995), and numerous articles on Celtic saints. Consultant on this subject.

REV. AYLWARD SHORTER, W.F. Long experience of African Missions and author of many books on the subject. Former President of Missionary Institute London, now Principal of Tangaza College, Nairobi. Consultant on missionary saints.

DOM ALBERIC STACPOOLE, O.S.B. Monk of Ampleforth Abbey. Fellow of the Royal Historical Society. Secretary of the Ecumenical Society of Our Lady. Editor of several works, including *Vatican II by Those Who Were There* (1985). Engaged on a study of St Anslem. Consultant on feasts of Our Lady.

DOM HENRY WANSBROUGH, O.S.B. Monk of Ampleforth Abbey, currently Master of St Benet's Hall, Oxford. Member of the Pontifical Biblical Commission. Author of numerous works on scripture and Editor of the *New Jerusalem Bible* (1985). Consultant on New Testament saints.

SR BENEDICTA WARD. Anglican religious. Lecturer at Oxford Institute of Medieval History. Author of numerous works on hagiography, spirituality, and mysticism. Consultant on Middle Ages and age of Bede.